Japan

Japan

CASSELL BUSINESS BRIEFINGS

Japan

Michael Jenkins

JAPAN BUSINESS CONSULTANCY

with

Joyce Jenkins

JAPANESE LANGUAGE ASSOCIATION

and with contributions from
Tim Barker and Teresa Castelvetere

Cassell

Villiers House
41/47 Strand
London WC2N 5JE

387 Park Avenue South
New York
NY 10016-8810

First published 1993

British Library Cataloguing-in-Publication Data
A catalogue entry for this book is available from the British Library.

Library of Congress Cataloguing-in-Publication Data
Jenkins, Michael.
    Cassell business briefings : Japan / Michael Jenkins with Joyce Jenkins.
        p.   cm. — (Cassell business briefings)
    Includes index.
    ISBN 0-304-32637-2
    1. Japan—Economic conditions—1989-   2. Japan—Social conditions—1945-   3. Japan—Politics and government—1945-
4. Japan—Commerce. I. Jenkins, Joyce. II. Title. III. Title: Japan. IV. Series.
    HC462.95.J46   1993
    330.952—dc20   93-25809
                                                                  CIP

ISBN 0-304-32637-2

Typeset by Colset Private Limited, Singapore
Printed and bound in Great Britain by Biddles Ltd,
Guildford and King's Lynn

Contents

PART FOUR

Culture

PART FIVE

The Economy

PART SIX

Doing Business in Japan

PART SEVEN

Directory

PART EIGHT

Appendix

Foreword

Japan is the world's second largest national market and perhaps its most demanding and sophisticated. Japan sets world standards in quality, service, technology and management expertise. No British company with global aspirations can afford to miss the opportunity to establish a long-term presence in the Japanese market.

It is not only in Japan itself that the benefits of partnership with Japanese companies are to be found. No less than 41 per cent of Japanese investment in the EC has come to the UK – giving us a market of 200 Japanese manufacturers on our doorstep. Japanese companies are to be found running major projects around the world, sometimes with funding from Japan's huge programme of development aid. These too present extensive opportunities for British contractors and suppliers.

For all these reasons, I and my Department are committed to helping British business people push forward with a positive strategy for Japan. We have already made a start with the Opportunity Japan and Priority Japan campaigns. Now, we are forging ahead with a programme to promote partnership with Japan in a range of key business sectors, led by export promoters seconded in from the private sector. This book will help you take advantage of the opportunities Japan offers for British business today.

Richard Needham, MP, Minister for Trade,
Department of Trade and Industry

Preface

The sheer pace of change in Japan has been one of the hall-marks of the country's development since the 1950s. The signs are that the 1990s will be a turbulent decade for Japan as it comes to terms with an ageing society, a growing labour shortage and the aftermath of the economic excesses of the 1980s.

By the year 2000 Japan will have undergone significant economic, social and political changes. In order to reflect these changes, this book will be revised at regular intervals: updates in electronic form will be made available on application to the publisher.

Although every effort has been made to ensure that the statistics used in this book are accurate and consistent, the reader should be aware that differing methods of data collection in Japan and other countries may make absolute comparisons difficult.

Where deemed familiar to the reader, names of people, places and things have been given their usual spelling, e.g. Tokyo, not Tōkyō, and Noh rather than nō.

Acknowledgements

I would like to thank Teresa Castelvetere for writing the sections on history and politics; Tim Barker for the section on religions; Matthew Dando for preparing the Directory and the Appendix; and Joyce Jenkins for producing the General Overview and the Gazetteer in Part One, and the sections on society and culture.

Thanks are also due to the following people for helping to type and produce the manuscript: Anna Jenkins, Siân Bohana (Japanese Language Association) and Yiping Ge (Japanese Language Association). My appreciation too to my colleagues Julie Jessett, Tim Orchard and Philip Fuji at Japan Business Consultancy and to colleagues at Bath College of Higher Education for their support during the writing of this book, and to James Norris for designing the main map of Japan. My thanks to Peter Falzon in Tokyo for providing me with a base from which to gather information in Japan.

This book is dedicated to my father, Lyn Jenkins, whose enjoyment of Japan was an encouragement. Thanks also to my mother Shirley for her support, and to my daughter Maia, without whom this book would have been produced sooner.

Michael Jenkins
March 1993

About the Authors

Michael Jenkins is Manager of Japan Business Consultancy in Bath. He worked with Toyota Motor Corporation in Japan and has been advising companies on how to do business with the Japanese since his return to the UK in 1988.

Joyce Jenkins is Director of the Japanese Language Association, a national organization which promotes the teaching of Japanese throughout the UK.

Teresa Castelvetere is a Japanese Labour History specialist from Adelaide, Australia. She has conducted postgraduate research in Japan and at Harvard.

Tim Barker is a graduate of Chinese and Japanese and is currently Lecturer in Japanese Studies at Bath College of Higher Education. He is a specialist in Japanese religion and society.

PART ONE

Introduction

JAPAN

Hokkaidō

- ASAHIKAWA
- HOKKAIDŌ
- SAPPORO
- HAKODATE

- AOMORI
- AOMORI

Tōhoku

- AKITA IWATE
- AKITA
- MORIOKA

- YAMAGATA MIYAGI
- YAMAGATA SENDAI

SEA OF JAPAN

Chūbu

- NIIGATA
- NIIGATA

- FUKUSHIMA
- FUKUSHIMA

- TOCHIGI
- NAGANO GUNMA UTSUNOMIYA
- KANAZAWA TOYAMA MAEBASHI MITO

Kantō

Chūgoku

- ISHIKAWA
- FUKUI
- FUKUI
- TOTTORI
- SAITAMA
- IBARAKI
- NAGANO
- TOKYO
- TOTTORI
- GIFU
- KOFU URAWA
- TOTTORI
- YAMANASHI
- SHIMANE
- MATSUE
- NAGOYA
- YOKOHAMA
- OKAYAMA
- KYOTO SHIGA
- GIFU
- CHIBA
- OKAYAMA
- KYOTO OTSU
- AICHI SHIZUOKA KANAGAWA
- YAMAGUCHI
- HIROSHIMA
- HYOGO OSAKA
- NARA MIE
- HAMAMATSU
- SHIZUOKA
- YAMAGUCHI
- OKAYAMA
- KOBE OSAKA
- OKAYAMA
- NARA
- FUKUOKA TAKAMATSU WAKAYAMA
- KAGAWA TOKUSHIMA YOKUSHIMA

Kinki

- FUKUOKA
- MATSUYAMA TOKUSHIMA KOCHI WAKAYAMA
- SAGA OITA EHIME KOCHI
- FUKUOKA SAGA OITA
- NAGASAKI
- SAGA KUMAMOTO

Shikoku

- NAGASAKI
- KUMAMOTO
- KUMAMOTO MIYAZAKI
- KAGOSHIMA MIYAZAKI
- KAGOSHIMA

PACIFIC OCEAN

Kyūshū

0		200km
0		125miles

1 General Overview

Japan is above all a land of contrasts and paradoxes. Spectacularly modern technology is often juxtaposed with ancient traditions. The 'economic miracle' of the twentieth century is based on technology, but Japan's past was founded on agriculture. Although the country itself is rich in scenic beauty, with great ranges of mountains and hills and magnificent coastlines, it is poor in resources and in land suitable for agriculture or building.

The Japanese like to think of themselves as unique: according to ancient myth, the Yamato race (Japanese) are descended from deities and the emperor is the god on earth (see: Religion). There is a tendency in the west to nurture this view and it is very hard to find a westerner who does not view Japan and its achievements with either uncritical admiration or total damnation, regarding the Japanese people as inhuman economic ants.

Certainly the achievements of the Japanese people are remarkable: they have brought the country, in little more than a century, from self-imposed isolation and postwar devastation to a place of prominence and economic might among the nations of the world. But what is perhaps most remarkable is the way the Japanese have managed to import, master and improve on the technologies of the west, while retaining their traditional culture running alongside aspects of western/international culture which they have adopted. The other remarkable feature is the political and social changes which, accompanying economic and technical modernization, have transformed Japan from a feudal society into a stable, basically free, democratic, egalitarian one in little over a century. The democratic system in Japan may have many drawbacks and may operate quite differently from our own, but it does produce the necessary

3

decisions to run the country efficiently and fairly openly (see: Politics). Japan is the only major non-western country that has become a fully industrialized and modernized society.

As with any country, a look at Japan's geography, climate and history may help provide some insight into the national characteristics and culture which makes Japan the country it is today.

GEOGRAPHY

Japan is an archipelago which consists of four main islands – Hokkaidō, Honshū, Shikoku and Kyūshū – and numerous smaller ones. Hokkaidō is the northernmost of the main islands; Honshū is the biggest and most densely populated; Shikoku is tucked in close to the southern end of Honshū, facing out to the Pacific Ocean; and Kyūshū, just a short hop away in the south, lies directly opposite the Korean peninsula (see the map on page 2).

Japan, with a land area of 146,000 square miles (378,000 square km), is slightly larger than the United Kingdom, and from north to south the country extends a total of 1,860 miles (3,000 km). The northern islands are off the coast of Russia; Honshū and Kyūshū curve down the coasts of North and South Korea; and a string of islands extends down the coast of mainland China towards Taiwan. Tokyo, the capital, is located on approximately the same latitude as Gibraltar, and is situated in one of the world's most earthquake-prone areas. Minor earthquakes are experienced in Japan almost every day (particularly in the Tokyo area) and schools, offices and factories have regular earthquake drills in preparation for 'the big one'. An earthquake on the scale of the one which destroyed Tokyo in 1923 is expected at any moment.

Japan is volcanic, its most famous active volcano being Mt Fuji, which last erupted in 1707. Over 80 per cent of the land is mountainous and unsuitable for farming or building; over two-thirds is given over to forests, and only 14 per cent of total available land is farmed. The coastal plains are therefore very densely populated, with most of the population of 124 million living on a narrow coastal plain stretching from the Kansai region in the west (the urban sprawl which encompasses Kobe, Osaka and Kyoto) to the Kanto region in the east (Tokyo, Yokohama and environs). Land prices in Japan are among the highest in the world, reflecting the dearth of land suitable for building purposes. The renting of homes has therefore become the norm.

Japan lacks natural resources and depends heavily on the rest of the world for the bulk of its energy and raw material needs (see: Natural Resources; Energy Resources). Despite high rainfall levels, the country does not have enough reservoirs to make hydroelectric power a primary source of energy. Atomic energy and the last of the existing coal mines, together with imported oil and natural gas, are the main energy sources for Japanese industry.

CLIMATE

Japan, situated in the temperate zone, has a fairly mild, wet climate and is subject to distinct seasons – four main seasons, spring, summer, autumn and winter, and two semi-seasons: the rainy (*tsuyu*), which falls between spring and summer, and the typhoon, which separates summer and autumn. Weather conditions vary widely in Japan between the north and the south of the country and between the Sea of Japan side and the Pacific side of the archipelago. Hokkaidō and the islands in the far north suffer almost Arctic conditions in the winter and remain cool in the summer, while Okinawa and the islands in the far south enjoy a tropical climate and are warm all year round. In the winter it is theoretically possible to go skiing in the mountains in Hokkaidō one day and then fly down to Okinawa to enjoy good windsurfing and scuba-diving the next.

Spring in central Japan (April and May) is relatively short and is the cherry-blossom (*sakura*) season, celebrated by eating, drinking and singing under cherry or plum blossom which, after dark, is illuminated by red lanterns hung on the branches of the trees. This centuries'-old tradition of cherry-blossom viewing is known as *yozakura* and the parties held under the trees are called *hanami*. The spring gives way to heavy rains which fall during *tsuyu*.

Tsuyu (in early June) affects most of Japan, with the exception of Hokkaidō in the far north. After the rains, steely grey clouds and soaring temperatures herald the extremely humid Japanese summer.

The heat and humidity of the summer (mid-June to September) continue unabated until the early weeks of September, when the typhoon season arrives with gale-force winds and torrential rains to clear the closeness of July and August. When the storms abate they often leave in their wake warm, dry days and long, balmy evenings for the end of summer – rather like an Indian summer in Britain or the United States.

The Japanese autumn starts in October and continues through November. In October temperatures start to drop steadily, the air becomes crisp and clear and the leaves on the trees turn brilliant shades of red, orange and yellow before dropping to the ground. The autumn is one of the most pleasant seasons in Japan. As temperatures are mild during the day, there is little rainfall, and the scenery is spectacular, with the hillsides covered in brightly coloured trees against a background of brilliant blue skies.

Winter (December–March) in Japan is also pleasantly crisp, with blue, sunny skies and little rain. Temperatures fall to freezing point at sea-level on Honshū and Shikoku and to well below freezing point on Hokkaidō and in the mountains of central Japan (see: Miscellaneous). The dryness of the atmosphere, however, and the sunshine during the day, make winter pleasant for walking around in Japan. Snowfall is quite high in Hokkaidō, on the Sea of Japan side of the country, and in the mountains of central Japan. Skiing is very popular during winter, and the slopes at weekends and holidays start to resemble rush-hour at Shinjuku station.

HISTORY

The early dwellers of Japan are believed to have been the Jōmon people, who were hunter-gatherers and fishers and who lived in caves. From around 300 BC, however, wet-paddy rice agriculture and metal-working technology were introduced into northern Kyūshū from the Korean peninsula, and an agricultural civilization possessing bronze and iron began to spread through the Japanese archipelago. Agrarian values, ceremonies and customs were developed and formed the rudiments of modern Japanese culture. The independent tribes scattered throughout Japan were consolidated under the Yamato clan and by the sixth century AD had formed a more-or-less unified state covering over two-thirds of Japan.

Knowledge and technology from the Chinese continent had been spreading during this period. The Chinese writing system was adopted in the fifth century AD and Confucianism and Buddhism in the sixth century AD. Between the seventh and ninth centuries, the Japanese made a concerted effort to emulate the institutions and arts of China, further centralizing the state and strengthening imperial authority. Buddhist culture and art flourished, with *kanbun* (writing in the Chinese style) remaining the leading form of literary expression. Buddhist monasteries of the age were full of sculptures and art in the Chinese style. Missions to Tang-dynasty China stopped after 894 and Japan remained a remote land with a cultural base quite different from that of China, so although the Chinese influence remained and was refreshed from time to time by periodical contact with the continent, the Japanese social and political system developed into something entirely different from those of China.

With the development in the tenth century of the *kana* Japanese phonetic writing system, based on Chinese characters (see: Language), which made the written expression of Japanese possible for the first time, a uniquely Japanese culture developed.

Feudalism went through various stages and the inability of the imperial court to control outlying regions led to widespread unrest and the emergence of a strong warrior class. A military court was established in Kamakura which challenged the imperial court in Kyoto. From the twelfth to the sixteenth century, power was transferred from the imperial court to the military with different warlords seizing power and no strong central government. Battles between competing warlords were frequent into the latter half of the fifteenth century (see: History). Nevertheless, trade with Ming China flourished during this period, and Portuguese and Spanish traders also contributed to Japanese culture in the mid-sixteenth century with the introduction of firearms and Christianity.

Then, in the seventeenth century, following decades of civil war, Tokugawa Ieyasu made himself shogun and established his government in Edo (Tokyo) in 1603. The shogunate kept the emperor, the nobility and the religious institutions under tight control and strictly regulated the lives of the common people. In the latter half of the seventeenth century, the third shogun cut the country off from foreign commerce and plunged Japan into isolation for over two hundred years. During these years Japan had the chance to cultivate its own cultural heritage, and advances were made in education and scholarship, with schools set up for samurai children and for those of townspeople. However, the country also fell technologically far behind the west, as was demonstrated in 1853 when Commodore Perry of the American Navy arrived and forced Japan to open up for trade. The Japanese realized that they were unable to compete with the western military and economic technology, and within fifteen years an ambitious group of young Japanese swept away the shogunate and restored the Meiji emperor. This created a more centralized nation which then rushed to catch up with the industrialized west. Industry was promoted, western culture was encouraged, a constitution was drawn up, a parliament was established and gradually Japan became a more modernized country, entering into international trade and political life and becoming both an economic and a military power. A period of wars followed, with victories in the Sino-Japanese and Russo-Japanese wars, while Japan sought to establish hegemony over all East Asia. Japan's imperialistic tendencies intensified following the end of World War I, culminating in the loss of World War II, which left the Japanese all but destitute and forced them to start all over again. The atomic bombing of Hiroshima and Nagasaki brought the end of the war and saw Japan in a state of almost complete ruin, with over two million of its people killed and most of its major cities destroyed. The economy and the country at large were paralysed and seemed incapable of supporting the population.

The so-called 'economic miracle' which followed and which made the country the formidable economic power it is today can be attributed to several factors. One is an educated and highly motivated workforce. Another is the 'Japan Inc.' ideology, in which government, industry and media work closely together to produce sophisticated industrial and economic policies, while at the same time pushing the idea of national commitment to commercial and industrial growth as necessary to the country's survival (see: Japan Inc.). It is also the case that, as the Japanese had to build up their industries from scratch after the war (in terms of both physical buildings and company structure), the resulting industries were more modern and efficient.

However, the main factor in Japan's economic recovery and success has undoubtedly been the lingering influence of the seven-year postwar Allied Occupation. This lasted from 1945 until 1952, when Japan was given its sovereignty under the terms of the San Francisco Peace Treaty. As well as carrying out wide-ranging reform to government at many different levels (including the removal from the emperor of executive powers, the abolition of the dogma of his divinity, and the introduction of a new democratic Constitution), the United States, represented by General Douglas MacArthur, instigated the Marshall Plan. This economic aid package, along with the United States military expenditure in Japan during the Korean War (1950–3), is probably the largest single factor responsible for the recovery of Japan's postwar economy. In the course of it, the United States left Japan with an addition to its cultural legacy second only to that of China.

RELIGION

The Japanese tend to avoid identifying with any single religious doctrine but do have a strong-rooted, almost mystical reverence for ceremonies as a means of supplicating the gods for rewards and protection. Japan has many religions, each of which may have many gods. The Japanese tend to choose ceremonies from different religions to celebrate different phases in life. For example, while most Japanese would consider themselves to be adherents both to Shinto – the Way of the Gods – which is the indigenous religion of Japan, and to Buddhism, it is not uncommon to find elements of Christian religious practice, especially at weddings or at Christmas. A couple may, for instance, be married according to Shinto ritual, but increasingly the wedding reception may be conducted with the bride in white and the groom in a dinner jacket. Alternatively, some ceremonies may take place in a mock-up of a parish church on the roof of the sixteenth floor of a hotel. These 'churches' are not consecrated, but this is of little concern to the participants. Funerals, by contrast, tend to be a mixture of Shinto and Buddhism. Most Japanese will visit Shinto shrines at New Year, make trips to Buddhist temples in spring and autumn to visit the family grave, and feel a close affinity to Inari – once an agrarian deity which is now popular throughout Japan as an all-purpose god. In a 1989 survey asking, 'What do you believe in?', only 7.5 per cent cited anything which would tie them to a specific religion.

Religious sects abound, ranging from the Buddhist Soka Gakkai (which also has a political arm) to the unique Tenrikyo, founded this century by a Japanese housewife, which takes as its main tenet cleanliness and the banishment of dust, as a parable for the cleansing of sin.

THE JAPANESE PEOPLE

There are various theories about the origin of the Japanese people, but the commonly accepted hypothesis is that the early Japanese came to the islands around 18,000 years ago at the time of the last glacial period, when great migrations were being made all over the world in search of food. At that time Japan was linked to the Asian continent by various land bridges, and from the north there came a Mongoloid race with flat features, adapted to the hard northern climate. From the south came the older Mongoloid race of round-faced people who populated much of the southern Asian continent. The intermixing of these two races resulted in a race of people who were hairy, short of stature and round-faced – the prototype Japanese. Over the centuries, tall, narrow-faced peoples from China and Korea immigrated to western Japan and were gradually assimilated into the indigenous race, resulting in the modern Japanese. Even now, studies have shown that people in the north tend to be short and round-faced, while people in the south tend to be tall and narrow-faced.

It is often said that Japan is a homogeneous society made up only of the Yamato race, and indeed there is a marked lack of ethnic diversity across the country. This can lead to problems for those who are considered ethnically different.

In fact the country also has a large Korean population and a substantial Chinese one. The Korean people are mainly descendants of those brought to Japan as forced labour after the occupation of Korea in 1910. Although they have been brought up speaking Japanese and many have adopted Japanese names, so are virtually indistinguishable from native Japanese, they still are registered as 'aliens' and have been discriminated against legally and socially. 'Koreans', for example, are still forbidden by law from becoming civil servants or teachers in the public sector. A person of Korean descent will have virtually no chance of marrying a 'true Japanese'. As a result, the Korean community tends to stick to itself and is responsible for the running of many of the bars and games parlours, in addition to being behind many of the *yakuza* gangster groups. The issue causes considerable embarrassment to the Japanese, and, despite regular protests, tends to be glossed over in any information about Japan.

There are also a number of indigenous peoples left in Japan. Hokkaidō, the northernmost island, is home to the Ainu, a Mongoloid people with their own language and culture who used to inhabit territory as far south as modern-day Sendai (in the north-east of Honshū). Clashes with the expansionist Yamato resulted in the Ainu being driven back into the northern reaches, and today the Ainu tend to live in specially designated communities, similar to Native American reservations in the United States. These communities have become tourist attractions and the traditional crafts which the Ainu produce are prized as souvenirs.

The Burakumin is another minority group which the Japanese would like to pretend does not exist. At the last estimate there were three million Burakumin in Japan. They can be found all over the country and are the descendants of those who worked with animal skins and offal, who were regarded as outcasts in the caste system which developed between the sixteenth and nineteenth centuries. This system placed warriors at the top, followed by farmers, craft-workers and merchants. The Burakumin were at the very bottom, and strong prejudice against them still persists. As recently as the early 1970s, books were published with biographical data on all the Burakumin families so that people could make sure of not marrying a member of this group. The Burakumin are still trapped in a vicious circle of economic and educational disadvantages: unable to send their children to good schools, they cannot get jobs and are often seen begging and living on the street.

Modern Japan also has a growing South-east Asian population of migrant workers who come to work in the sectors where there is a lack of Japanese labour, such as in the construction industry and in entertainment. Many of these people are working illegally, and are employed by unscrupulous dealers who exploit the fact that officially they do not exist and therefore do not have any human rights. Various official and voluntary bodies have been set up to try and improve conditions for these people and to regularize the terms under which they work.

POLITICS

Japan is governed by a parliament headed by a prime minister. The prime minister has a cabinet of ministers chosen to head the various ministries, such as the Ministry of Education, the Ministry for International Trade and Industry, etc. The lower house in the parliament is known as the National Diet or simply the Diet, and is counterbalanced by a House of Councillors. In spite of a number of serious scandals involving senior politicians during the late 1980s, which rocked the ruling Liberal Democratic Party (LDP) and resulted in the resignations of two prime ministers, the LDP has ruled Japan since the end of the American Occupation, with the exception of a short period in the late 1950s (see: Major Political Parties).

The periodic scandals have called into question the moral integrity of Japanese politics (and politicians) and have prompted a certain disillusionment with the LDP among the Japanese voters, but no serious contenders for government have emerged and Japan is basically a one-party state. The opposition parties have not enjoyed much popular support among significant sectors of the population. The Social Democratic Party of Japan and the former Communist Party of Japan have been at loggerheads over dogma and both have suffered from their anti-American stances. Widespread discontent over fiscal reforms and the introduction of the hated consumption tax has worked against the LDP and the party's one-time invincibility has been called into doubt.

Japanese politics are characterized by factionalism (see: Politics), which extends across the political spectrum. The leader of the LDP is chosen by the leaders of the rival factions within the party and usually goes on to become prime minister.

NIHONGO – THE LANGUAGE OF JAPAN

Standard Japanese is the language used throughout Japan today with some regional variations in terms of accent, slang and certain vocabulary items. As is the case in most countries, there are some dialects, such as those spoken in the north-east and the far south, which are almost completely unintelligible to speakers from outside these areas. English is the most commonly studied foreign language and is studied by all high-school students. Despite this, very little English is used outside main tourist areas, and increasingly it is expected that foreigners wishing to do business with the Japanese should have Japanese-speaking staff and should produce their materials in Japanese. Nevertheless, the Japanese will generally be pleasantly surprised by any foreigner who has made the effort to master some of their language.

Learning some basic survival Japanese is not particularly difficult for English speakers, as the pronunciation of Japanese is probably as easy as that of Spanish and there are no sounds in the language which do not have a near-equivalent in English. Verbs come at the end of the sentence and do not distinguish between singular and plural. Japanese has various tenses as well as personal pronouns (I, you, he, she, etc.), although these are not used as freely and as frequently as they are in English.

Japanese, like some other Asian languages including Thai and Korean, has various registers of politeness, which mean that different verbs and nouns are used according to the relationship between speakers. There is however a standard polite form which is acceptable at any level, so there should be no problems as long as you keep to the polite forms, until you are fluent enough to try other styles of speech (see: Language).

By all means try to master a few phrases of Japanese prior to a visit to Japan, since this will be much appreciated by your Japanese colleagues. They will admire you for having made an effort and, whatever happens, it should help to break the ice. For a list of useful phrases and when to use them, see: Key Phrases.

2 Gazetteer

Japan is divided into nine large regions, subdivided into 47 smaller prefectures, generally called *ken* in Japanese. The prefectures are the official administrative units of Japan, and 43 of them have -*ken* added to their names in Japanese (for example, Aichi-ken). Some of the metropolitan areas of the largest cities are prefectures in terms of administrative structure, but are not called *ken*. *Tō*, meaning 'capital', is added to Tōkyō to mean 'Greater Tokyo', and *fu* (also meaning 'prefecture') is added to Kyōto and Ōsaka. Hokkaidō, which is an island and a district as well as a prefecture, is known as *Hokkaidō-dō* (Hokkaido island).

The regions, which are areas defined by geographical or historical divisions, are:

- **Hokkaidō** (the large northern island);
- **Tōhoku** (the north-eastern part of Honshū Island);
- **Kantō** (the area around Tokyo);
- **Chūbu** (the central Honshū area, around Nagoya);
- **Kansai**, also known as Kinki (south-west Honshū, around Osaka);
- **Chūgoku** (the southernmost section of Honshū);
- **Shikoku** (the large island off the Pacific ocean coast of Honshū);
- **Kyūshū** (the southernmost of the main islands);
- **Okinawa Islands** (the group of islands at the southernmost tip of the Japanese archipelago).

TOKYO

Tokyo is the capital of Japan and its largest city. It has spread out to encompass Yokohama, Japan's second largest city, and the metropolitan area of Tokyo and Yokohama combined has a population of around 17 million. This makes it the third largest metropolitan area in the world after Mexico City and New York City. In land area it covers over 800 square miles (2,100 square km).

Situated in East Central Honshū at the edge of Tokyo Bay, Tokyo is the administrative, financial and cultural centre of Japan, as well as being a major industrial and transportation centre. It is home of the world's first public monorail line and is linked to the rest of Japan by the high-speed *shinkansen* – bullet train.

It was founded in 1457 as Edo, by the local lord, Dokan Ota, and was a minor castle town until 1590, when it was made capital of Tokugawa Ieyasu's shogunate. During the 250 years of the Tokugawas' rule, the population expanded rapidly and by 1700 had reached 1 million – the largest city in the world. The population included visiting *daimyo* (feudal lords) and samurai, who were forced to spend part of each year in the capital under surveillance. Merchants and artisans were brought into the city to service the enormous population, and the eastern marshes (present-day Tsukiji, Shimbashi and Nihonbashi) were drained and reclaimed for their use. The merchants thrived commercially during this period, although they were regarded as very low in the hierarchy of Tokugawa society. The samurai class, conversely, became more and more impoverished.

In 1868, when the emperor was restored to power, he made Edo the nation's capital and renamed it Tokyo, meaning 'eastern capital'. The city continued to grow and prosper, but over half of it was destroyed in the great earthquake and fire of 1923. Heavy Allied bombing in World War II also devastated much of the city, including most of its industrial plants. Left intact were the imperial palace and surrounding embassies, the Diet (parliament) buildings, a number of famed landmarks such as the Meiji shrine and other ancient temples, and many office buildings.

Frequent rebuilding should have made Tokyo one of the world's most modern cities, and in some senses it is. Individually many of the buildings are miracles of modern technology – earthquake-proofed, incredibly high, 'intelligent' buildings which can be programmed by computer to switch heating on and off, open and close doors, etc. Parts of the transportation system are also state-of-the-art – the monorail to Haneda airport was the first of its kind. The fully automated ticket machines at stations are incredibly efficient compared to their British and American counterparts, and underground trains can take you right to the basements of many of the main buildings. But many stations still employ armies of men to stand at ticket gates and clip tickets, with old-fashioned punches, although a programme to institute automatic barriers in all underground stations is currently under way.

The rest of the city is equally contradictory. Buildings have sprung up willy-nilly and residential areas appear next to business, shopping and even industrial areas. Streets are often very narrow, without pavements and sometimes with open drains running down the side.

Although the overall impression of Tokyo is of size and crowded hustle and bustle, and much of it is concrete jungle, it is a city that breaks down into distinct areas, which are like a collection of small villages, each with its own character. They include the following:

- **Akasaka** This is a high-class entertainment area, where politicians and company directors dine, served and entertained by geisha girls. The bars, cabarets, discos, night-clubs and restaurants in this area are among the most exclusive in town.

- **Akihabara** This is Tokyo's electronics district, where you can pick up the latest in technological gadgetry and duty-free purchases can be made. Beware of prices – Japanese goods are often more expensive in Japan than at home!

- **Aoyama** Much of Aoyama is residential and several embassies are situated here. It is also full of high-class antique shops, restaurants and boutiques.

- **Ginza** This is Japan's most famous shopping district, full of department stores and expensive boutiques, shops and restaurants, as well as art galleries, theatres and cinemas. On Sundays the main street is closed to traffic and crowded with pedestrians. At night Ginza's expensive hostess bars open for lavish entertaining on expense accounts.

- **Hirō** This is home to many foreign executives – a cosmopolitan residential area.

- **Kabucho** Home to the Tokyo Stock Exchange, Kabucho is Tokyo's main financial district.

- **Kasumigaseki** The National Diet and the prime minister's residence can be found here, as well as government offices, ministries and agencies.

- **Marunouchi** Literally translated as 'within the circle', Marunouchi is the area around the Imperial Palace and

Tokyo Station, which is encircled by the Marunouchi Railway Line (the first line to be built). Anything within the Marunouchi line was considered to be in the city. Marunouchi is now the business centre of Tokyo and home to the headquarters of most major Japanese companies, in particular, banks and financial firms. The neat, tree-lined avenues are deserted at night.

- **Nihonbashi** This is an important commercial district with a number of banks, including the Bank of Japan. There are also a number of national government offices and the main branch of one of Japan's best-known department stores, Mitsukoshi.

- **Nishi Azabu** Down the road from Hirō, Nishi Azabu has many fashionable bars and restaurants.

- **Roppongi** The back streets of this area are home to many embassies and expensive residences. The main street is packed with restaurants, discos and night-clubs where the young, international set eat, drink and dance into the early hours of the morning. The prestigious Okura hotel is here, as is the Ark Hills development, a business centre which houses many foreign companies.

- **Shibuya** This is an up-and-coming fashion centre for young, trendy Japanese.

- **Shinagawa** A number of large hotels are situated in Shinagawa, which is a pleasant, green district. It is also a hub on the transportation network, with good connections to all parts of Tokyo and out to Yokohama and beyond in one direction and to Narita Airport in the other.

- **Shinjuku** This is where documentary makers film scenes showing the crowded hustle and bustle of Japan. Its station is one of the largest and arguably most confusing in the world. (Do not arrange to meet someone 'outside the station' or you could be lost forever!) Shinjuku is one of the liveliest areas of Tokyo, with the narrow streets on the Kabukicho side bright with neon-lit amusement arcades, *pachinko* parlours, and signs offering massages and other pleasures. The main streets are full of department stores and boutiques, while on the west side of the station are to be found the skyscrapers of Sunshine City and the New Metropolitan Centre (a space-age building housing the metropolitan government offices), which dominate the Tokyo skyline.

Transportation

Tokyo is serviced by a massive JR (Japan Railways) network of **subway** lines, as well as by a number of private subway lines. Some stations are terminals for both JR and private lines and sometimes you have to change stations to change lines. The subways are clean, efficient, safe and – usually – the quickest way to get around. Needless to say, they get very crowded, so avoid rush-hour (07.30–09.30 and 17.00–19.00) if possible.

Subway stations are marked by a dark blue circular symbol. Station names are written in Japanese and Romanized script, but maps and ticket machines are often in Japanese only, as are station maps. You can buy bilingual maps to plan your route, and can (if you have time) match the characters for where you want to go from the bilingual map to the station route map to find out what price you should pay. Another method is to pay the cheapest fare, then settle up the difference when you get off at the other end. There is usually a 'fare-adjustment office' – *kaisatsuguchi* – near the exit barriers. Usually if you stand and look at your map for long enough, someone will take pity on you and will point you in the right direction – whether you like it or not!

The **bus system** in Tokyo is extensive and buses often go to places that cannot be accessed by trains. However, unless you are going to a major destination (whose name you can read and understand in Japanese), they can be quite difficult for foreigners to use. Destinations are usually written only in *kanji* and names are announced in Japanese. Buses are usually of the 'one-man' variety, with fares collected by the drivers, who do not have much time to waste on foreigners who do not know where they are going. Many buses stop running around 22.00.

Taxis can be flagged down in the street if their red light is lit, or can be taken from taxi ranks at hotels, stations and department stores and some main streets. You may have difficulties flagging one down, as many taxi drivers panic at the foreseen difficulties of communicating with foreigners and speed on by. The Japanese address system, whereby houses are assigned numbers in the order in which they are built, rather than in a sequence along a street, means that taxi drivers are unlikely to be able to find an address unless it is a famous landmark. The Japanese give detailed instructions to anyone who is likely to be visiting them. Ask for these to be written down (in Japanese) so you can show your taxi driver. Taxi fares are increased by 20 per cent between 23.00 and 05.00. The minimum taxi fare in Tokyo is ¥480 (US$4.48) for the first 0.8 miles (2 kilometres), and ¥90 (US$0.84) for each additional 400 yards (370 metres).

Driving in Tokyo is not for the faint-hearted. The roads are crowded, the traffic system is complicated and road-signs are in Japanese only. However, if you are in Japan for long periods and feel up to tackling it, an international driving licence will enable you to hire a car. This will give you access to the countryside and to areas which are a bit off the beaten track and uncrowded. The main car-hire firms have branches in Tokyo. Ask at your hotel. The Japanese drive on the left.

Tokyo is linked to the rest of Japan by an extensive, efficient **railway** network, which includes JR lines and private railway lines. The famous bullet train (*shinkansen*) and its successor the *nozomi* run on JR lines, and are fast and luxurious. Trains leave from Tokyo Station, sometimes with stops at other major Tokyo stations.

There are two types of *shinkansen*, *hikari* ('light') and *kodama* ('echo') on the Tokaido Sanyo *shinkansen* line, and *aoba* and *yamabiko* on the Tohoku line. The *hikari* are the super-express trains which only stop at major stations, while the *kodama* stop at a few more stations. Ordinary trains also run on the same lines, but stop at every station, so are much slower. If you want to travel to a minor station, the fastest way is to get a *shinkansen* to the nearest major station and then change to an ordinary train. Ordinary trains are cheaper because you do not have to pay the express surcharge.

Tokyo Station is a vast complex, with several exits connected by passageways and large underground shopping complexes. The original red-brick structure, built in 1914, can still be seen on the Marunouchi side of the station. The *shinkansen* tracks are on the Yaesu South side – make sure you get the taxi driver to take you to the right side! The Marunouchi subway line can be joined from the north side of the station and from there you can connect to any of the JR subway lines. If you arrive in Tokyo your *shinkansen* ticket entitles you to travel on any of Tokyo's JR subway lines to your destination.

Airports
Tokyo has two airports, Narita (some 40 miles or 66 km north of the city) and Haneda (in the city). All international flights, with the exception of China Airlines, the carrier of Taiwan, fly from Narita and most domestic flights leave from Haneda. A limousine bus connects the two airports and takes about two hours.

Narita Airport was completed in 1978, in the teeth of much protest from local farmers, who lost fields in the process. The protests over the years have been violent and security approaching the airport is tight. There are now two terminals, Terminal 1 (the old one, divided into north and south wings) and Terminal 2 (the new one). This has helped ease some of the congestion – a welcome development, as passage through Narita was beginning to become quite time-consuming and unpleasant. The airport has the usual collection of coffee-shops, bars and restaurants – beware, most of them close at 20.00 – as well as shops selling gifts, electronic goods and duty-free items, and several banks. Make sure you check which terminal your flight leaves from. The Narita Express (see below) stops first at Terminal 2 and then Terminal 1.

Passengers leaving from Narita have to pay a ¥2,000 (US$18.66) passenger service **tax** (¥1,000 (US$9.33) for children aged 2 to 11). There are various ways of travelling between the city and Narita:

- Limousine **buses** run to a number of points in Tokyo, including the Tokyo City Air Terminal (ten minutes' walk from Ningyocho Station on the Hibiya line and a short taxi ride from Tokyo Station, where the bus makes a stop). There are also buses direct to major hotels, which depart every few minutes, and to Yokohama City Air Terminal, Shinjuku Station and Haneda Airport.

- The **Keisei Skyliner train**, which runs from Keisei Ueno Station to Keisei Narita station, takes about an hour and is comfortable and reliable. All seats are reserved. From Keisei Narita, it is a short shuttle ride to the airport.

- The **JR Narita Express** departs from Yokohama, Shinjuku, Ikebukuro and Tokyo Station, from where it takes about an hour to reach Narita Airport. All seats are reserved. It is worth booking in advance, as this is one of the most reasonable and convenient ways of getting to the airport. Japan Rail passes can be used on this service.

- A **taxi** from Narita into the centre of Tokyo or vice versa will be very costly and time-consuming (over ¥20,000 or US$186.57).

Haneda Airport is very central and is connected by monorail from Hamamatsucho Station (JR, Yamanote line). Trains leave every few minutes and take approximately fifteen minutes.

The limousine **bus** departs every 40 minutes and stops at major hotels. There are also buses to Narita and to Yokohama. **Taxis** to and from Haneda Airport are not particularly expensive, but it takes about 45 minutes to get to or from Tokyo Station.

The facilities at Haneda are fairly limited, and all coffee-shops, restaurants and bars close at 20.30.

Sightseeing

For those with limited time, sights not to be missed in Tokyo include:

- **Asakusa Kannon Temple** The oldest temple in Tokyo, Asakusa Kannon, officially known as Sensoji, was first built in the seventh century to house an image of Kannon, the Buddhist goddess of mercy. The temple has a five-storey pagoda and is famous for its huge red lantern (4 feet or 1.2m tall) which hangs in the temple gateway – 'Kaminari-mon' or 'Lightning Gate'. The tiny stalls in the narrow streets around the temple are always thronged with people and are a good place to buy souvenirs.

- **The Imperial Palace** The official residence of the emperor, the palace itself is only open twice a year, on New Year's Day and on the emperor's birthday (23 December). However, it is pleasant to walk around the East Garden, which is an attractive park with landscaped lawns and flowers. The koi carp in the moats are also quite impressive.

- **Meiji shrine** The shrine was built in the early twentieth century to commemorate the Emperor Meiji. It is set in wooded parkland among trees, streams and flowers. Although always full of pilgrims and visitors, it gives the impression of fresh air and tranquillity in the middle of the bustle of Tokyo. It is particularly popular in June, when its famous irises bloom. It is also nice to visit at the Shichigosan (Seven–Five–Three) Festival, when it is visited by families with children aged 3, 5 and 7 all dressed in traditional Japanese style.

- **Goto Art Museum** This contains Japanese and Chinese paintings, calligraphy and ceramics. The thousand-year-old Genji Monogotari scrolls are also displayed here for one week in May.

- **Tokyo National Museum** This houses the largest collection of Japanese art in the world, only a fraction of which is on display at any one time. There are also excellent temporary exhibitions.

- **Tokyo National Museum of Modern Art** This houses an extensive collection of Japanese art from the Meiji period onwards.

- **Japan Folkcrafts Museum** This has a changing display of furniture, ceramics and textiles, set in an old wooden house, brought in pieces from the countryside and reconstructed here.

If you have a bit longer to spare, it is well worth taking a day-trip to **Kamakura**, one of the old capitals of Japan, which is about an hour away from Tokyo on the Yokosuka Line. It is an attractively situated town, on the sea, with wooded hills on three sides. Hundreds of temples dot the hillsides. Well worth seeing are the Daibutsu – a great bronze Buddha cast in 1252 – and the Zeni Arai Benten – the 'Money Washing Temple', where money washed in the spring and dried in incense smoke is reputed to double in value. It is just as well Japan has a low crime rate, as any aspiring bank-robber would have easy pickings here from all the people carrying baskets of ten-thousand-yen notes!

Nikko is a bit further from Tokyo, taking 1 hour 45 minutes from Asakusa Station by the Tobu private line. Nikko is full of historical sites, the most popular place to visit being the great Toshogu shrine, built in 1636 by Shogun Iemitsu in honour of his grandfather Tokugawa Ieyasu. After visiting the shrine, visitors often take a bus to visit Lake Chuzenji and the Kegon waterfall, which spills out of one end of the lake in a spectacular 316-foot (96-metre) drop.

OTHER MAJOR CITIES
Osaka

Osaka, capital of the Kansai area, is Japan's business capital. It is thought of as a 'city of merchants', with natives of Osaka having a national reputation for being money-grabbing. A standard greeting is *'Mo kari makka!'* – 'Made any money?'. A huge industrial and commercial city, Osaka produces about a quarter of Japan's industrial output, including textiles, iron and steel. The city's airport and docks handle 40 per cent of the country's total exports. It is also home to Japan's pharmaceutical industry and some of the great business and banking houses have their origins here; for example, Daiwa, Sanwa, Marubeni and Sumitomo. New developments include the Kansai International Airport and the Osaka Business Park.

Osaka is accessible to the rest of Japan by **rail, bus or air**. JR railway lines and private lines (the most famous being the Hanshin and Hankyu lines) link it with major cities and there is an extensive **subway** network of JR and private lines. Osaka's subway system is marginally less confusing for westerners to use than Tokyo's. All the station names are given in Roman script and maps are easily available. From Osaka to Tokyo takes about three hours by *shinkansen*.

Taxi drivers in Osaka tend to be friendlier and more likely to stop for foreigners than Tokyo taxi drivers. However, they are equally unlikely to be able to speak English or to be able to find an address without specific directions in Japanese.

Itami – Osaka International Airport – handles flights from Europe, North America and Asia, as well as connections to every major Japanese city. The airport is quite central, and it takes only about half an hour to get to the centre of the city. Because of this, take-offs and landings are only permitted between 06.00 and 21.00, and all the facilities at the airport close at 19.30. Nevertheless, travelling via Itami Airport is relatively hassle-free, and if you have business in Osaka or Kobe, it may well be worth flying directly into Osaka. You can then go on to Tokyo by train, or fly into Haneda and avoid the long trek into Tokyo from Narita.

Limousine **buses** leave Itami every 7–8 minutes between 07.00 and 21.30, stopping at major hotels and stations. The journey takes about half an hour – up to an hour in rush-hour traffic.

Kobe

Kobe, also in Kansai, is a thriving industrial city and Japan's busiest port. It has the largest container capacity in the world, and its industries, which include shipbuilding and iron and steel production, are mainly related to the port. As Kobe was one of the first ports to be opened to trade with the west in 1868, many westerners settled here and set up businesses. As a result, a flourishing foreign community grew up and Kobe still has a very international flavour. In Kitano – one of the high-class residential areas with consulates, night-clubs and restaurants – streets full of old western-style houses built by early foreign residents can be found.

Kobe's situation, squeezed between the sea and the mountains, means that the city can only expand into the sea and several artificial islands have been created to house residential, industrial and cultural areas.

Kobe is easily accessible from Osaka's **Itami Airport** (see above). Limousine **buses** run to and from Kobe's Sannomiya Station and take around 40 minutes.

The *shinkansen* from Osaka and Tokyo stops at Shin-Kobe station (check that the train actually stops; not all of the *hikaris* do).

Kobe is linked with Kyoto and Osaka by the private Hanshin and Hankyu lines and by JR ordinary **trains** and *shinkansen*. Sannomiya Station, in one of Kobe's busiest shopping areas, is the terminal for JR lines and private lines. Train lines run east and west, parallel to the coast through the city, with a few lines going north to south. (Kobe is a long, narrow city, so north-south distances are fairly short and manageable on foot, or by taxi.) A driverless monorail connects Port Island with

Sannomiya Station, taking a circular route around Port Island. One of the city's best hotels, the Portopia, is situated here. Station names and announcements are in English as well as Japanese.

Sightseeing: Kansai area

Osaka is not a great place for sightseeing. The castle is worth a visit, although the original buildings were destroyed and have been replaced by a reconstruction. It does have a number of interesting museums and shrines – details will be available from your hotel or tourist information office.

Kobe is worth a visit, as it is attractively situated between the mountains and the sea. Visitors generally go up Mount Rokko by cable car to see the views from the peak across the city and the Inland Sea to Shikoku Island. On the other side of the peak there is a ropeway to Arima Spa, a famous hot-spring resort.

Himeji is also accessible from both Kobe and Osaka and is the home of the 'White Heron' castle, considered one of the most beautiful in Japan and featured in the 'Shogun' films. Himeji is about an hour to the west of Osaka by train.

Kyoto

Kyoto is a must for any visitor to Japan. Even if you have no other cause to visit the Kansai area, it is worth making a special trip. It takes about two and a half hours to get to Kyoto by *shinkansen* from Tokyo. From Osaka or Kobe it takes about half an hour by ordinary JR train or private line (even less by *shinkansen*). At first sight, Kyoto looks like any other Japanese city, but beyond the bustling main streets lie over 1,600 temples and several palaces, set in hilly woodlands. Kyoto was the capital of Japan and the home of the imperial family from 794 until 1868. Although the centre of administrative power moved to Tokyo, Kyoto remained the home of traditional culture and the arts.

It is impossible to visit all the sights in Kyoto in one visit, but the tourist information office outside the station is very good at suggesting possible routes to take in a few of the major attractions.

Nara

Nara can be reached in under an hour from Kyoto, and is well worth a day-trip. The JR line takes 50 minutes and the Kintetsu–Nara line takes 35. Nara's main claim to fame is its huge deer park with over a thousand tame deer. You can walk through the park to visit many of the places of interest, including the Todaiji temple, which has both the world's largest wooden structure and the world's largest bronze Buddha (weighing over 7.2 tons and over 50 feet or 15.5 m high, dating from AD 752).

Nagoya

Nagoya, a prosperous commercial and industrial city, is Japan's fourth largest city – with a population of over 2 million – and third largest port. Conveniently located in the centre of the Tokaido industrial belt, its heavy industries include automobile manufacture and its light industries include porcelain, ceramics and pearl jewellery, for which the area has been famous since the twelfth century. Nagoya is home to the renowned Noritake company and to Mikimoto Pearls. The city was virtually destroyed during the war and has been completely rebuilt, in a neat grid, with wide boulevards, which make it quite easy to find your way around the central district on foot.

It is possible to **fly** direct to Nagoya – (Nagoya International) Komaki Airport – from an increasing number of international destinations, including Hong Kong, Seoul, Bangkok, Manila and several European, Australian and US destinations, as well as from major Japanese cities. The airport is conveniently situated and passage through it is quick and efficient. Facilities are fairly limited. A large new airport is in the feasibility study stage. From Tokyo, it is probably as easy to take the *shinkansen*. From the airport, there are buses into the Meitetsu Bus Centre, near Nagoya Station. The trip takes about 40 minutes. Taxis are marginally quicker, but much more expensive.

Nagoya is two hours away from Tokyo and 50 minutes from Kyoto by *shinkansen*. It is linked to smaller surrounding towns and suburbs by JR lines and by the Meitetsu and Kintetsu private railway lines. Nagoya is a good place to stay if you have business in the area, and if you have meetings in both the Kansai and Tokyo areas. Toyohashi, outside Nagoya, is equidistant from Tokyo and Osaka on the *shinkansen* line, and its recently built Holiday Tower Hotel has very reasonably priced, comfortable accommodation and business/conference facilities. Nagoya has an efficient, modern **subway** system, which is not too difficult for foreigners to use. English maps are available from the Tourist Information Centre.

The extensive **bus** system may be difficult to use, unless you have good Japanese. However, there is a circular bus with a fixed fare, which follows a route round the centre of the city, and is quite convenient.

Sightseeing: Nagoya region

The region around Nagoya has a rich history. Japan's most famous warlords – Oda Nobunaga, Toyotomi Hideyoshi and

Tokugawa Ieyasu – all came from the area, and some of the
greatest battles of Japanese history took place here. The city
grew up around the strongholds of the warlords and the great
castle built by Tokugawa Ieyasu in 1612 for his son. Unfortunately, most of Nagoya's historical sites were destroyed in
World War II. The present castle is a 1959 ferro-concrete copy.
It is still well worth seeing, set in beautiful grounds and housing
a collection of art treasures.

Also worth a visit are:

- **Atsuta shrine** This is one of Japan's three holiest
  shrines and home of the Sacred Grass-Mowing Sword
  (one of the emperor's pieces of ceremonial regalia). It
  was founded in the third century and its great wooden
  buildings stand in glades of ancient, towering cedars.
- **Tokugawa Art Museum** This museum, built on the
  site of the Tokugawa mansion, contains a collection of
  Japanese paintings, ceramics, lacquerware and prints.

The countryside around Nagoya is quite beautiful and
it is worth trying to get out of the city. Popular days out
include:

- **Gifu** Gifu City is about an hour away from Nagoya on
  the Meitetsu line. Situated on the Nagaragawa River,
  the town is surrounded by wooded hills and overlooked
  by a small castle. Parasols, lanterns and paper goods are
  made here. It is also the home of cormorant fishing
  (*u-kai*), which takes place in the summer months.
  Fishing boats paddle up and down the river, containing
  cormorants on leads. Lured by the light from torches
  suspended from the prows of the boats, the *ayu* fish rise
  to the surface and are snapped up and brought to the
  boats by cormorants, with rings round their necks to
  prevent them swallowing the fish. (They are rewarded
  with an occasional fish to eat.) Spectators can book
  places on boats which are paddled up and down while
  the visitors are served food and drinks.
- **Meiji Mura** A 60-minute bus ride out of Nagoya, Meiji
  Mura is a large hillside theme park housing 50
  significant buildings of the Meiji period (1868–1912).
  These include the house occupied in turn by novelists
  Mori Ogai and Natsume Soseki.
- **Inuyama** Just down the road from Meiji Mura is
  Inuyama, where you can see Japan's oldest surviving
  castle, dating from 1440.

- **Ise** Nagoya is also a convenient place from which to visit the Grand Ise Shrine – the heart of the Shinto religion and the most important shrine in Japan. Situated in the Ise Shima National Park, the shrine itself is quite plain and the wooden buildings have been ceremonially rebuilt every twenty years. The shrine in fact consists of two separate shrines about a mile (two kilometres) apart, the Naiku (inner), dedicated to the sun-goddess Amaterasu, and the Geku (outer), dedicated to the goddess of farms. The sun-goddess is the supreme deity of the Shinto religion and the mythical forebear of the emperor of Japan. Within both shrines there is an area which is reserved for the emperor and shrine officials, within which are kept the three sacred treasures of the imperial family – mirror, sword and jewel.

- **Toba** Any bus trip or tour to Ise is likely to include a stop at Toba to see the women pearl divers. There are about 3,500 of them; well-wrapped-up, middle-aged ladies who float their wooden buckets on the surface, then double up like ducks and disappear under the surface for whole minutes at a time. In fact, they rarely dive for pearls now, but they collect sea vegetables on the bottom. They dive every 40 minutes and can be watched from Pearl Island, which is a kind of shrine to the memory of Kokichi Mikimoto, the father of the cultured pearl. The process of producing cultured pearls can be watched, with explanations in English.

Sapporo

Sapporo is the capital of Hokkaidō, the large northern island of Japan, and its cultural, economic and political centre. The island was settled by the Japanese as late as the nineteenth century. It is sparsely populated, with 22 per cent of Japan's total land area but only 5 per cent of its population. The majority of the population is Japanese (of the Yamato race), but there are a few inhabitants of indigenous race – the Ainu, Gilyak and Oroke. Hokkaidō produces much of Japan's food, including most of its dairy produce. Other products include potatoes, sweetcorn, wheat and beans. Key industries are fishing and forestry, with 70 per cent of the land under timber. Sapporo is a centre for winter sports.

Sapporo can be reached by *shinkansen* from Tokyo in around ten and a half hours. The 21-mile (33.6-km) Seikan tunnel connecting Hokkaidō with Honshū was completed in March 1988. It is also possible to travel by **ferry** (33 hours from Tokyo to Kushiro, and 31 hours from Tokyo to Tomakomai).

Most visitors **fly** in, however. The journey takes 1 hour and 30 minutes from Tokyo and slightly longer from Osaka. Chitose Airport, 25 miles (40 km) south of Sapporo, is a large, efficient, modern airport with a few international flights and regular connections to major cities in Japan. JAL and ANA operate bus services at fifteen-minute intervals during plane arrival and departure times. The buses stop at major hotels and take slightly longer than an hour. There are also trains to and from the airport station. The express takes around 35 minutes and the ordinary train about 50 minutes. Taxis take around 45 minutes and are quite costly.

Sapporo is conveniently laid out in a regular grid and streets are numbered north and south and east and west, so it is quite easy to find your way around. The **subway** is efficient, quiet (it runs on rubber tyres!) and quite straightforward for foreigners. As with other cities, the **bus** system is extensive, but difficult to use unless your Japanese is good and you know where you are going.

Sightseeing: Sapporo region

Sapporo has few historic sights, but the spectacular mountains, hot springs and lakes of Hokkaidō are within easy reach. It is also worth seeing the relics of Ainu culture in the Batchelor Museum of Ainu Artefacts. This contains over 20,000 Ainu and Gilyak artefacts collected by Dr John Batchelor, an English clergyman who lived in Sapporo in the late nineteenth century. The collection is in the old wooden house that was his home.

A worthwhile day out can be spent at Shikotsu-Toya National Park, 45 miles (72 km) south-west of Sapporo. Lake Toya, within the park, is a circular volcanic lake, and there are also mountains, forests, volcanoes and hot springs. The most famous hot spring, Noboribetsu, has one part called 'Hell Valley', which is a spectacular cauldron of hissing, boiling streams and sulphurous fumes.

Fukuoka

Fukuoka is the capital and the economic, cultural and communications centre of Kyūshū, Japan's large southern island. It is a flourishing modern business city and port, with a pleasant, semitropical climate. Its proximity to Asia made it a leading trading port and a major route through which Chinese culture filtered into Japan in ancient times. Main products include electrical appliances, tools, textiles and foodstuffs. The major corporation in Fukuoka is Nishietsu, which runs the buses, a private railway, department stores and hotels. A number of consulates, including the American and the Korean, are based in the city.

Fukuoka is seven hours' journey from Tokyo and around four from Osaka by *shinkansen*. The journey is not much cheaper than by plane, unless you have a Japan Rail Pass. There are international and domestic services to and from Fukuoka **Airport**, which is conveniently situated about a 10–20-minute drive from the city centre. The flight from Tokyo takes about 1 hour and 45 minutes. From Osaka the train is as convenient.

Taxis from the airport to the city are quite affordable, but there is also a bus service to Hakata Station, from where you will have to take another bus or a taxi to your destination.

Fukuoka is not a large town, and is laid out more or less in a grid pattern, making it quite easy to walk around. Traffic is not nearly as heavy as in Tokyo or Osaka, so **taxis** are a reasonable and quick alternative for longer distances. Taxi drivers are friendly and usually able to find the major restaurants, hotels and offices.

Fukuoka's **subway** is gradually being extended, and is very modern, clean, efficient and relatively uncrowded. All signs are in English and Japanese. Fukuoka is serviced by JR lines and by the private Nishietsu lines. The **train** is the best way to travel to the suburbs and surrounding small towns.

Sightseeing: Fukuoka region

There is little to see in Fukuoka itself, but there are many interesting places to visit just outside the city, and if you have a few days spare, you can explore Kyūshū.

3 History

ANCIENT JAPAN

The earliest accounts of Japanese history to have been produced by Japanese writers claim that a unified state was created by the Emperor Jimmu as early as 660 BC. Jimmu is heralded as a direct descendant of the sun-goddess (Amaterasu Omikami) and the first emperor of Japan. Chinese historical records, however, make the earliest references to Japan – in the first century AD – and they describe a country made up of many tribes at war with one another. Various theories exist regarding the origins of these early inhabitants of the Japanese islands and the process of the formation of the earliest Japanese 'state'.

Archaeological and anthropological studies provide information which helps us to construct a picture of the early settlements. The main wave of immigrant settlers to Japan appears to have come from the regions to the north of China and from Korea. They are likely to have been pushed into mass emigration as a result of Chinese military campaigns. Attempts to unify and expand the Chinese empire northwards drove these groups of Mongoloid peoples down the Korean peninsula and across the waters to western Japan. There are also signs of Malayo-Polynesian influences in the social structure and language patterns of the Japanese, suggesting another possible wave of migration.

Jōmon (7500–200 BC) and Yayoi (300 BC–AD 33)

Pottery, tools, weapons, burial mounds and rubbish tips are some of the richest sources of information we have about these early settlers. The two main groups about which we have some knowledge are the Jōmon (7500–200 BC) and the Yayoi (300 BC–AD 33).

The name 'Jōmon' derives from the twisted rope patterns

they made on their clay pots. The Jōmon people were Stone-Age hunter-gatherers, but evidence from old settlement sites and the shell mounds (basically rubbish tips) suggests that they eventually began to establish more permanent settlements.

During the third century BC another wave of immigrants – the Yayoi – who used bronze and iron and cultivated rice, began to overshadow the Jōmon as the dominant culture. There was no destruction of the earlier culture and replacement by the new one; instead, in a pattern repeated throughout Japanese history, there was a layering effect, with the new elements, initially at least, coexisting with the old. The discovery of Chinese objects dating from various periods at Yayoi settlements suggests that this group of Mongoloid settlers had contacts with Chinese civilization.

Rice cultivation demanded a high level of social organization to guarantee the labour needed for irrigation projects, planting and harvesting. Permanent, well-organized communities were needed for this level of cooperation. The existence of some sort of hierarchy and the ability to gather massive amounts of labour power is suggested also by the development, between AD 300 and 645, of the Kōfun or tomb-culture period. This saw the erection of large, earthen burial mounds for tribal leaders – construction schemes comparable to the Egyptian pyramids. This practice of building tombs and the clay figurines which were placed on them confirm the existence of a warrior elite in society and also Korean influences (burial mounds were built in Korea too). One of the many tribes in this social structure managed to prevail over the others (though it is not clear exactly how) during the fourth century AD, and began the first attempt at creating a unified state.

Yamato (*ca.* AD 300–538)

The Yamato state, the first Japanese state, emerged from a social and political structure based on tribes or clans and supported by a rice economy. Each clan had a chief, whose position was hereditary, and everyone in the clan worshipped a common deity who was regarded as the founding ancestor of that clan. The chiefs' positions as heads of the clans (also their basis for political, social and economic power) rested on the claim of descent from the clan deity. As a powerful clan managed to overpower and subdue other nearby clans, these were incorporated into the victorious one, which thus grew bigger and stronger. The clan which managed to win some form of supremacy or at least recognition above most of the others worshipped the sun-goddess, and it attempted to consolidate political power in the form of the Yamato state. Along with recognition of its superior position *vis-à-vis* the other clans came acceptance of its deity as supreme also. Thus, the sun-goddess came to represent the socio-religious position of the head of the sun-line clan and also of the Yamato state. There was a fusing of religious and political symbols. The heads of the sun-line clan became the emperors and empresses of Japan, and it is through this claim to descent from the sun-goddess that the Japanese imperial family purports to have the longest unbroken imperial line (see: Religion).

In the early Yamato period, the social and political structures of the new state were recognizably Japanese in influence – for example, stressing hereditary over meritocratic principles. These Japanese features were not replaced completely by new ideas on government and administration, adapted from the Chinese model, but they became one of many layers of practice. In the fifth and sixth centuries the Yamato state sent numerous expeditions to Korea. These were not only military campaigns: they also resulted in the movement of considerable numbers of teachers and skilled craft-workers from Korea to Japan. It was in this period that Japan began to learn about Chinese writing, Confucian and Buddhist texts (see: Religion) and Chinese ideas on government. To the head of the Yamato state, Chinese ideas about centralized state power, the emperor as Son of Heaven, and a system of court titles and ranks that would make the members of other powerful clan families – currently holding court titles – 'officials' of the emperor were very appealing. It is important to remember that the imperial family faced challenges to its power from these other families and was eager to centralize power as much as possible.

The introduction of Buddhism to Japan, via Korea, sparked a major conflict among the large clan families. The imperial family favoured its introduction, as an ideology that could be used to bolster the power of the ruler of the state. Buddhism was in fact used by the imperial family as a state cult without any apparent sense of conflict with their own Shinto underpinning. Other clan families, however, opposed the introduction of Buddhism. They felt threatened by the idea that Buddha would be placed above all local deities – that is, over their own ancestral deities. The introduction of Buddhism was secured when one, of what would be many, astute political manipulators of the imperial family (the Soga clan) supported the imperial family in this dispute. The main opponents were defeated in battle and the Soga gained a strong court position from which they were able to dominate the imperial family.

Asuka (538–645)

In the sixth century, Shōtoku Taishi, a descendant of both the imperial and Soga families, became regent and worked earnestly to increase the power of the emperor and the imperial family. It was Shōtoku Taishi, during the Asuka period, who introduced many elements of Chinese government in an attempt to centralize political power in the imperial institution. After his death, however, the power struggles between the powerful families resumed. The Soga family was defeated by another powerful family – the Fujiwara – who went on to control the imperial family for approximately five centuries. Continuing Shōtoku Taishi's political and administrative programme of centralization was also in the Fujiwaras' own interests. Gradually, greater centralization, a census and law codes were developed, and in 710, Japan had its first permanent capital at present-day Nara.

ARISTOCRATIC JAPAN
Nara (710–84)

The reorganization of Japan's political system into a centralized state system continued in the Nara period. Despite the gaps between the theory of political change and the actual extent of changes, the reforms of the Nara period (known as the Taiho Law Codes) did help to decrease the power of many clan families and strengthen the official power of the emperor. That Japan's rulers borrowed from China in this period is not surprising given the splendid nature of Tang China, which was a cultural magnet for many countries. The highly centralized Chinese capital of Changan, with its elaborate official court and system of court titles, was an attractive model for Japanese emperors and also for those powerful families that stood to gain from a strengthening of the imperial institution. It was around this time that the leaders of the sun-line clan came to be called *tenno* – similar to the Chinese son of heaven.

The modifications made to the Chinese concept of the emperor by Japan's rulers are representative of a process of selective borrowing and skilful adaptation of foreign concepts that Japan has displayed in successive historical periods. In the Chinese system, the emperor held a mandate from heaven and could be deposed if events suggested that he had lost that mandate – for example, misrule, large-scale social upheaval or natural disasters. In Japan, the position of the emperor remained hereditary and, although often manipulated by powerful court families, he could not be deposed. (There were some very powerful empresses in Japan, but most of the time Japanese imperial rulers were men.)

Most of the information available about the lives of the Japanese people in the Nara and the subsequent Heian period is about the lives of aristocratic elites. There are court records, poems, songs, novels and paintings that depict their lifestyles, pastimes, religious practices, court rituals, and political and romantic intrigues. Few records exist of the lives of ordinary people whose activities produced the silk, rice and other products that supported the nobility's sumptuous lifestyle. It can, however, be surmised that tremendous agricultural activity was being undertaken to produce this surplus.

The introduction of Buddhism had been undertaken as a means of helping to bolster a new official ideology, but it spurred many other cultural developments as well. The Korean and Chinese teachers who had been brought to Japan to teach about Buddhism, and the Chinese writing system so that the Japanese, who had no writing system, could record Buddhist texts and legal codes, often became high-ranking members of the Japanese nobility. The use of Chinese characters to write down Japanese words (the two languages belong to separate families!) has produced over time one of the most difficult languages to read and write. Many Korean and Chinese skilled artisans also came to Japan to sculpt religious icons, build temples and teach Chinese. Nara was a period of tremendous cultural activity fed in large part by the brilliance of Chinese culture at the Tang court.

A knowledge of the Chinese literary classics became a must for nobles who wished to be held in high regard. Only men were expected to be able to write and read Chinese characters. These were seen as too hard for women, but some brilliant female authors appeared in the Heian period, who had secretly learnt the characters and could read the Chinese classics. The newly acquired writing system was used to compile records of Japanese literary works – for example, the *Manyōshū*, an anthology of Japanese poems (see: The Arts). The first official histories were also commissioned by the imperial court during the Nara period. These were the *Kojiki* and the *Nihon shoki*. The claim that Jimmu founded the Japanese nation in 660 BC is to be found in these works. The motivation for writing these histories is clear when seen in the context of a period of considerable efforts to emulate China and also to increase the prestige of the imperial family.

Temple architecture and bronze-casting were some of the artistic and technical skills introduced to Japan alongside Buddhism. The Tōdaiji temple in Nara (see: Gazetteer) is a fine example of the early patronage of Buddhism by Japanese emperors and the skills of the craft-workers who built it. Buddhism gained official status as emperors sponsored the erection of temples and the court adopted Buddhist rituals. The ease with which Buddhism incorporated aspects of other religions made its coexistence alongside Shinto possible. The sun-goddess was presented as yet another manifestation of the Buddha. As with the adaptation of Chinese Confucian concepts of the Son of Heaven, sponsorship of Buddhism provided the Japanese ruler with another set of ideas and images that added (religious) weight to his power and prestige. In time, however, the power of the Buddhist monks, who had taken advantage of their close relationship to the imperial court, grew so great that the court decided to move the capital away from the influence of the great temples that it had built.

This move out of Nara and eventually to present-day Kyoto signalled the beginning of a new era – the Heian period, after the old name for Kyoto ('Heian' means 'City of Peace/Tranquillity'). Although a new period name is used, there was no sudden change in policies and practices. While there were new developments in the Heian period, trends of Chinese borrowing and adaptation continued for some time.

In summary, by the end of the Nara period the imperial court had restyled itself along Chinese lines but without forgoing all the structures of political rule upon which the Yamato state had been established. Court ranks and titles were adopted but remained on a hereditary basis, and members of powerful families were appointed to them purely on the grounds of existing wealth, social standing or services to the imperial court.

Heian (794–1185)

The Heian period is sometimes subdivided into Early Heian and then the Fujiwara period. The name Fujiwara was granted to the aristocratic family that had helped to rid the imperial family of the Soga family's influence. By the middle of the ninth century, the Fujiwara exerted such a hold over the emperor that the rest of the Heian period (858–1185) bears their name. Thus, while the move away from Nara had been calculated to free the imperial court from the influence of the Buddhist monks, it had not diminished the threat from other powerful families seeking political power. The Fujiwara had been particularly loyal and trusted advisors to the emperor since their part in overthrowing the Soga family; they were given high court titles and positions of state, and they provided concubines for the emperors. It was by placing his infant nephew on the throne and then naming himself regent (ruler on the infant emperor's behalf) that the head of the Fujiwara family inaugurated the centuries of Fujiwara dominance of the court that were to follow.

There were also other court families with political aspirations, and the social and economic forces which had brought the Fujiwara to power were working to increase the wealth and power of these families in the capital and in the provinces.

These social and economic forces grew out of a system of private landholding (shōen) in which the lands of various ranks of the nobility, religious institutions and others rewarded by the court were exempt from central government administration and taxation. The reforms mentioned earlier had aimed to increase the centralized power of the emperors and had declared all land registered by the census to be the property of the emperor. These lands became the source of the central government's and the imperial family's revenues. Naturally, as the amount of land held in a private capacity by nobles, temples, shrines and others increased, the income of the imperial family decreased. The Fujiwara, not surprisingly, held the largest amount of private, tax-free land.

It was not only court families who benefited from this process but also the newly emerging provincial warrior families who would eventually become a provincial aristocracy. These provincial families benefited in two ways from this process of increasing decentralization represented by the shōen: they stepped in to fill a vacuum created by the declining effectiveness of central government, policing and maintenance of law and order; and they acted as administrative officials, tax collectors and policemen on the estates of court families. In this way, powerful provincial families developed strong bands of fighting men who helped to keep the peace and to fight rival local powerholders. Fighting and disorder was aggravated by the breakdown of central government's local machinery and the rush to aggrandize landholdings in the provinces. This situation also drove small landholders to place their lands in the hands of large, private landholders in return for protection. An additional factor that helped the growth of these local officials and warriors, at the long-term expense of the central government, was the more personal nature of the bond that developed between the local lord and his officials and warriors. Direct personal loyalty in return for rewards formed a stronger bond than loyalty to a far-away emperor or court noble.

Although the power of the imperial family and its wealth declined throughout the Heian period, its symbolic importance did not. The closeness of religious and political functions in the person of the emperor gave him a powerful legitimizing role. The Fujiwara (like the Soga before them and many shōgun – supreme military commanders – after them) might have had the power to force their control on the emperors, but they recognized the value of claiming to derive legitimacy for their political actions from the imperial institution.

This period, in which power moved gradually away from the imperial capital, none the less saw a flourishing of the literary arts in Japan. There was also considerable diffusion of court culture to other parts of Japan as contact developed between the court and the developing provinces. During the Heian period there was a more conscious creation of Japanese styles. Chinese influences did not disappear, but artists no longer looked solely to China for models of good art. The type of Japanese painting developed in this period is tellingly named *Yamato-e* (Yamato paintings). Two great classics of world literature – *The Tale of Genji* and *The Pillow Book of Sei Shonagon* – were also written in this period by Japanese court women (see: The Arts). The creation of a phonetic script, in the ninth century, helped this development of a more 'native' literature and also enabled more women to write. (The authors of the books mentioned above were both accomplished in Chinese writing and were familiar with Chinese classics.) On the subject of women, it is interesting to note that in Heian Japan women could still inherit property.

The end of the Heian period and of the 'Aristocratic Age' did not come suddenly but was in the making for a long time. As well as a general decline in the power of the centre *vis-à-vis* the provinces, there were several challenges to Fujiwara control of the court. The first came from powerful emperors born of non-Fujiwara mothers, who attempted to reassert the authority of the imperial family. The second was a direct challenge to the power of the central government (Fujiwara and imperial families alike) from the leaders of the two most powerful military families in the provinces – the Taira and then the Minamoto. This sort of challenge from the provincial aristocracy is not surprising given the growth of private landholdings, the declining power and authority of central government in the provinces, and the loyal followings built up by provincial lords. The Taira and Minamoto family heads commanded strong, loyal followings because of their proven valour in the field, their ability to reward their faithful vassals and also, ironically, their noble descent. 'Taira' and 'Minamoto' were surnames given to some of the excess imperial offspring who were sent to the provinces to make their way in the world.

THE AGE OF THE SAMURAI

Rivalries and conflicts were rife in Kyoto towards the end of the Heian period. The first emperor of the Heian period had sponsored two new Buddhist sects in Kyoto, as a counter to the power of the Nara sects. Each had its headquarters on mountains just outside the new capital. The power of the Nara sects diminished by the end of the Heian period, but Buddhist monasteries were causing trouble for the court once again. Large groups of monks, and troops gathered by them, fought in the streets of Kyoto. At the same time there were succession disputes within the imperial family and rivalries between court families – in short, a state of chaos in the capital. Provincial warriors had been relied on for some time to quell disturbances in the capital, and in 1160 the Taira and the Minamoto were enlisted on opposite sides, in a court battle for imperial succession. The Taira side won, and by executing the Minamoto leaders they gained supremacy. An infant male of the Minamoto family was spared death and he later returned to exact revenge on the Taira.

The head of the Taira family was rewarded by the successful emperor with the rank of counsellor. This was the first time that such a high court appointment had gone to someone from the provinces. The Taira slotted themselves into the lifestyle of the imperial capital and began playing marriage politics with the imperial family, just as the Fujiwara had done. It was not long, however, before a court plot was hatched to get rid of them. A call for help in fighting the Taira was answered by the infant who had been spared by them twenty years before – Minamoto no Yoritomo. The battle between these two big military families is known as the Gempei War (1180–5), and the decisive battle, which saw the total defeat of the Taira, was at Dan-no-ura. This military clash has inspired many works of art – paintings, kabuki and Noh plays, such as *The Tale of the Heike*. The battle saw the clash between the new powers from the provinces and the now very courtly looking Taira forces. This was the end of an era.

Kamakura (1185–1333)

The Minamoto had their power base in Kamakura and their leader, Yoritomo, anxious to avoid the 'effete' influences of courtly life on his warriors, made this the new political capital of Japan. Yorimoto was also wise enough to see the advantage in consolidating his control over wider political power and wealth by building up local power bases. Yoritomo recognized that, as the only real power in the country able to maintain order and collect taxes, the imperial court would value his services more than if he were to become another court power.

Yoritomo built Kamakura into the first *bakufu*, or military government. Meanwhile the imperial court bestowed numerous military titles on him, which gave him the power to appoint military governors and other local officials. By using these appointments skilfully he was able to build an administrative network that covered most provinces and was directly responsible to him. These powers also enabled him to reward loyal followers with appointments and, as his power and prestige grew accordingly, increasing numbers of samurai placed themselves in his service and their properties under his protection.

The system of military government built up by Yoritomo did not replace the old imperial government: they existed alongside each other and the leaders of the Kamakura government continued to receive titles from the old government. In 1192, Yorimoto was given the title of Shogun by the emperor. Although Yoritomo had enough military and administrative power to control the court, the latter's stamp of legitimacy was not insignificant.

The samurai, who formed the ruling elite until 1871, grew out of the development of powerful local interests. *Bushi* is another word for warrior and forms part of the name given to the code of samurai behaviour – *bushidō* (the way of the warrior). The word 'samurai' denotes one who serves. The samurai class was made up of many levels from the shogun down to the foot soldiers. It was a landed class that trained itself in the martial arts, archery and swordsmanship. *Bushidō* stresses that a samurai should live as if already dead, since death in the lord's service is his goal: life is short and its beauty is in falling (like the cherry blossom).

Yoritomo died in 1199 and was succeeded by his wife, Hōjō Masako. The Hōjō family continued to preside over the Kamakura government until its end in 1333, but unlike Yoritomo they could not claim direct loyalty from his vassals. The Hōjō ruled through offspring of Minamoto and Fujiwara matches; the marriage politics at court continued. Yoritomo's administrative network was so strong that the Hōjō were able to exercise effective control over Japan even after his death. Japan therefore enjoyed political and military stability in this period. Economic developments in this and the following Ashikaga period were also impressive: in agricultural productivity, commercialization of agriculture, the appearance of elements of a market economy, increased use of money, and significant growth in foreign trade.

As is often the case, currents of change were building up beneath the surface of political stability. The various levels of officials who had been appointed by the *bakufu* in the provinces – for example, military governors and land stewards – demanded more recompense for their efforts. These powerful individuals, who had been building up strong loyal followings as they amassed more land and wealth, sought a greater share of political power. Many vassals of the Kamakura shogun found it advantageous to transfer their loyalties to the local power-holders – usually from the military governor and land steward groups – as the economic returns from the positions they had been granted earlier declined. In this way, large military families increased their bands of loyal retainers and their ability to challenge the authority of the Hōjō family.

The growing tension in relations between the Kamakura *bakufu* and its vassals were exacerbated by the expensive military campaigns against the invading Mongol armies. In 1274 and again in 1281, Kublai Khan sent large armies to Japan to force it to submit to his rule. These armies were held back by Japanese armies but were forced to abandon their campaigns when typhoons wrecked most of their ships. These winds were named the *kamikaze* (divine winds). Once the fighting was over there was relief but also considerable dissatisfaction among the warriors who had fought the Mongols. Unlike past battles, these produced no spoils of war to be handed out, and this helped to weaken further the bonds between the Kamakura government and its vassals, many of whom now headed powerful military families themselves.

Ashikaga/Muromachi (1338–1573)

It was ultimately another attempt by an emperor to reassert imperial control that gave one of these military families – the Ashikaga – a chance to wrest political power from the Kamakura government. Ashikaga Takauji was the general sent by the Kamakura government to suppress an uprising by the Emperor Go Daigo in 1331. When Ashikaga got to Kyoto (still the site of the imperial court), he betrayed the Kamakura government and helped the emperor secure his hold over Kyoto. Go Daigo hoped to reassert fully the old centralizing power structures. In 1335, however, Ashikaga removed Go Daigo and had him replaced by an emperor from another line. Then in 1338, Ashikaga proclaimed himself shogun and, by locating the seat of his military government in Kyoto, dealt a decisive blow to the political power of the imperial court. The Ashikaga period is also known as the Muromachi period because the Ashikaga headquarters were in the Muromachi quarter of Kyoto.

Yoritomo had built the Kamakura shogunate on the strength of loyal bonds with vassals: he had won this loyalty by displaying his own military power and through his ability to grant lucrative appointments to loyal vassals. These ties weakened after Yoritomo's death and, while general political stability remained, rival powerful military figures were appearing in other areas. When Ashikaga Takauji created his shogunate he could not claim that he was the unchallenged military leader or that he had a widespread loyal following. The same social forces that had produced his family's power and wealth were still at work in the country and benefiting other powerful families.

After the collapse of the Kamakura government, the struggles to build up the size of landholdings (*shōen*) and of one's military following gave further encouragement to smaller landholders to ally themselves with a powerful local lord for protection. This process encouraged the growth of regional lord–vassal bands and also the appearance of strong local military leaders. Lacking the centralized administrative power of the Kamakura shogunate, the Ashikaga could only maintain stability for as long as they were able to keep up an alliance with other powerful military families.

Much is made of the code of unquestioning loyalty among samurai, but as events such as Takauji's treachery show, this loyalty was not unconditional. There were also destructive rivalries within the large military families. The Ashikaga family suffered an internal succession dispute which led to the Ōnin War of 1467–77. This war destroyed most of Kyoto and also the power of the Ashikaga. Following the Ōnin War, the economic and political power of the imperial and other court families as well as of the Ashikaga declined drastically. By contrast, though, the military and economic power of strong military leaders throughout Japan increased. Throughout the rest of the Ashikaga period and the subsequent Warring States period (Sengoku), conflict and fighting continued between rival branches of families, monasteries and military officials, rival contenders for the imperial throne and rival local power-holders.

These high levels of domestic warfare required a strong economic base to provide the food for the armies, their armour and weapons and the transportation of large amounts of goods. The high levels of agricultural productivity, commercial production and foreign trade mentioned with reference to the Kamakura period had been accompanied by new cultural developments. Zen Buddhism, which had been introduced during the Kamakura period and whose meditative and austere aspects appealed to the samurai, gave rise to a cultural explosion in the troubled years of Ashikaga Japan. Zen monks took part in politics and foreign affairs, and influenced literature and architecture. Zen also influenced painting styles (*suiboku-ga*, black-ink painting) and landscape gardening. The relocation of the political capital away from Kyoto also helped to broaden the audience for artistic works. Picture scrolls, which grew in popularity in the Kamakura period, depicted a much wider variety of topics than ever before and were used, in particular, to extol the warrior ideals or spread new religious messages. The Kamakura and Ashikaga shoguns were generous patrons of the arts, as were many other wealthy individuals, thus helping the growth of Noh, kabuki and the tea ceremony (see: The Arts).

Sengoku (1467–1568)

Although the Ashikaga period is said to span the years 1338–1573, the Ōnin War of 1466–7 plunged Japan into civil warfare which lasted until the unification attempts of three of Japan's great military figures, beginning in 1568. The instability of life during constant warfare did not bring a halt in economic or administrative developments. There was considerable commercial activity to supply the military campaigns, and significant consolidation of landholdings, leading to more efficient local administration and the growth of large urban towns. The old *shōen* – private landholdings – were being replaced by fiefs, and the old military governors were replaced by a new class of local lords – the *daimyō* of the Warring States period.

The new *daimyō* who emerged from this process of local reorganization placed the utmost emphasis on military organization. They built castles and encouraged self-government at the village level. The appearance of large castle towns indicates the change in the nature of warfare – from individual combat by samurai to the deployment of large armies, which had to be housed and fed. The introduction of firearms in the mid-sixteenth century also later influenced fighting styles and the design of castles. It was contacts with European traders and Christian missionaries from the mid-sixteenth century that introduced the Japanese to firearms. These early missionaries were Jesuits who impressed many top samurai with their austerity and learning. Christianity achieved considerable success initially, but was banned in 1613 because of suspicion by the new government of the commercial and military help that contacts with these foreigners could give rival military families (see: Religion).

Unification (1568–1603)

As the fighting continued throughout the Warring States period, powerful *daimyo* began forming regional alliances as a means of increasing their chances of taking over the territory of other, rival *daimyo*. One who was very successful in using alliances to support his moves towards gaining control over all of Japan was Oda Nobunaga – the first of the great unifiers. Oda entered Kyoto, installed his own choice of shogun and then set about brutally suppressing all opposition. His slaughter of Buddhist communities is a vivid example of his brutal single-mindedness. By 1573, Oda felt strong enough to expel the shogun from Kyoto. The changes begun by Oda in reorganizing village administration, tax collection, new land surveys, the unification of weights and measures, and the abolition of guilds and regional trade barriers were important steps towards national unification, and were continued by Oda's successors.

Oda and his son were killed by one of Oda's own generals, a reminder of the still fluid power balance at this time. After further intrigue, Hideyoshi Toyotomi, the second great unifier and Oda's most trusted general, killed the regents for Oda's young son and heir and seized power. Continuing the old tradition of stamping new political power with an old symbol of legitimacy, Hideyoshi assumed a court title which suggested that he received the support of the emperor. His real ability to exercise power lay in his ability to conclude powerful alliances, including one with Tokugawa Ieyasu, one of Oda's old allies and the third figure in the unification story. Via important military successes and the submission of many other opponents, Hideyoshi finally succeeded in achieving the military unification of Japan. This success put him at the head of a group of vassals of very disparate degrees of loyalty. Hideyoshi's counter to this problem was to move the *daimyo* lords around according to their loyalty and in a fashion that would keep the most loyal closest to him, thus guaranteeing maximum protection.

Hideyoshi's continuation of Oda's reform programme brought Japan even closer to national unification. The main changes were a thorough and systematic resurveying of land; the introduction of a new system of land ownership and village organization; the removal of the samurai from the villages, where they could build independent bases of wealth; the disarming of all but the samurai; and the implementation of a rigid social hierarchy. This period, not surprisingly, experienced massive urbanization. Samurai moved into castle towns, as did other groups supplying their needs – artisans, craftworkers and merchants. While these domestic reforms were to have a long-lasting influence, Hideyoshi did not create a stable political structure, and when he died in 1583 the ambition of various political figures who outlived him was only temporarily held in check by his system. The man who finally emerged victorious was Tokugawa Ieyasu.

Tokugawa (1600–1868)

Tokugawa Ieyasu met with initial opposition from some powerful military families, but he also received pledges of support from many others before the Battle of Sekigahara in 1600, at which Tokugawa forces defeated their military opponents. Hideyoshi's heir was allowed to remain in Osaka Castle, but in 1614, betraying his promise to Hideyoshi, Tokugawa Ieyasu decided to destroy the Toyotomi house. The defences of Osaka Castle were formidable and it was only by further treachery and broken promises that it was taken. Hideyoshi's heir committed suicide.

Having succeeded in gaining control over a militarily united Japan, the Tokugawa regime began moulding a stable social and political system. Like Yoritomo, Tokugawa Ieyasu decided that his headquarters should be in the region where his wealth and power had nurtured the strongest loyalty among his vassals, thus Edo (present-day Tokyo) became the new seat of government. The imperial court stayed in Kyoto and, despite its poor financial situation and lack of any real power, its traditional position as the source of titles and ranks kept it symbolically relevant to political power. Ieyasu became the prominent military figure after the battle of 1600, and in 1603 he assumed the title of shogun (originally granted by the imperial court to its officials).

Ieyasu extended the reforms which Oda and Hideyoshi had begun as the means of stabilizing the social order and thereby his own grip on power. It is important to remember that the Tokugawa period lasted 268 years and that, therefore, many aspects of the original system developed in the early 1600s changed. Even more significant are the social and economic changes which political stability and peace brought to communities throughout Japan and, inevitably, to the functioning of the Tokugawa system itself. The features of the Tokugawa system of control were developed over several decades. Among them were: a rearrangement of *daimyō* territories, creating a buffer zone of loyal *daimyō* around Edo; the alternate attendance system, which required *daimyō* to make official visits to the shogun every other year and to leave hostages in Edo; and the seclusion policy, which restricted trade contacts to one island near Nagasaki, expelled foreigners from Japan and outlawed Christianity.

Severe repression of Japanese Christians was carried out with the help of Buddhist temples. All citizens had to register with a local temple and display their lack of Christian beliefs by trampling on a holy picture (an act known as *fumi-e*).

The above measures sought to restrict the access of potential rivals to outside financial or military help and to deplete their wealth, which might otherwise have been used to fund campaigns against the government. Remembering the steps in their own defeat of rival *daimyō*, the Tokugawa also forbade any *daimyō* alliances or marriages between *daimyō* families without Tokugawa approval.

In an attempt to prevent social mobility, a rigid system of social stratification (begun by Hideyoshi) was imposed. The four groups, in descending social status, were samurai, peasants, artisans and merchants. Confucian concepts were now written up into stringent codes of behaviour for various social groups. As in any political system, there is a gap between ideology and practice, and as time passes the increase in ideological rhetoric often belies the need to counteract the growth of new forces. The stable political order of the Tokugawa period helped to encourage economic changes that in turn gave rise to new political and social aspirations, which did not fit into the official ideal of social order.

The best example of a measure that was designed to ensure stability but instead helped to create economic and political change was the alternate attendance system. Under this requirement, each *daimyō* had to maintain a residence in Edo, attire himself appropriately, entertain in suitably lavish fashion when in the capital, and undertake the long and costly procession to Edo every other year. This generated an enormous amount of economic activity: road systems had to be maintained, inns appeared along the main routes to Edo, residences had to be built, and food supplies had to be gathered and transported over long distances. Ultimately, the alternate attendance system helped to create a national economy, national transportation routes and a system of credit, and increased crop specialization and commercial activity. These developments, in turn, nurtured the growth and increasing wealth of what, ideologically at least, was the most despised social group – the merchants.

As the Tokugawa period progressed, the highest group in the social hierarchy, the samurai, experienced the impoverishment of significant numbers of its members. There were, of course, many levels of samurai, but in the Tokugawa period they were all residents of the castle towns and dependent on their *daimyō* for stipends, which were in return for their now largely bureaucratic services. Many *daimyō* found themselves in financial difficulty as a result of expenditures forced on them by the shogunate or because of financial mismanagement of their territories; consequently, many *daimyō* borrowed from and became indebted to merchants. In difficult times *daimyō* often cut samurai stipends, throwing this group – especially the lower samurai – into economic distress. Increasingly, the lower samurai made straw sandals or other objects to sell, taught the children of samurai or wealthy commoners, and some even married into wealthy merchant families in order to exchange their status for financial comfort.

The countryside also underwent considerable change in the Tokugawa period. Some regions became major centres for the production of specialized crops and commercial products – for example, soy sauce, sake and silk – for urban areas and saw a greater introduction of a money economy. Wealthy peasants and merchants began engaging in moneylending, and the consequences led to a growth in the distinctions between wealthy and poor peasants and in the numbers of landless tenants. Agricultural productivity rose throughout the Tokugawa period, but not all areas experienced this growth and not all peasants enjoyed its fruits. There were famines, floods, exploitation and infanticide. Peasants in desperate conditions rebelled and presented petitions to the authorities even though the fate of leaders of these movements might be death, despite the acknowledged justness of their cause.

The impetus for challenging the Tokugawa system finally came from the lower levels of the samurai class. Encouraged to study in this period of peace, they had time to ponder the gap between ideology and practice, and also between the Confucian principles regarding the behaviour of lords who deserved loyalty and the behaviour of Tokugawa or other officials in their own domains. Increasingly, some of these high officials and *daimyō* were judged to be lacking in the qualities that would deserve the loyalty of the samurai beneath them. They could no longer claim respect for military valour. Many lower samurai, by contrast, actively urged or themselves carried out administrative reforms that strengthened their domains financially and administratively. This was happening in the domains that led the challenge against the Tokugawa government.

MODERN JAPAN

On top of this growing ferment in Japanese society there was now imposed a foreign dimension – the arrival in 1853 of the black ships from the United States of America. Since the time of the Seclusion Edicts (1639), anyone approaching Japanese shores had been executed, but now a barbarian (westerners with their strange ways and ignorance of what was considered civilized learning) arrived, refusing to state his business at Nagasaki and demanding that his message be transmitted directly to the shogun. This was Commodore Matthew C. Perry, who presented his demands and then announced that he would return in a year's time for the response. The weakness of the Tokugawa shogunate was exposed by its reaction to the need to devise a response to these demands, which included trading rights and other guarantees. In the climate of dissatisfaction that already existed, the Tokugawa government's attempt to survey the opinions of *daimyō* on the question of whether Japan should agree to treaty relations with the United States or not was interpreted as a sign of its incompetence and indecisiveness.

There was a range of opinions as to whether Japan should open up to the outside world or not. Some of the samurai were very xenophobic and wanted the barbarians to be sent away. Others grasped the possibility of using an anti-treaty stance as a position from which to attack the shogunate. In fact, once treaty relations were established and foreign powers were trading in Japan, members of this latter group still continued to attack the government, while recognizing the superior military power of the foreigners. Various samurai decided to enlist the help of the militarily advanced westerners to develop a better military capacity. Some of these samurai patriots, in other words, were very pragmatic. Some groups favoured opening Japan up to foreign contact from the outset. This group was also made up of samurai patriots – some of whom felt that the foreigners had superior knowledge, which Japan needed if it was to develop into a great nation. Others also felt that this superior knowledge had to be acquired, but as a means of eventually ridding Japan of the foreigners and their demands.

When Perry returned, the shogun agreed to the demands and the first treaty, opening two ports to limited US trade and allowing US consular representation, was signed. It was not long, of course, in that age of imperialism, before Britain, Russia and other countries also signed treaties with Japan. In 1858 a series of 'unequal treaties' was signed, fixing Japanese tariffs at low levels and establishing the principle of extraterritoriality – the practice of trying foreign nationals who have committed a crime in Japan in the home countries of those nationals. These treaties aroused the indignation of many, particularly the self-styled samurai patriots, who resented the weak Tokugawa government for allowing this slur on Japan's sovereignty and pride. The fervent desire to get rid of these treaties galvanized Japan's political leadership for several decades with a sense of mission and the need to 'catch up'. The immediate task was the overthrow of the Tokugawa government.

It is at this point that the imperial court was presented with an opportunity to make a political comeback. The government had tried to enlist the court's support by getting it to agree to the unequal treaties, but the latter had refused to give its backing. The outcome of the approach to the court had been to damage the government's image and prospects even more. The young samurai activists, who resented the tenor of the unequal treaties and who wanted to bring down the Tokugawa government, declared themselves to be loyal servants of the emperor. They had a strong symbolic focus for their efforts in the person of the emperor: a symbol, moreover, unsullied by contemporary politics. These activists assassinated government officials and foreigners and attempted to stage a coup. The government responded by trying to punish samurai in the most recalcitrant domains, and battles were fought between Tokugawa and anti-Tokugawa forces. The anti-Tokugawa forces were victorious, and finally, on 3 January 1868, an alliance of powerful domains successfully carried out a palace coup. They announced the end of the Tokugawa government and the restoration of imperial rule.

Meiji (1868–1912)

The leaders of the new government, samurai from the main anti-Tokugawa territories, continued to use Edo – now Tokyo (meaning eastern capital) – as the capital. The emperor was moved to Tokyo and gave his reign-name to this period of Japanese history – Meiji (enlightened rule). Throughout the Meiji period, Japan's leadership gradually developed an emperor system and emperor ideology that stressed the unique nature of the Japanese state and the duty of all subjects to give unquestioning loyalty and service to all imperial causes. Since the government leaders were driven by the dual aims of catching up with the foreign powers in order to be rid of the unequal treaties and also surpassing these nations to prove Japan's true world status, there were many imperial causes demanding the people's energies. One of the cries of the period was 'rich country – strong military', and Japan achieved considerable success in its attempts to achieve both of these goals. A new national education system and conscription provided two influential organizations for moulding loyal subjects.

Various cultural missions were sent abroad to learn about the social, economic and political systems of the powerful European countries and the United States. Opinion regarding which were the models for Japan to adopt was divided, but some of the prevailing choices were the French education system and the Prussian army and constitutional systems. In a way reminiscent of the Nara period, the ruling elite of Meiji Japan embarked on another wave of political and cultural borrowing. As with ideas imported in the past, there was some adaptation to Japanese needs and some layering of the new on top of the old. Meiji period changes to the social and political order were significantly different from those of other periods in that some radical reforms were carried out. Social distinctions were abolished and positions in the bureaucracy were open to all on the basis of merit, as demonstrated in examinations. Members of the old samurai class were ordered to stop wearing swords and to shave their top-knots; samurai stipends were commuted to lump-sum payments in government bonds, which they were encouraged to invest in new industries and government projects; and the old *daimyō* territories were dissolved and a modern system of prefectures established.

It looked as if the government leaders had legislated themselves out of their old social status, but as far as many other members of the old samurai class were concerned, the former samurai of the main anti-Tokugawa territories had created a monopoly on political power for themselves. Some of these disaffected members of the former samurai class and wealthy landlords built the first political opposition in modern Japan on their calls for a broadening of the base for political participation. This was by no means an appeal for universal suffrage but rather for inclusion of their groups in the political process. The adoption of constitutional government itself had not been the result of pressure from below but a measure deemed necessary by the new government to convince the foreign countries of Japan's equal status.

About a decade after the beginning of the Meiji period, the government promised that there would be a constitution (see: The System of Government). This step was probably taken to impress the foreigners and to assuage the growing calls for political participation in Japan. When the Meiji Constitution was presented to the people of Japan in 1890, it was as a gift from the emperor to his subjects. The Constitution spoke of the duties (not rights) of the subjects. The government, suspicious of letting constitutional government run a free course lest it endanger the national goals of catching up with the foreign countries or loosen their own grip on power, enacted the Peace Police Law in 1900. The Constitution had opened the way for the formation of political parties; this law severely restricted participation in political meetings and banned labour organization. The political parties that survived this repression had no ideological platform other than opposition to the government and were regularly bought off in deals and compromises.

The successes in achieving economic goals in the Meiji period were based largely on the strong economic base inherited from the Tokugawa period: a high level of commercial activity, the establishment of a national infrastructure, and rising agricultural productivity. Government revenues that financed the massive military campaigns and industrialization projects of the Meiji period came from the new land tax and the textile industry. Textiles and in particular silk were the main areas of industrial activity in this period. Japan had an existing skills base and resources in this area, and with government help in applying the latest technology it was possible to maximize this domestic advantage. Japan also benefited from a silkworm disease that hit Europe around the beginning of the Meiji period, thereby creating tremendous demand for Japanese silk. From the 1890s to 1914, silk represented more than 30 per cent of Japan's exports by value. The textile industry was staffed mainly by female workers, a group whose contribution to, and exploitation in the name of, national development is usually ignored.

Other major developments in this period were railways and a modern banking system. The countries that had imposed the unequal treaties on Japan admired all of Japan's achievements, but did not agree to remove the treaties altogether until

1911. By that time Japan had presented what was perhaps a more significant credential to the club of imperialist powers – military might and colonial acquisitions. In 1895 Japan defeated China in the Sino-Japanese War and exacted heavy financial and territorial prizes, including Formosa (Taiwan), the Liaotung Peninsula and a large indemnity. In 1905 Japan defeated Russia in the Russo-Japanese War, becoming the first Asian power to defeat a European power – the source of much pride for Japanese and many other Asians. It was as a result of this victory that Japan acquired the southern half of Sakhalin (still disputed territory today) and further interests in Korea and Manchuria.

Japan had shown its mettle in both conflicts but the jubilation following each success was tempered as a result of intervention by the other imperialist countries to reduce Japan's spoils of war. In 1895 Russia, Germany and France forced Japan to give up the Liaotung Peninsula, and in 1905 the United States mediated a peace treaty between Russia and Japan which failed to give the large indemnity that the latter sought. Japan had spent heavily to finance these wars and territorial expansion, and this in turn was creating domestic social tensions as worsening conditions in the countryside and urban areas were neglected.

The social problems that accompanied industrialization in other countries had begun to appear in Meiji Japan also: urban slums, exploitative working conditions and the resultant clashes between labour and capital. While the leaders of government, bureaucracy and big business were looking to the experiences of the industrialized countries for lessons in what to adopt and what to avoid, intellectuals and social activists – Christians, socialists, labour organizers and others – were studying social reform ideas from abroad. Organized labour activity remained on a fairly limited scale in the Meiji and following Taisho period, but this was mainly as a result of official repression. Attempts to organize labour also suffered at times from the elitist appearance of the mainly intellectual leadership and their failure to raise the consciousness of significant numbers of workers. This type of activity was made extremely difficult and dangerous by Clause 17 of the Peace Police Law (1900), which made strikes and other types of labour union organization illegal.

Increasing frustration led many intellectuals and labour activists to feel that if they were to change the state of things they would have to become politically active. Socialist and anarchist ideas spread among social activists and official repression increased. This situation gave rise to two main trends among those interested in social reform: co-optation and increasing radicalization. In the first case, labour activists were co-opted into working with groups of government, bureaucracy and big business leaders to develop and promote harmonious relations between labour and capital. The other (very diverse) group, which wanted significant changes to the organization of political and economic power in order to change the unfair conditions of labour and rural tenants, was hounded by the thought police. It is telling that the major proponents of labour legislation were not the labour activists – but social bureaucrats whose main concern was to ensure smooth social relations and high industrial productivity.

Taishō (1912–26)

With the death of the Meiji emperor in 1912, the new era of Taishō began, but according to many Japanese writing at the time, the emperor's death also marked the end of old and familiar ways. Despite the many achievements of the Meiji period, there was considerable unease about the pace and nature of change. The main themes of the Taishō period were the growing nationalism fuelled by Japanese resentment of the international community's responses to Japan's imperialist activities; mounting social and political tensions and their suppression; the growth in party politics and a political crisis; and the shift to heavy industry as a result of the boost provided by World War I.

In 1902 Japan had signed the Anglo-Japanese Alliance, but when World War I began, Japan's cabinet voted by only a narrow margin to support the Allied side. This proved a fortunate move by Japan, as this far-away war gave Japanese industry a boost in its role as supplier of its allies' war needs. Japan also acquired German territories in Asia and the South Pacific. The extent of the benefit to Japan is reflected in the fact that it achieved its first impressive export surplus in this period.

This war also brought problems in foreign relations for Japan. Japan issued a set of demands (the Twenty-one Demands) to China, including recognition of Japan's new control over former German territories in China; an extension and a strengthening of Japan's privileges there; and considerable Japanese control over Chinese political, economic and administrative policy. China was forced to agree, but the other imperialist countries were very critical of Japan's behaviour. The United States, in particular, began to proclaim itself a champion of the Chinese people, and as Japanese activity in China increased, tensions between Japan and the United States grew also. Another issue causing resentment in Japan was the failure of the new League of Nations to agree to the insertion of a racial equality clause in its charter.

Domestic social and economic problems also followed the

boom years of World War I. Gaps in living standards between various social groups grew perceptibly wider as the financial gains from the increased exports and general economic activity were not shared out evenly. Inflation and rising prices were not matched by rising wages and the large urban populations suffered under this post-boom recession. In 1918 rice riots erupted in various areas of Japan, and men and women attacked the homes of rice merchants and other figures they saw as responsible for rice hoarding, high prices and therefore their misery. These riots scared the Japanese ruling classes, especially given the events in Russia just the year before. Anxieties mounted as labour unrest increased throughout 1919 and 1920, with the biggest pre-World War II labour strike occurring in 1920. In the countryside, where increasing numbers of tenants were being made landless, tenant uprisings also rose dramatically in these years.

The appearance of the Japan Communist Party in 1922 (see: Major Political Parties) was viewed with dismay by the authorities, who targeted it for especially brutal repression. This background of economic recession, social tension and heightened anxiety on the part of the ruling classes was significant in influencing the response of the police and military to the massive earthquake that struck the Kanto Plain (the eastern plain which includes Tokyo and Yokohama) in 1923. The shock of the earthquake itself, and the fires that spread from the lunchtime cooking fires which were burning when it hit (around midday), caused enormous numbers of deaths and huge destruction. In the chaos that followed, rumours were spread about Koreans living in Japan having poisoned the water. Police and vigilante groups went on a rampage, killing large numbers of Koreans. This disaster was also used as an excuse by the thought police and military police to round up and/or murder communists and other 'radicals'.

The introduction of universal male suffrage in 1925 is considered to have been partly a calculated attempt to defuse some of the mounting social tension, by giving more men a feeling that they had a say. It was also partly a response to growing public pressure. Aware of the potential dangers that truly open political debate and the emergence of mass parties could pose to their vision of the best course for Japan and to their own power, Japan's leaders simultaneously passed the Peace Preservation Law of 1925. This outlawed organizations that wanted to change the system of government or abolish private property, or even discussed these matters. The ambiguous wording of this law made it easy to use against any person or group regarded as an 'enemy of the state' by the police – in particular labour activists and communists.

At the time of the establishment of the Meiji political system, cabinets had been viewed as being composed of men whose interests were above mere factional party loyalties. They were responsible only to the emperor, not to the Diet (Japan's parliament). Once political parties began to establish themselves, their growth was opposed by many of the original Meiji leaders, but the parties were able to take advantage of the constitutional provision allowing the House of Representatives a veto power over the proposed budget. This led to a situation in which cabinets acknowledged the advantage of making deals with certain parties in order to secure their support in the Diet. This co-optation of the political parties and the growth of pork-barrel politics which it encouraged tarnished the image of the parties in the mind of the public. The political parties experienced their high point between 1918, when the first 'commoner' prime minister was appointed, and 1932, when the first military man was appointed as prime minister. This growth of parliamentary politics – in contrast to control of the government by the exclusive group of the original Meiji leaders – was seen by some as the rise of the power of the ordinary people and consequently called 'Taishō democracy'.

The readiness with which most political parties dissolved themselves when ordered to do so in 1940 – as part of a national reorganization to mobilize the nation more effectively for the war effort – and their failure to counter the rising power of the military in government during the 1930s and 1940s suggest that parliamentary politics were flawed. The parties had failed to develop a large mass base, and instead were seen as related to powerful local figures, big business and others who could deliver funds or votes. As far as most people were concerned, the parties appeared to be self-seeking, corrupt organizations that bore no relation to them.

Shōwa (1926–89)

Emperor Hirohito took over from the Taishō emperor, who died in 1926, and adopted the reign-name Shōwa. The Shōwa period ended in 1989 with the death of the Japanese emperor most widely known abroad. A major reason for this was the tragic occurrence of the Pacific War.

Throughout the 1930s nationalist sentiment and militarism grew, and in contrast to the weak government and the corrupt party politicians, the emerging ultra-nationalist figures appealed to many. Some right-wing groups, including young army officers, called for a Shōwa restoration – echoing the events of 1868 – which would reassert the dominance of the emperor. These groups claimed that it was they who were the true servants of the imperial will, not the corrupt advisers who were serving only their own interests. The early Shōwa period saw a series of attempted and actual assassinations of political figures and an attempted *coup d'état*.

Meanwhile, the Kwangtung army – a division of the Japanese army in Manchuria – staged an attack on the South Manchuria Railway and claimed that this had been the work of Chinese troops. Using this as an excuse, the army then occupied Mukden in 1931; an event that is known as the Manchurian Incident. This development embroiled Japan more deeply in Asia and highlighted the inability of the government in Tokyo to control the army in the field.

The Manchurian Incident led to the estrangement of Japan from the other big powers and to Japan's withdrawal from the League of Nations when the other members demanded that Japan remove its forces from Manchuria. Japan annexed Manchuria in 1932 and its activities there increased tensions with China. The second Sino-Japanese War finally broke out in 1937.

Japan's army and government leaders had counted on a short war and a speedy victory, but the war dragged on. The speed of initial victories in cities such as Nanking – the scene of dreadful atrocities against civilians – could not be sustained: resistance by communist-led forces was too strong and China too vast. Japan found itself committing vast amounts of resources to the China war and also drifting towards open confrontation with the United States over China. The United States demanded a withdrawal of Japanese troops from China, while Japan sought US recognition of its objectives there. Neither side appeared able to compromise and the futile negotiations turned into a waiting game. Japan began its preparations for a southward advance into South-east Asia as a means of cutting the supply lines to China and also of securing badly needed raw materials. This Japanese move threatened US access to those rich raw material supplies, such as tin and rubber. The rapidity of Japan's early successes belied the vast amounts of human, capital and material resources that would be needed for the successful achievement of the country's goals in Asia.

Japan occupied most of East and South-east Asia, and the people at home heard glowing reports of the successes of the imperial forces, but not everyone was convinced by the propaganda. By the time of the Battle of Midway in 1942, Japan had begun to lose ground and Allied air attacks on its navy and airforce were increasingly successful. The result for the Japanese homeland was a cutting of supply lines: food and raw materials previously taken from colonies and occupied areas no longer reached Japan. Long before the atomic bombs were dropped on Hiroshima and Nagasaki on 6 and 9 August 1945, massive bombing raids over Tokyo and other large cities killed hundreds of thousands of civilians and levelled large areas of residential as well as industrial buildings. Some of the US advisers who discussed the merits of using the newly tested atomic bomb favoured a total blockade of Japan, arguing that it would be forced to surrender before long and that this alternative would not cost many more Allied lives. This alternative was not accepted.

Japan finally accepted the terms of the Potsdam Declaration – unconditional surrender and military occupation – and on 15 August 1945 the emperor broadcast this news to the Japanese people. Photographs of this day show people kneeling and sobbing, but written accounts suggest that many people could not understand what the frail voice was saying because of the unfamiliar style in which the emperor spoke. The surrender was not in fact 'unconditional' as the Japanese leaders insisted on keeping the emperor as head of the nation. The emperor survived without ever being made to answer for his 'war responsibility', largely as a result of high-level US support.

In September 1945 the seven-year occupation of Japan began. This was meant to be an Allied Occupation but was mainly a US affair, dominated by the personality of General Douglas MacArthur until his sacking in 1951. A group of Japan experts had been gathered during the war to draw up policy initiatives for its eventual occupation. The most important decision taken by the US regarding the nature of the occupation was to retain the existing government structure. Japan was to be ruled indirectly via its government and Diet. It was thought that a purge of militarists from public office would be sufficient to remove the dangerous elements that threatened the goals of the occupation.

The two broad objectives of the occupation were demilitarization and democratization. Satisfied that rapid demobilization of Japanese troops and the purge would achieve the first objective, the occupation administration began its democratization programme. Some of the main reforms were the encouragement of a labour movement; the writing of a new constitution and the removal of the emperor's 'divine' status; the reform of the education system; the decentralization and strengthening of local government; and land reform. There had been plans to dissolve the *zaibatsu* (large financial conglomerates), but these were abandoned. Divisions within the occupation administration's thinking about how best to proceed with the democratization programme and the intensification of Cold War tensions led to the abandonment of many occupation reforms.

There has been a tendency to view the occupation period as one in which US administrators gave the Japanese people a democratic society. Recent research, however, seeks to highlight the role of the Japanese people themselves and their own attempts to build a more democratic society.

Communist victory in China in 1949 and the outbreak of the Korean War in 1950 led to the military hardliners in the occupation administration stressing the need to build Japan into a strong ally against communism in the Pacific. The democratic reform programme, which had already been diluted and even abandoned by some, was now replaced with a policy of strengthening Japan. The militarist purge was replaced by a 'red purge' in 1950, which was used to get rid of communists and organized labour in general.

The importance of Japan as a US ally in the Pacific is reflected in the treaties that marked the end of the occupation. The San Francisco Peace Treaty became effective in 1952, ending the occupation and removing Japan's 'enemy' status. When Japan signed this treaty in 1951 it was compelled to sign the US–Japan Security Treaty also. The Security Treaty gave the US the right to station troops in Japan and made it necessary for the Japanese government to request US permission before granting any other country the right to have bases there. There was considerable opposition to this treaty in Japan, where some feared that the country would be drawn into US military conflicts or begin to rearm itself.

The new Constitution, written in 1946 by a group of US occupation officers with some Japanese input, contains a clause forbidding the use of force to settle international disputes or the maintenance of an army.

Heisei (1989–)

Japan has a self-defence force but, as events during the Gulf War demonstrated, the constitutional provision against the deployment of a Japanese military body has been impossible to ignore. In 1989–90 the Japanese government found itself caught between pressure at home to respect the constitutional restriction and growing pressure from other nations – especially the US – for Japan to share more of the burden of resolving international conflicts. In 1992 the Diet managed to pass a bill that will allow the self-defence forces to take part in United Nations peace-keeping operations.

The death of Emperor Hirohito in 1989 saw the end of the Shōwa and the beginning of the Heisei (peace and prosperity) era. Japan's economic performance since the mid-1950s has led to the growth of a very narrow image of that country and its people: an image defined in economic terms. Alongside economic developments there have been changes in social, political and cultural trends also. As in earlier periods of history, Japan in recent decades has experienced the growth of new artistic movements and new religions; pressures to change its political system; social tensions because of economic inequalities, racism and discrimination; and environmental pollution. Japan is also attempting to adjust to a potentially prominent role in the international context. At various points in its history Japan has sought to minimize the impact of outside forces and at others it has embraced them. As its economic role in the international community increases, its own fate also is bound up increasingly with that of other countries.

PART TWO

Politics

4 Introduction

Japan's first political parties appeared in the early 1880s and stood for opposition to the government's monopoly on political power rather than for any democratic ideologies (see: History). The activities of these parties were frequently suppressed by the early Meiji government, which wanted to keep control over the pace and nature of political and economic developments. The government and its supporters were keen to see Japan win high standing in the eyes of the imperialist powers that were active in Asia and had already imposed unequal treaties in Japan. Although the development of a modern, democratic form of government was an essential step in winning this recognition, the government leaders were not prepared to risk letting any other group steer Japanese social and political development away from their vision of a strong army and a rich country.

Thus, the Meiji Constitution (see below), which they helped to draft and which the emperor granted as a gift to his subjects in 1890, was careful to spell out the duties and not the rights of the people. The ability of the parties to act as an effective opposition was impeded by constitutional provisions which located all sovereignty in the emperor and made the cabinet responsible only to him. This left the Diet – the parliament supposedly representing the people – in a very weak position, and the political parties were cast not as loyal servants of the throne but as self-interested and disruptive elements.

Unfortunately, their inability to oppose the government effectively, and also a degree of self-interest, led the early political parties to act in ways that discredited them in the eyes of the people as well. There was considerable co-optation of parties by the government, bribery and corruption, and an overall lack of ideological commitment. The period from about 1912 to the late 1920s is usually referred to as one of 'Taishō Democracy' because of the appearance of party governments and increased calls for broader political participation by the people in politics.

Ultimately, however, the parties proved too weak to oppose the rise of ultra-nationalism and militarism. This weakness was the result of constitutional provisions, such as that which placed the navy and army ministers above the Diet by making them responsible only to the emperor, and also the result of the failure of the parties themselves to attract a mass base of support among the people.

As army and navy ministers were appointed to head the government, the power of the parties declined even further. The parties that had been formed to represent the interests of workers, farmers and the poor were increasingly suppressed (they had been since their inception) and finally forced to dissolve themselves. This process of pressing all political bodies into loyal service to achieve Japan's imperial war aims culminated in 1940 in the creation of the Imperial Rule Assistance Association.

This organization was full of too many competing views to achieve its purpose of concentrating all national political power, but it did successfully terminate any potential power that the opposition parties might have had. The political landscape confronting the Allied Occupation Forces who began arriving in Japan in August 1945 was one devoid of political parties or indeed any groups representing the interests of groups such as labour, rural tenants or women. This did not mean that Japan had not had a history of labour, women's or rural political activism – far from it.

In the years immediately after surrender, groups of Japanese citizens – workers, farmers, housewives – acted to attempt to reshape their society. Whereas in the past their activism had been constrained by imperialist ideology and official suppression, now it was subject to the approval or disapproval of the largely US occupation forces.

5 The System of Government

Japan's present system of government is based on the political reforms of the old Meiji Constitution, which were carried out during the occupation period (1945–52). It is not, however, just the sum of the various reforms imposed by a foreign power. Social practices and expectations that had flavoured Japan's pre-1945 political development continued to influence the particular nature of Japanese democratic government after the war years. Indeed, as the membership of the newly formed Liberal Democratic Party (LDP) showed, in 1955, the very personalities that had played a significant role in politics before the occupation and its political reforms continued to do so in post-occupation Japan. The basic aim of these occupation-period reforms had been to root out and prevent a regrowth of ultra-nationalism and militarism. In order to achieve this, the reformers sought to establish a 'democratic' system of government in Japan.

The US decided to make the occupation primarily its own operation. Various Allied forces and personnel did participate but the authority of the US occupation commander was absolute. This commander (General Douglas MacArthur, 1945–51) also had authority over the Japanese government, which continued to be designated an 'enemy' until 1952. In preparing the occupation strategy for Japan, the US government decided to keep the Japanese bureaucracy in place and to use it to implement political and other reforms. In other words, the occupying forces sought to democratize Japan via a system of indirect military rule.

Some scholars have viewed this decision to utilize the existing bureaucratic structure as a key to the 'success' of the policies to democratize Japanese politics, and society in general, because of the home-grown flavour of reforms implemented by

Japanese rather than US officials. Others have questioned the degree of democratization actually achieved, citing the incompatible interests of the US reformers and the Japanese bureaucratic elite that was to carry out the reforms. The dearth of occupation officials with sufficient knowledge of either Japanese language or politics and society undoubtedly made this decision to use the existing bureaucratic system appealing. It is certain, however, that the purge of militarists and ultra-nationalists from public office carried out by the occupation officials was ineffective. Standing between the occupation reformers and the Japanese public and responsible for the translation and implementation of reform directives was the Japanese bureaucratic elite. This was largely the same bureaucracy of the pre-war and war years and it wielded considerable power over the extent and nature of democratization.

What, then, is the system of government that Japan has today and how does it differ from the pre-1945 system? Government in Japan is based on the Constitution drafted in 1946 largely by US occupation officials and then ratified by the Japanese Diet (parliament) in 1947. MacArthur, the Supreme Commander for the Allied Powers (SCAP), had asked the Japanese government to draft a new Constitution for Japan, but rejected the product because it still resembled Japan's old Constitution. In essence, the Japanese drafters had been unable to bring themselves to remove sovereignty from the emperor and place it with the people.

Japan's first Constitution – the Meiji Constitution – had been promised to the people in 1881 by a government made up mainly of former samurai from the major two domains (precursors of Japan's modern prefectures) that had brought down Japan's last shogunate, or military government under a shogun (see: History). This rather exclusive group had been in power for thirteen years by then, and as far as other former members of Japan's elite warrior class could tell, they showed no signs of sharing their power with anyone else. The initial calls for a parliament and democratic constitution came from this group of disaffected citizens, who formed an anti-government movement, the Jiyu Minken Undo (People's Rights Movement), 1871–90. Before long, rich farmers joined the call for broader participation in government and a constitution. This movement should not be confused with calls for universal suffrage or even for universal male suffrage, as it was initiated by the wealthy and privileged who wanted a share of the new political power. It is also necessary to remember that suffrage in many other democracies at this time was also strictly limited.

By 1881, the time of the government's announcement of plans for a parliament and a constitution, this anti-government movement had grown considerably larger and had a more varied membership. The government's announcement can thus be seen as, in part, a response to this growing pressure. Another important stimulus for the development of a parliament and a constitution in this period was the need to prove Japan's ability to stand on an equal footing with the imperialist powers of the time, as a modern nation. This was not only a question of national pride but an essential step in getting rid of the unequal treaties (see: History) that had been imposed on Japan.

Having announced their intentions, the leading members of the government began to study the available models of government earnestly. The one that impressed the government leaders most was the Prussian model. In 1889 the Meiji Constitution was 'granted' to the people of Japan by the emperor, with whom sovereignty rested and who was to be the sole initiator of constitutional amendments. The Constitution created a bicameral Diet (parliament) and a cabinet, but the latter was answerable only to the emperor, by whom it was appointed. The emperor was also given the power to make laws, apart from the Diet, and sole control over the army and navy. In other words, the Diet created by the Meiji Constitution was extremely weak. The major criticisms of the Constitution have focused on its creation of what is called the emperor system or *tennosei*: a system of government in which politics was controlled by elite bodies that stood outside of the parliament and were supposedly responsible to the emperor alone. The main offenders were the armed forces and the bureaucracy. In the emperor system, the emperor was the highest power in Japan and all decisions were taken in his name.

When Japan finally agreed to surrender in 1945 – a move that had been held up for a long time by the inability to secure a guarantee that the emperor would not be tried as a war criminal or removed as head of the nation – it was because of fears of 'revolution from below'. Those Japanese with the power to negotiate feared revolution more than surrender. Early in the occupation, SCAP identified a group of Japanese 'liberals' whom it felt it could rely on to help in the occupation's democratization programmes. These may have been people who had been harassed by the Japanese military and were therefore seen as anti-militarist, or they may have espoused various 'liberal' doctrines before 1945, but, ultimately, SCAP felt that it had to write Japan's new Constitution itself.

Some of the most important changes in the new Constitution were the provisions which located sovereignty with the people and made the emperor a symbol of the state, made the Diet the highest state body and created a cabinet responsible to the Diet, and renounced war as a means of settling disputes with other countries. This new Constitution also included a requirement for a two-thirds majority before it could be amended in any way.

The Diet created by the 1947 Constitution is made up of two houses, the House of Representatives (four-year terms) and the House of Councillors (six-year terms). Unlike the pre-1945 situation, the Diet is now the sole law-making body in Japan. Bills need the approval of both houses to become law, but in matters of the budget and international treaties, the view of the House of Representatives prevails in the case of a dispute.

This new authority did not necessarily bring the Diet power, but rather *functions*, that is, to pass bills put to it by the LDP. The weakness of the Diet has been largely a result of the dominance of the LDP (see: Major Political Parties).

THE PRIME MINISTER

The prime minister heads the cabinet and appoints ministers, all of whom are responsible to the Diet. A new cabinet must be formed after each House of Representatives election, but in fact cabinet reshuffles occur on an almost annual basis. This is the result of the factional politics of the ruling LDP. In other words, the leaders of factions want and need to give cabinet posts to their supporters as a reward and also to encourage further support once their power to reward is displayed. One important result of this constant reshuffling of cabinet ministers is the non-existent or minimal impact of ministers on their ministries. In this situation, the bureaucracy is the body that provides continuity of policies and indeed the expertise to initiate policies (see: The Bureaucracy).

Recent years have seen the biggest shake-up of Japanese prime ministers, ousted in the wake of sex- and finance-related scandals. Some of the best-known personalities in Japanese politics are included in Table 1.

VOTING

Any Japanese over twenty years of age has the right to vote in Japan. The Japanese electorate is divided into multi-member constituencies, and parties are able to run more than one candidate in each district. This system sees candidates from the same party competing against each other for votes. Voting is often for a particular person rather than a party or its policies (see: Major Political Parties). This system has also enabled LDP voters to punish the government for scandals or bad economic developments, without always damaging the party's electoral performance, by voting for an LDP candidate other than the incumbent. This means in turn that there are not many safe

TABLE 1 Japanese prime ministers since 1946

Date of initial cabinet formation	Name of prime minister
22 May 1946	Yoshida Shigeru
22 May 1947	Katayama Tetsu
10 March 1948	Ashida Hitoshi
15 October 1948	Yoshida Shigeru
10 December 1954	Hatoyama Ichiro
23 December 1956	Ishibashi Tanzan
25 February 1957	Kishi Nobusuke
19 July 1960	Ikeda Hayato
9 November 1964	Sato Eisaku
7 July 1972	Tanaka Kakuei[a]
9 December 1974	Miki Takeo
24 December 1976	Fukuda Takeo
7 December 1978	Ohira Masayoshi
17 July 1980	Suzuki Zenko
27 November 1982	Nakasone Yasuhiro[a]
6 November 1987	Takeshita Noboru[a]
3 June 1989	Uno Sousuke
9 August 1989	Kaifu Toshiki
5 November 1991	Miyazawa Kiichi[a]
9 August 1993	Hosokawa Morihiro[b]

[a] See: Key Political Personalities. [b] Of the Nihon Shinto (Japan New Party)

seats, since voters can vote to oust the incumbent as a protest move without hurting the party itself.

THE JUDICIARY

Under the Japanese Constitution the judiciary is totally independent of the executive and legislative branches. At the top of the judicial system sits the Supreme Court, with a series of high courts, district courts and summary courts below it. Japan also has a system of family courts and conciliation commissions which encourage out-of-court settlements for civil and family matters. Some commentators see the frequent use of this mechanism for out-of-court settlements as a reflection of Japanese culture. It is less commonly mentioned that pressure from the legal establishment itself to settle out of court accounts for the high levels of recourse to these conciliation commissions. As its name suggests, the Supreme Court is the highest legal power in the land. The chief justice and indeed all other justices in the Supreme Court are selected by the cabinet, but the chief justice is appointed by the emperor.

LOCAL GOVERNMENT
One of the major concerns of the occupation reformers, eager to democratize Japan, was the decentralization of governmental power. Before 1945, and especially under the political regime of the war years, power rested squarely in the hands of the central government in Tokyo. The new Constitution of 1946 sought to strengthen local government, seeing this as a means of broadening the levels of participation in government and thereby democracy. The Constitution thus provided for local government officials to be elected directly by the people in their communities and also sought to increase the autonomy of these local bodies.

As with some other areas of the democratization programme, the political reforms of the occupation period regarding local government could be used to bolster some of the surviving pre-1945 views of how government should function. For example, the powers and autonomy of local government are weak – despite the aims and provisions of the 1947 Constitution – because local government is financially dependent on the national government. In addition, the national government sends its representatives to fill positions in the prefectural administration and also submits 'model' laws which the local governments are encouraged to adopt.

6 The Bureaucracy

The bureaucracy might not normally be discussed alongside the cabinet and judiciary, but in the case of Japanese government structure it cannot easily be omitted. There are two levels of political appointment in the bureaucracy, the cabinet minister and the parliamentary vice-minister. Beneath these is the administrative vice-minister, who is the senior member of the ministry's bureaucrats. The Conference of Administrative Vice-Ministers plays a vital role for the cabinet as it is at the meetings of the former that most policy decisions are made before being sent on to the cabinet for routine approval. In a system where, as already mentioned, cabinets are frequently reshuffled, the bureaucracy's knowledge is crucial when making policy. Another avenue for the power of the bureaucracy to influence the government is the strong tendency for retired career bureaucrats to enter politics. Considerable numbers of LDP members, cabinet ministers and also prime ministers have hailed from the bureaucracy. The influence of the bureaucracy in Japanese government and politics raises questions about the nature of Japanese democracy. Bureaucrats are *not* elected by the people and are not answerable to them.

Bureaucrats are a highly educated elite in Japan and they have generally commanded a respect among the people that the politicians have failed to win. Serious questions arise, however, about the impact of the relationship between the bureaucracy and the LDP on the working of democracy in Japan. Many former bureaucrats have become LDP politicians (see: Major Political Parties). Apart from this obvious connection, the Japanese bureaucracy – like many others – has a type of negative or invisible power that it can use to influence the policy decisions and actions of the government.

If the bureaucracy does not agree with a particular policy or wishes to exert influence on its minister, it can adopt delaying tactics in its administrative handling of bills. The fairly short 'reign' of ministers in combination with delaying tactics can successfully stymie the passage of legislation that is not strongly pushed by the LDP. This question of the strength of political will and commitment to policy decisions is of course a vital element in deciding the fate of legislation. As a party that has stood largely for economic growth and that has not been strongly committed to many new policies, the LDP has not had to make many policy decisions. The bureaucracy has supplied most of these.

Who accepts responsibility for policy decisions in this situation? Ultimately, it is the government (LDP) politicians who must take responsibility at elections and not the bureaucracy. As pointed out above, however, in a system where the incumbent LDP member can be thrown out by the electorate voting for another LDP politician running in the same district, individuals and not the party are hurt. Since 'the party' has also been the government in Japan for almost four consecutive decades, this means that neither the bureaucracy nor the government has been forced to take ultimate responsibility for its decisions. Some might argue that as a country that relies on 'consensus decision making', responsibility is shared in Japan. In the case of democratic government, however, the separation of power and responsibility should not occur.

Another feature of the Japanese political system that gives rise to questions about whether Japan is indeed a democracy is the virtual one-party rule that has continued from 1948 until recently. The LDP has formed the government without interruption in this period, and the opposition parties have inevitably fallen into the trap of being seen less and less as contenders for government and more as a permanent opposition. An implication of not being able to hold a government accountable by 'kicking the rascals out' is that democracy – in the form of responsible government – cannot exist.

This unbroken hold on political power has not been underpinned by continued LDP majorities in elections. Yet, despite opposition to government initiatives – for example, the proposed introduction of a 3 per cent consumption tax in 1989 – the people have not brought the government down. Major political crises in Japan since 1948 – pollution, revision of the Security Treaty, and bribery and corruption cases involving senior LDP politicians and prime ministers – have generated considerable popular anger and even some electoral defeats for the government. Why have they not led to a change of government? The answer to this continued LDP power lies in the structural weakness of the opposition, which is too fragmented to defeat the government, and also in the ability to hold power and attract further support that the almost continuous favourable economic conditions have afforded the government in power – the LDP.

7 Major Political Parties

The main political parties in Japan are the Liberal Democratic Party (LDP), the Social Democratic Party of Japan (SDPJ, formerly the Japan Socialist Party – JSP), Komeito (the Clean Government Party), the Japan Communist Party (JCP), and the Democratic Socialist Party of Japan (DSPJ). Table 2 shows the ratio of votes polled in the 39th election for the House of Representatives, and Table 3 shows the configuration of seats held by each of the political parties and groups in the Japanese Diet as of 1992. New Japanese political parties which contested the July 1993 elections include the Japan New Party (Nihon Shinto) and the New Born Party (Shinseito).

THE LIBERAL DEMOCRATIC PARTY

The LDP was formed in 1955 by conservatives from the Japan Liberal Party and the Japan Democratic Party. In these years immediately after the occupation, Japan's conservatives were deeply divided on issues of ideology and personalities, but one development helped to encourage the merger that led to the establishment of the LDP. This was the reunification of the JSP, which the conservatives feared would give the opposition parties – until then even more divided than the conservatives – the electoral strength to take government. The LDP was formed just one month after the reunification of the JSP, and the size of its subsequent majorities in both houses left no possibility of the opposition winning power.

Various factors have contributed to the LDP's ability to maintain its majority for most of its existence. One of these has been the tendency for conservatives running as independent candidates to give their support to the LDP. In fact, once successfully elected, so-called independents are usually endorsed by the LDP. The LDP has also been able to rely on considerable

TABLE 2 Voting for the House of Representatives, 1990

Party	Votes polled		
	Number (1,000)	Share %	Persons elected
Liberal Democratic Party	30,315	46.1	275
Soc. Dem. Party of Japan	16,025	24.4	136
Kōmeitō	5,243	8.0	46
Japan Communist Party	5,227	8.0	16
Democratic Socialist Party	3,179	4.8	14
Social Democratic Federation	567	0.9	4
Rengo	–	–	–
Japan New Party	–	–	–
Others	340	0.5	1
Independent	4,808	7.3	21
Vacancies	–	–	–
Total	*65,704*	*100.0*	*513*

The number of eligible voters on the day (18 February 1990) was 90,322,908, making the turn-out rate 73.31 per cent.
Source: Secretariat, House of Representatives and House of Councillors, Japan.

financial support from big business and electoral support from rural constituencies. These two pillars of LDP power have also been the location of some of the biggest political scandals in Japan – senior LDP members accepting massive bribes from business and the extension of a major railway line to an isolated rural village, examples in the best tradition of pork-barrel politics.

In the parlance of political scientists, the LDP is known as a 'pragmatic' rather than a 'programmatic' party. A pragmatic party's goal is to win power, and if it perceives that it is losing ground with the voters it will attempt to move to a position that they will support. In the case of pragmatic parties the voters choose leaders rather than a set of policies. By not tying itself to any ideological platform the LDP has been able to adopt as its own any major political issues that have appeared and threatened to attract electoral support. One example of this is the appearance of mass citizens' movements to protest against the rising levels of environmental pollution in the 1960s. The LDP eventually responded by formulating pollution control measures, though there were broader considerations behind the party's actions than just the citizen protests. The issue and to some extent the citizens' movement was co-opted by the government and did not develop into a basis for opposition to the LDP at election time. Thus, despite its commitment to economic and industrial expansion, the LDP was able to implement tough pollution control laws and measures for industry.

The LDP, as the party in power throughout Japan's economic rebirth after the war years and the occupation, naturally benefited from this association for some time. It has presented itself as the party of economic growth, higher living standards and democracy, and as the best equipped to improve international relations. Alongside its claims of support for free enterprise, the LDP – largely via the bureaucracy – has also presided over attempts to plan and regulate economic and industrial development (with varying degrees of success). The party has considerable flexibility as a result of its pragmatic nature.

Historical as well as economic factors may have helped initially to create a more 'favourable' view of the LDP than of opposition parties. The specific historical factor present here is the 'illegal' status assigned to the left-wing and independent labour movements that developed in Japan from the late 1890s onwards. A Japan Socialist Party was legally formed in 1906 but then banned in 1907; the JCP was formed in 1922 but remained illegal until the occupation period, when it reformed as a legal party (1945). In contrast to the 'illegal' or 'radical' aura that the pre-1945 experience had bestowed on the names of the opposition parties, the LDP's name and membership were easily associated with those who had held power before 1945. The prominence of many LDP members in government and the bureaucracy during the war years ceased to be a stigma in many minds long before the end of the occupation (1952). There was thus a sense of the familiar for some voters once the occupation was over. This association with power and credibility as a party able to govern increased, to the disadvantage of opposition parties, the longer the LDP stayed in power.

As the LDP's tenure increased so too did the perception of this party as the one able to provide strong patronage and to reward loyal voters. Varying degrees of this patron–client relationship exist throughout the world's democracies, but in Japan it is promoted by the local support groups of the LDP members – the *kōenkai*.

The *kōenkai* is the 'personal' support organization of the local LDP member and relies on as many personal links as possible to increase membership and thereby local voters for the particular member. Since there is often more than one LDP candidate in a particular constituency, two or more *kōenkai* may be at work building support for their own member and simultaneously splitting the conservative vote. Old school friends, neighbours and acquaintances of the member or his relatives are approached to join. The *kōenkai* also spends as much money as it has at its disposal to attract membership. By providing buses for outings by local groups, banquets and even presents, the *kōenkai* attempts to oblige the recipients of this largess to vote loyally on election day.

This type of machine requires a lot of money, and even if the means of acquiring this money erupts into a political scandal, the LDP member concerned may still be re-elected because of the personal and local benefits that members of his *kōenkai* have derived. LDP members are helped in their ability to present themselves as effective local patrons by the continued rule of their party and its strong links with the bureaucracy. When a member of a *kōenkai* comes to its office with a problem regarding taxes or local facilities, it is likely that the *kōenkai* officials or the LDP member himself will know someone in the bureaucracy who can be approached to help solve the problem.

The factions
Another aspect of LDP organization is the role of the factions. As a result of the practice of running multiple LDP candidates in each district, the party's organization on the local level is necessarily weak. The existence of factions compensates for this. Unlike the party, each faction usually backs only one candidate in each district. An LDP candidate's funds will come mainly from his *kōenkai* and from his faction. Being a member of a powerful faction also lends the local candidate the potential political clout that helps his image as an effective local patron.

Factions take their names from the leader, and each leader aspires to become prime minister one day. A faction leader who appears to have good prospects of becoming prime minister will attract an increasing membership. Each faction is a well-organized unit that plays power politics as it attempts to jostle its way towards the prime ministership or a top ministerial position for the faction leader. Policy issues are not a prominent concern of LDP factions, and a variety of other explanations has been offered for their existence. One is the cultural argument, which sees the existence of factions as a reflection of the way Japanese society is organized. That is, the tendency to be in a group where patron–client relations occur (boss–worker, school senior–junior) has simply been translated into the political structure. Another explanation is based on the concrete role that they play. This includes choosing the prime minister – a function performed by the factions – and providing financial and career support for the multiple LDP candidates who run in each district.

The nature of factions and factional politics is changing all the time – originally, for example, a faction leader was supposed to retire after one term in office, but this has not always happened. By retiring after just one term, each leader makes way for other powerful faction leaders to reward his followers with the ministerial appointments and favours that are the prime minister's to give. There has been repeated talk of getting rid of the factions, but it is difficult to see how this could be achieved, given their role in providing financial support for candidates and a fairly secure route to top political positions.

The strength of factional politics is one of the main problems identified by critics of Japanese democracy. The type of horse-trading that factions engage in inevitably produces prime ministers who are strongly mired in a network of domestic give-and-take. The appearance of a strong prime minister who is interested and skilled in international politics is unlikely. Factional politics also leads to a lack of responsiveness to the electorate in the party. In other words, if there is a scandal or other major crisis that threatens the party's electoral performance, it is quite easy to replace the incumbent prime minister with the faction leader next in line. This does not represent an attempt to correct the specific problem against which the people protested and, in terms of being able to hold government accountable, it is not particularly democratic either. However, the inability of the Japanese electorate to effect a change of government has as much to do with the state of Japan's political opposition as it does with the structural strengths of the LDP and the largely favourable historical and economic environment in which it has operated.

THE SOCIAL DEMOCRATIC PARTY OF JAPAN (FORMERLY THE JAPAN SOCIALIST PARTY)

In contrast to its experience as an illegal and then severely restricted party before 1945, the JSP became very popular early in the occupation period. The elections of 1947 are the only time that a conservative government has not been elected. The newly reconstituted JSP won this election, becoming the largest single party in the Diet, and formed a coalition with the Democratic Party. Within a year, however, this cabinet resigned as the result of criticism from its left wing for its inability to carry out socialist policies. The party also suffered as a result of revelations that JSP members had been implicated in a major corruption scandal. At the subsequent election, in 1947, the JSP's seats in the Diet fell to one-third of their level in 1946. Ideological differences surfaced again, and in 1951 the party split over the issue of whether or not to ratify the Security Treaty with the US. Signing this treaty, which gave the US continued power to make unilateral decisions about US bases and military activities in Japan, had been made a condition for ending the occupation and reinstating Japan's 'sovereignty'.

It was the left wing of the JSP that opposed the proposed treaty and its implications for Japanese rearmament. This group argued instead that Japan should adopt a neutral position in international affairs. The San Francisco Peace Treaty and the US–Japan Security Treaty were both signed in 1951 (see: History). The JSP remained divided until the reunification of 1955, which spurred the conservative parties to unite and form the LDP, as a counter to the possible resurgence of socialist power. Unlike the LDP, the JSP has always been a programmatic party and as such it is prone to severe ideological factionalism and splits.

The next occasion for a party split came in 1960, over the issue of the renewal of the Security Treaty. The more right-wing leaders of the JSP broke away and formed a new party – the Democratic Socialist Party (DSP).

Despite its continued position as the second largest party in the Diet, the JSP has remained unable to replace the LDP. The reasons usually offered for this failure to win government include the rigid ideological positions taken by party members, which have led to major intra-party divisions. Some commentators argue that the remoteness of the possibility of ever winning power has acted to encourage ideological rigidity and a lack of concern with developing policies that would make it popular with the electorate. The continuing failure of the JSP to appeal to a significant segment of the electorate has helped to keep the LDP in power even though there has been a gradual decline in the conservative vote. The continuing lack of electoral popularity of the DSPJ (as it became in 1989) has been accompanied by the appearance of many new opposition parties. This trend has of course helped to fragment the opposition vote even more, thus ensuring the survival of the LDP. This ability of the LDP to stay in power (without achieving a majority of the popular vote at any national election since 1963) raises further questions about the type of democracy operating in Japan.

There have been some interesting developments recently – particularly at the time of the Gulf War (1989–90) – which suggest that some changes in the Japanese political system may be on the way. In the 1989 House of Representatives election, the JSP, now newly named the Social Democratic Party of Japan (SDPJ), enjoyed an increase in its vote while the LDP failed to gain a majority. The electorate had voted against the ruling LDP for three main reasons: the increasing incidence of corruption by serving politicians; the proposal to introduce a sales tax; and proposals to remove existing protection for beef and citrus. What had made the SDPJ (the old JSP) a more viable avenue for expressing disaffection with the ruling party?

The three factors listed above (corruption, sales tax, protection) had caused non-traditional LDP voters to desert the party, but at the same time the SDPJ had begun to make itself more attractive to the electorate. The party's move to a social democratic rather than a Marxist ideological stance, and the appearance of a party leader who was popular with the voters – Doi – helped it to win more votes. It began to look like a strong opposition party that would vie for power. Then, just as the issue of the Security Treaty in 1951 and its revision in 1960 had caused ideological splits and upheavals in the party, the Gulf War shifted the focus away from the progress the SDPJ had been making in remodelling itself. The party once again concentrated on the constitutional issues and its opposition to Japanese rearmament or any changes to the constitutional limits on the use of Japanese troops overseas. The importance of the issue of amendments to the Constitution not only for the SDPJ but also for many Japanese people should not be underestimated. The point being emphasized here, though, is the electoral cost of the party's apparent ideological step backwards without presenting any policies for countering international criticism of Japan during the Gulf War crisis.

As the domestic and international environment keeps changing, the LDP's ability to rely on traditional voters will decrease because the interests of voters are also changing all the time. Japan's more prominent international profile calls for stronger prime ministers who can take a lead. Increasing numbers of young Japanese have priorities and aspirations different from those of their parents, who were the traditional LDP voters. There is also the hope that a less fragmented opposition may develop and even that a new centrist party with appeal to members of the major parties who want change may appear. Change has been occurring slowly over the past five decades, but as long as there is no opposition capable of effectively challenging the LDP's power, Japan's political system will continue to be characterized by one-party rule.

THE JAPAN COMMUNIST PARTY (JCP)

The Japan Communist Party (JCP) was founded in 1922 but remained illegal until 1945. The JCP was severely suppressed by the government, with mass arrests and brutality against its members in 1923–4 and 1928–9. This suppression weakened the party tremendously, as did numerous ideological disagreements. When the occupation forces freed all political prisoners, those communists who had survived the war years in gaol were among the few in politics to be able to deny any collaboration in the war effort. The JCP enjoyed some popularity in the immediate postwar years and actively led some labour and other popular protests. In 1950, however, the party split because of ideological issues and was weakened by the 'red purge' initiated by the occupation authorities against suspected communists.

Although ideological splits continued to weaken the JCP, its successful attempts to build a new grass-roots organization in the late 1960s won it some fresh electoral support. The late 1960s and the 1970s saw massive citizens' protest movements against the increasing levels of pollution and the lack of government action to recognize and punish the offending industries or to support the compensation claims of victims. Places such as Minamata and Yokkaichi have given their names to diseases and terrible suffering by victims of industrial pollution.

The JCP, being a very programmatic and autonomous party and having built a strong local organization, responded to the pollution issues before any other party. JCP lawyers helped people with their grievances and local issues were raised by JCP members in the Diet.

Unlike the LDP, which is backed by the power and money of big business, and the SDPJ, which is backed by the large labour federations which are able to supply block votes, the JCP is truly autonomous. It is the only one of the three to rely on party membership and sale of its newspaper, *Akahata* (Red Flag), for funds. Its lack of institutional ties enables it to act on any important issue without fear of compromising its base of financial support. As well as this ability to respond quickly to local issues, the JCP differs from the LDP and SDPJ, which have strongly centralized power but weak local organizations, in the opportunity it offers people to participate in party decisions on policies and candidates at the local level.

KŌMEITŌ (THE CLEAN GOVERNMENT PARTY)

Of the other main parties, one of the most interesting is Kōmeitō or the Clean Government Party (CGP). It is not an autonomous party but the political wing of the Buddhist religious organization Sokagakkai. This is the most successful of the new religions that have sprung up in Japan since the end of the war. While Kōmeitō is no longer officially part of the Sokagakkai, the latter continues to provide funds and officials to the party. Kōmeitō's political platform rests on calls for social renewal, a new welfare system, abolition of income tax, and no use of nuclear power. Its strongest political characteristics seem to

TABLE 3 Diet membership, as of 27 July 1992

	House of Representatives	House of Councillors
Liberal Democratic Party	277	108
Soc. Dem. Party of Japan	137	71
Kōmeitō	46	24
Japan Communist Party	16	11
Democratic Socialist Party	13	7
Social Democratic Federation	4	1
Rengo	0	12
Japan New Party	0	4
Others	1	7
Independent	6	7
Vacancies	12	0
Total	*512*	*252*

Source: House of Representatives and House of Councillors, Japan.

be opposition to communism and support for 'humanitarian socialism'. The base of Kōmeitō support is to be found in the Sokagakkai membership: all members must join Kōmeitō.

THE 1993 LOWER HOUSE ELECTIONS
On 18 July 1993 elections for the Lower House of the Diet were held in Japan. These elections had been forced by the departure from the LDP of a group of dissatisfied members who wanted immediate action on electoral reform and other matters. This split led to the formation of the Shinseito ('New Born' Party) led by Hata Tsutomo (former Finance Minister). For the first time since 1955 the LDP lost its majority in the Lower House at these elections.

8 Foreign Relations

The parochial nature of Japanese politics does not make international relations a top priority for the majority of Japanese politicians despite the fact that Japan's internal well-being is inextricably linked with the fate of its overseas partners. The Japanese foreign minister is a politician by profession, not a diplomat, and he is chosen to be foreign minister by factional discussions. In the frequent cabinet shuffles that are a hallmark of the Japanese political system, even would-be foreign affairs specialists will find their aspirations blocked by a move to a completely different ministry after only one or two years at most in the job. Added to these difficulties, the Foreign Ministry itself suffers from a lack of manpower, a lack of foreign affairs and country-specific specialists, a poor information-gathering system and constant competition with MITI (the Ministry of International Trade and Industry) and others. The number of Japanese diplomats at home and abroad in 1991 were as shown in Table 4.

On top of these disadvantages, the Foreign Ministry has a poor PR record: it is held to be very 'closed' and conservative.

THE ROLE OF THE UNITED STATES IN JAPANESE INTERNATIONAL RELATIONS

Outside and inside Japan, Japan's record in international relations has had a reputation for being dominated by American foreign policy. This was illustrated by the way in which Nixon went about recognizing the People's Republic of China in 1972: the first the Japanese knew of the move, so it goes, was when they read about it in their morning papers. (Not surprisingly, Japan quickly followed suit and recognized China shortly afterwards.)

There are signs that Japan is getting frustrated by the role

TABLE 4 Number of diplomats at home and abroad, 1991

Country	Number of diplomats	
	At home	**Abroad**
Japan	4,328	1,743
USA	15,900	10,000
UK	8,204	5,375
Canada	4,608	n.a.
France	6,632	2,873
Italy	4,855	n.a.

Source: Tokyo Business Today.

of second-class citizen in international affairs. Its economic might, particularly in the late 1980s, signalled a growing interest in turning economic influence into political influence, as emphasized by books such as *No to ieru Nihon* ('The Japan that can say no'), written by the right-wing journalist-turned-politician Ishihara Shintaro and Morita Akio, chairman of Sony Corporation. As Ishihara states emphatically in the book:

> unless Japan can convey its views forcefully, other nations will assume that with enough pressure, Tokyo always caves in. This perception endangers our foreign relations. If we continue this kowtow diplomacy, one day it will be too late to say no. Nobody will take us seriously.

Any Japanese aspirations for a greater say in world affairs took a knock during the Gulf War (1989–90), when the country's politicians showed themselves to be indecisive and divided. Admittedly, history was not on their side, for Japan's Self-defence Forces Law at the time banned any kind of overseas troop deployment (this has since been modified to allow Japanese troops to be stationed overseas in a peace-keeping but non-combative role). There was strong political opposition from across the political spectrum to any kind of personnel transfers: this mirrored Japanese public opinion too – that this was a foreign war concerning a small country of limited interest to Japan. After an initial attempt to thwart foreign criticism by paying its way out, Japan made US$4 billion available to underwrite the costs of the war: this was later (under pressure from the United States) increased to US$9 billion. People in Japan were angry about these payments, but there was no real alternative if Japan was to be seen to be sincere about its commitment to a greater say in international affairs. The debacle showed that calls for greater awareness of *kokusaika* (internationalization), which enjoyed a kind of heyday throughout the 1980s, were really empty platitudes.

Deciding a role for Japan in the international arena of the twenty-first century will be a tall order unless there are some fundamental changes in the way politics is conducted in Japan. There will also need to be changes in the way the various ministries in the bureaucracy exercise their influence on foreign policy: this is unlikely to happen without the much-needed reform of the political system.

Society

9 Introduction

HOMOGENEITY?

Most discussions of Japanese society begin with mentioning the homogeneity of the Japanese race, and the ensuing racial harmony which has resulted in such a close-knit, efficiently run society. In fact, this homogeneity is a bit of a myth (see: Introduction – General Overview). The origins of the Japanese people are quite diverse, with influxes from the Korean peninsula and China at various periods of history, as well as the original tribal inhabitants, such as the Ainu in Hokkaidō. From north to south, Japan has such a wide variation in climatic conditions that it is not surprising there should be cultural and racial differences, and, as with other countries, there is regional rivalry, with most Japanese in everyday conversation insisting on their regional 'uniqueness'.

Nevertheless, despite a number of racial, cultural and linguistic differences that divide the Japanese, to an outsider Japanese society does present a remarkably united front. Many different explanations are given for this, but some of the contributing factors which are most widely accepted are examined below.

GEOGRAPHICAL SITUATION

Japan, a series of islands separated by a stormy stretch of water from the Asian mainland, has been able to prevent wholesale immigration or invasion. (The only challenger to this was Kublai Khan in the thirteenth century, who sent a fleet of ships to invade Japan, which was destroyed by a fortuitous typhoon, dubbed *kamikaze* – 'divine wind' – by the Japanese.) Large-scale immigration to Japan ceased by the eighth or ninth centuries, and, with the exception of the arrival of around half a million Korean slave-labourers earlier in the twentieth century, nothing much has happened to disrupt the Japanese view of themselves as a single, unified and homogeneous people.

Japan was nevertheless in the fortunate position of being close enough to China and Korea to allow trade when it wanted to and for generations of scholars and priests to make the journey to the continent, bringing back practical and philosophical elements of Chinese and Korean culture, which contributed to Japan's civilization. In such a way, Japan was able to benefit from China's cultural influence, without having to suffer the turmoil of its history. Because of its geographical position, Japan was able also to cut itself off completely from unwanted foreign influence. In the seventeenth century, when the ruling Tokugawa shogun became suspicious of the intentions of the west, he was able to impose a policy of isolation, preventing visitors from entering the country and Japanese citizens from leaving. This state of affairs lasted for 250 years, until Japan's complacency was shattered by Commodore Perry and the US Navy, who forced Japan to open its doors to foreign trade and influence (see: History). This isolation and homogeneity have brought about a great capacity for concerted effort, and a close identification of individual Japanese with the Japanese as a people, which in turn has led to social harmony. However, the often-pointed-to weaknesses in the system are the low priority given to the development and expression of individual personality and the potential for national egotism and bigotry, such as that which welled up before World War II.

LANGUAGE

Although there are a number of regional dialects, the standard form of the Japanese language (*hyoojungo*) is used throughout Japan. The only exceptions are the Ainu people and the other indigenous peoples of Hokkaidō, who have their own languages, and the large Korean community, who tend to be bilingual.

CULTURAL BACKGROUND

One of the cultural elements brought over from China in around the sixth century was Confucianism, the ethics of which underlie much of Japan's culture. The importance placed on the group, rather than the individual, the emphasis on the importance of etiquette and form, and the necessity for everyone to have a recognized place and role in society, for example, are all basic tenets of Confucian philosophy. An equally significant import from China was the model of centralized government and its code of law and taxation system, which was then adapted to suit the Japanese.

Much art, architecture and learning was also imported

from China and again adapted and 'Japanized' to the extent that Japanese culture is basically uniform throughout the country.

JAPANIZATION

This art of taking foreign elements and ideas, adapting them to make them Japanese, and then making them work better than the original, is regarded as a crucial factor in the make-up of Japanese society. The Japanese have been assimilating imported ideas, without discarding indigenous customs and traditions, since Japanese history was first recorded.

GROUP ETHIC

For centuries the Japanese people have lived under centralized governments (not always national governments) and have been used to having their lives regulated in minute detail. This, and the importance placed on the group – the family, the school, the company, the nation – rather than the individual, are part of Japan's Confucian heritage. In a land with a large population and limited space, this accounts for much of Japanese society's appearance of uniformity.

EDUCATION

Throughout history, the Japanese have placed great importance on education. Warrior leaders in feudal times were often great scholars (in contrast with western military leaders of the same period, who were often illiterate and left learning to the priests). Japan has a very high literacy rate, a fact which was important in the period following the Meiji Restoration in 1868. It meant that new information and knowledge could be disseminated quickly, so the Japanese could learn about western technology. It also meant that they could carry out written commands and helped the new centralized government enforce social control.

Confucian ideals also stressed the importance of learning as a means of bettering yourself and raising yourself to a position of authority. These ideals are still seen as important in today's society and are demonstrated in the fact that the Japanese are almost always studying something – a foreign language, traditional arts, etc.

The Japanese have also always believed that education should be useful to society, and Japan's compulsory education system focuses on the subjects which are regarded as useful for the running of the country. It stresses, too, the importance of training in a variety of subjects, rather than specialization. Many Japanese manage to combine the two ideals by studying something for personal advancement, which also happens to be useful to their group.

10 Structure

The 'frame' concept is very important to an understanding of Japanese society. The anthropologist and writer Chie Nakane, in her book *Japanese Society*, argues that whereas westerners tend to be more concerned with who you are – a fixed entity – the Japanese will be more concerned with where everyone is and whom they are with – the social frame – which determines how you speak and act. In Japanese society, no one is in a fixed social position. Whether you are regarded as 'superior', 'inferior', 'insider', 'outsider', etc., will depend on whom you are talking to, when and where. Within the framework, there is always a hierarchy, but the hierarchy is not fixed and may vary depending on a number of factors. In some situations you can see the Japanese struggling to take account of different factors such as age, wealth, position in company, whether the person is male or female, etc., to work out the hierarchy in a particular situation in order to know how to behave.

The language used in any situation will reflect the hierarchical ranking. Seniors in any group will be spoken to using respect language by their juniors, and juniors can be addressed more familiarly.

UCHI AND *SOTO*: THE CONCEPT OF THE 'IN GROUP' AND THE 'OUT GROUP'

In Japan, as has been mentioned above, the concept of the group and the group identity is very important in the context of society. The identity of the group also depends on the context you are in – it can be your family, your class, your school, your company or your country. Your behaviour and language will change depending on whether you are talking to someone who is *uchi* – 'inside' the group – or *soto* – 'outside' the group – and this will obviously depend on the situation. Someone who is in your school, but not in your class, may be *uchi* on one occasion and *soto* on another.

RESPONSIBILITY IN RELATION TO ROLES

In Japan's shifting framework of society, people have certain roles in relation to others and recognized responsibilities in those roles. It is the recognition and acceptance of these responsibilities (*giri*) which helps keep the wheels of Japanese society running smoothly.

One of the most important of these relationships is the *senpai–kōhai* or senior–junior relationship. This applies when people have been in the same school, university or company, having joined in different years. Sometimes it is a formalized relationship – for example, a new pupil or employee may be assigned a *senpai* to show them the ropes. The *senpai* will then be in a position of superiority, but also of responsibility for the *kōhai*'s welfare and advancement for the rest of their lives. Sometimes the system is merely a kind of old-boy network, whereby people use the fact that they have been to the same school, etc., to gain an advantage.

THE FAMILY

The family unit is one of the cornerstones of Japanese society. It is the primary group to which all Japanese belong, and in a way it serves as a microcosm of Japanese society as a whole. There is a strong sense of loyalty to one's own family, and a strong differentiation between those who are 'in group' members and those who are outside the group. This is reflected in the language, in that different words are used to refer to your own mother, wife, children, etc., and to members of someone else's family. Less formal language is also used within your own family, although, as with other groups, there is a hierarchical ranking system, with the father as head of the household and seniors in the family – grandparents, older brothers and sisters – being addressed using respect language by their juniors.

The average Japanese family unit today consists of a mother, father and one or two children. In the countryside, and in wealthier families, the extended family is still quite common, with the eldest son and his family moving into the family home to look after aged parents. The family used to be known as *ie* (household) and was taken to mean all the people living together under one roof – not those, like younger sons or daughters, who had moved out and set up their own homes. Members of a household were – and are still to some extent – expected to subordinate their personal interests to those of the family as a whole.

The Japanese household is also taken to include all the

previous members of the family who have lived and died. The ancestors are still involved in the daily routine of the household and will have a shrine (*butsudan*) in most Japanese homes, which will be tended with offerings and consulted about major decisions. Visitors to the home will often pay their respects to the *butsudan* before greeting their hosts.

WOMEN'S ROLES

Women in Japan are often seen by westerners as downtrodden and poorly treated by Japanese men. However, in the family, no matter what sort of facade is maintained for the benefit of outsiders, the wife is, in practice, the wielder of power. The husband is the official head of the household, but the wife has complete control of the purse-strings and makes all the major decisions relating to household finances – often to the extent of giving her husband monthly pocket-money from his salary, which he hands over completely to her. Fathers also tend to have to work very long hours and spend little time at home, in order to be successful at work, and so women usually take full control of the upbringing and education of the children – a position of great responsibility anywhere in the world, but particularly so in Japan, where education is the key to future success.

As holders of the nation's purse-strings, women are increasingly recognized as a force to be reckoned with in Japan's consumer-led economy. Women are responsible for 80 per cent of Japan's domestic consumer spending, which in turn constitutes over 50 per cent of Japan's total GNP. The advertising and marketing worlds are increasingly aiming their sales pitches at women, who not only have their husband's money to spend, but increasingly their own salaries as well.

Women at work

In Japan, 41.3 per cent of women over the age of 15 are in full-time employment, in comparison with 41.2 per cent in the UK and 44 per cent in the US. This represents an increase of nearly 10 per cent since 1981. There has also been an increase in the number of married women who work: around 57.8 per cent of working women in 1991 were married. Nevertheless, the number of women between the ages of 25 and 45 at work plummets steeply, as women are still expected to take time out for child-rearing. Despite legislation such as the Equal Employment Law (1985) and the Childcare Leave Law (1991), the majority of women workers are in low-paid, unskilled work: the largest proportion (nearly 35 per cent) are clerical workers, known as 'OL' – 'office ladies' – who make tea and do routine office work. Fourteen per cent of women workers are in professional or technical jobs, while a mere 1 per cent are in managerial positions.

Women in education

A similar picture emerges in education. Although the percentage of women going on to higher education overtook that of men for the first time in 1989, the majority of women attend courses at two-year short-term universities – *tanki daigaku* – where they do a kind of finishing-school course, studying a number of general subjects in very little depth, rather than specializing in any particular field.

In a society where women are not expected to work if they have children, nor to demonstrate too much intelligence, many women seek to gain recognition from their children's achievements. This has resulted in a breed known as *kyooiku mamas* – 'education mothers'. These are mothers who encourage their children to study long hours, insist on sending them to cram schools and push them through 'examination hell'.

MARRIAGE

The rate of marriage is 5.8 per thousand population per annum, higher than France and Sweden, but lower than the US and the UK. The average age for women to marry is 23–4, for men 26–9. Women are jokingly referred to in reference to marriage as 'Christmas cake' – 'no good after 25'. Although an increasing number of Japanese marriages are 'love matches', still between 30 per cent and 40 per cent are *omiai kekkon* – arranged marriages. Often a family will wait and hope that their son or daughter will meet a suitable marriage partner of his or her own accord, but if they either show no signs of doing so by the appropriate marriageable age, or produce someone totally unsuitable, an *omiai* will be set up.

In an *omiai*, the services of a go-between who will look for a suitable match and will then perform a formal introduction are required. Sometimes the go-between will be hired on a formal basis and will take the prospective bride or groom's background, likes, dislikes, education, etc., into account to produce possible matches. Everything will be researched very thoroughly before any decisions are made, so there is no chance of marrying someone with congenital illnesses or whose background is not suitable. (Match-making is big business in Japan.) Sometimes the 'matchmaker' is a friend of the family, who will take on the job of introducing eligible partners and then negotiating wedding arrangements, settlements, etc., if the couple are mutually agreed on marriage. An individual may go through several *miai* or introductions before settling on a partner.

Whether the marriage is a love match or an arranged marriage, the wedding and reception are likely to be a lavish extravaganza. Weddings tend to be performed by Shinto priests and are usually held in hotels. For the religious ceremony the bride will wear a traditional white kimono and head-dress, with the groom also wearing traditional costume. Family and close friends only will attend at this point, but a large reception will be held afterwards, at which the bride and groom may appear in different outfits. A measure of the lavishness of the reception is the number of gowns the bride appears in. Usually she will change into a multi-coloured ceremonial kimono for the first part of the reception, followed by at least one western-style gown. A banquet will be served and the bride and the groom will make a dramatic entrance, sometimes theatrically staged – appearing through the floor in a cloud of dry ice or being lowered from the ceiling in a gondola. There will also be a candle-lighting ceremony, in which the bride and groom will go round the room and light the candle for each table, as well as a cake-cutting ceremony featuring a giant, plastic western-style wedding cake, which the couple will pretend to cut. Finally, all the guests will be given a bag full of presents to take away. The wedding is usually paid for by both sets of parents and the couple themselves – who pays for what is carefully negotiated. An average wedding costs around ¥7 million (US$65,000). The wedding industry is therefore thriving.

Wedding guests tend to give money presented in special ornate wedding envelopes, on which is written the name of the giver and the amount. The amount to give is more or less specified depending on the relationship to the couple.

The divorce rate is 1.27 per thousand population, just over a quarter that of the US (4.7) and around half that of the UK (2.86) (1989 figures).

THE HOME

The traditional architecture of the Japanese home also reflects social attitudes. Examples of this include the strong demarcation between 'inside' and 'outside', which is physically manifested by the *genkan* (entrance hall), a kind of no man's land between 'inside' and 'outside' where shoes are taken off before stepping 'inside' the house proper. Another example is the flexibility of space within the traditional home, with sliding panels (*fusuma*) changing the size and function of rooms to suit different situations. Traditionally there is no allocation of rooms for different purposes (dining, sleeping, sitting, etc.) or for individuals. The family as a whole is considered to be more important than its individuals, and would tend, for example, to eat together in one multi-purpose room, which could then be converted to a sleeping room, by folding away the low eating table and laying out futon and bedding, for the family to sleep together.

Japanese homes today range from large, traditional farmhouses in the country where several generations live together in one household, to small suburban houses and (by western standards) cramped apartments in the cities. Certain elements are common to most Japanese homes, however.

Tatami mats were the traditional flooring for Japanese houses and even modern, westernized apartments nowadays are likely to have at least one *tatami*-floored room. The mats are made of layers of thick rush matting edged with fabric, and come in standard sizes, so rooms are generally measured by the number of mats they have. Because the mats are so thick, they make a springy, insulated floor, which is warm in winter and cool in summer. They also make a comfortable base on which to lay futon bedding at night. Each *tatami* mat is approximately the size of one person's futon, so the number of mats in a room traditionally determined the number of people who could sleep in the room. *Tatami* mats can last for many years, not least because even slippers are taken off before stepping on them, so they are kept clean and undamaged.

Shoes, as mentioned above, are taken off at the *genkan*. This is an entrance hall, which is physically inside the house but set at the same level as the ground outside, with a step up into the rest of the house. Outdoor shoes are exchanged for slippers here by a complicated procedure involving stepping out of the shoes one by one and into the slippers which are laid out on the steps, without touching the floor of the *genkan* with stockinged feet, or touching the inside step with any part of the shoe. The *genkan* marks the symbolic division between *soto* – 'outside' – and *uchi* – 'inside' – as well as serving the purpose of preventing dirt from shoes being taken into the house.

Another aspect of cleanliness in the Japanese home is the use of the *o-furo* (bath). The Japanese tub is for soaking in: washing is done outside the bath, by either showering, or scooping water from the tub into a basin, soaping and sluicing off with more water scooped from the bath, before getting into the tub itself. Japanese bathrooms are fully waterproofed and have a drain set in the floor, so water can be freely splashed around. In this way, the actual bath water remains clean and can be used by the whole household to relax in after washing. The Japanese like to soak, up to their necks, in extremely hot water, so family bathtubs tend to be square and deep, and have a water heater at the side, which draws the water from the bath through, reheats it and circulates it. Thus the water can be kept hot for the whole family to use. There is also usually a lid for the bath, which keeps water hot between users. Traditionally the husband or any guests would be invited to bathe first, followed by sons, daughters and finally the wife, who would have had the task of preparing the bath in the first place.

The traditional structure of Japanese homes has been changing, reflecting corresponding changes in society. Younger people tend to prefer to sleep in beds, and to have separate rooms for different functions and for individual family members. However, most Japanese homes combine these western aspects with traditional Japanese aspects and retain a *genkan*, at least one *tatami* room and a traditional Japanese bath.

CLASS

The Japanese regard themselves as a more-or-less classless society, with everyone belonging to a huge middle class. In a government survey, 89.9 per cent of respondents felt they were middle-class, 0.5 per cent felt they were upper-class, 6.3 per cent lower-class and the rest 'didn't know'. (May 1991; Source: Prime Minister's Office). In terms of income and standard of living, this is largely true. The average family income for a non-promoted post is ¥278,000 (US$2,593) a month, with annual bonuses of ¥980,000 (US$9,141), a total of ¥4,316,000 (US$40,257) per annum. A company director earns around twice that amount (a much smaller differential than in western companies). In March 1992, 99 per cent of Japanese households owned at least one television and telephone, and 78.6 per cent owned at least one passenger car.

Unemployment has not been a great problem, although there is much hidden unemployment. Official figures (March 1992) put the unemployment rate at 2.1 per cent, in comparison with 7.3 per cent in the US and 9.4 per cent in the UK. In terms of education, 95.8 per cent of Japanese go on to senior high school and 36.8 per cent go on to full-time higher education (lower than the United States, but higher than the UK and Germany; see Table 5).

Education is the key factor in determining 'class' in Japanese society, and money tends to play a large part in what sort of education you receive. While not as class-conscious as their British counterparts, and despite their insistence that they are all middle-class, the Japanese can be quite snobbish, and tend to socialize with people who are of a similar status to them in the social hierarchy. A doctor and his family are unlikely to socialize with the family of a taxi driver or bar-owner, for example. Likewise, a company director would probably be horrified if his daughter announced she was going to marry a primary-school teacher. Doctors, lawyers, and *shachoo* (company directors) are the new samurai class in Japan. In addition

TABLE 5 Advancement rate to higher education

| | Year | Percentage of relevant age group | | |
		Total	Male	Female
USA[a]	1988	45.6	42.5	48.7
Japan[b]	1990	36.8	36.1	37.5
France[c]	1989	40.8	–	–
Germany[d]	1988	26.4	31.0	21.6
UK[d]	1988	26.5	27.7	25.3

Rate of junior high school graduates continuing on to senior high school (%)

Japan	1991	94.6	93.5	95.8

[a] Figures based on new entrants at 4-year and 2-year colleges (full time only).
[b] Figures based on new entrants at university level, junior college level, and senior level of colleges of technology.
[c] Figures based on students qualified to enter higher education (university level).
[d] Figures based on new entrants to higher education.
Source: Ministry of Education, Japan.

to being well-educated professionals, they earn vast amounts from salaries and private practices and are able to send their children to private schools, pay for extra tuition, and give them the necessary education to get them into top universities, and in turn into good jobs.

URBAN/RURAL COMPARISONS

Japan is largely an urban society, with a population density of 126 people per square mile (327 per square km), compared to a UK figure of 91 (235) and a US figure of 10 (27). In reality the figure should be much higher, as the bulk of Japan's population lives on the narrow coastal plain. Most of Japan's industry and cities are located there, and it constitutes only around 4 per cent of the country's total land area. The great ambition of most Japanese is to own their own home, and 61.3 per cent do so. Land prices in the 1980s were increasing so rapidly that it became more and more difficult to consider buying, and many people resorted to renting. This trend is now being reversed, as land prices have levelled out and are starting to come down. None the less, the average floor area of a Japanese home is 96.3

square yards (80.5 square metres), less than half the size of the average US home (162 square metres) (Source: Ministry of Construction, 1990). Figures are not available for the UK, but the average French home, at 105.5 square metres, is also considerably larger. Homes are larger in rural areas, but the working population of rural villages has been decreasing rapidly, as more and more young people reject the idea of working on the land and head for the cities. In certain areas, the situation has become so desperate that the local men, unable to persuade Japanese girls to settle for the life of a farmer's wife, have resorted to importing 'brides' from the Philippines.

Japan also has the highest life-expectancy rate in the world, at 75.86 years for males and 81.81 for females. This fact, and the steady fall in Japan's birth-rate from 36.3 per 1,000 in 1870 to under 11 per 1,000 in 1987, has led to the 'greying' of Japanese society, with the number of elderly people in proportion to the working population rising. This problem is of great concern to the Japanese. The land is already so crowded that it is not a viable option to try and encourage people to have more children, but it is becoming increasingly difficult to think of ways of supporting the elderly and physically fitting more people into Japan's crowded islands.

One result has been that the proportion of working women has been on the rise – whether the recession, with job cuts in all sectors, will affect this trend has yet to be seen.

Land-fill projects, such as the vast Tokyo Bay complex, are being used more and more to expand the areas which can be built on, and another solution which is being explored is colonies for elderly Japanese in foreign countries, such as Australia.

MALE/FEMALE COMPARISONS
Japan's population (as of October 1990) was 123,611,167; it was made up of 62,914,443 females and 60,696,274 males, despite the fact that each year more boys than girls are born (see Table 6).

HEALTH AND WELFARE
In Japan, although there are excellent medical facilities, doctors and hospitals available, there is minimal state provision for the elderly, the sick and the unemployed.

Traditionally welfare has been the responsibility of employers. Companies provide assistance with housing, medical, education and pension costs to life-time employees (see: Market Entry).

There is a national health insurance system, in addition to assisted medical insurance schemes provided by employers. In

TABLE 6 Japan's population by age and sex (as of 1 October 1990)

Age group	Total	Male	Female
0–4	6,509,996	3,337,729	3,171,967
5–9	7,485,530	3,835,026	3,650,504
10–14	8,548,436	4,384,951	4,163,485
15–19	10,034,657	5,141,504	4,893,153
20–24	8,827,647	4,487,660	4,339,987
25–29	8,094,526	4,095,197	3,999,329
30–34	7,809,011	3,940,200	3,868,811
35–39	9,027,579	4,541,293	4,486,286
40–44	10,686,873	5,369,719	5,317,154
45–49	9,042,647	4,499,227	4,543,420
50–54	8,110,208	4,012,193	4,098,015
55–59	7,744,933	3,797,013	3,947,920
60–64	6,761,488	3,247,563	3,513,925
65–69	5,115,353	2,202,117	2,913,236
70–74	3,826,119	1,565,121	2,260,998
75–79	3,024,951	1,201,428	1,823,523
80–84	1,836,836	680,610	1,156,226
85 up	1,124,677	358,173	766,504
Total	123,611,167	60,696,724	62,914,443

Source: Management and Coordination Agency, Japan.

both types of scheme, participants pay a proportion of their income in contributions for insurance. Under the employers' schemes, 100 per cent of costs are covered for the member and 70–80 per cent of a family member's costs. Under the national health system, the patient is liable to pay up to 30 per cent of costs. Approximately 25 per cent of the population is covered by the national health insurance scheme, mainly those working for small to medium-sized organizations which do not have their own insurance scheme.

There is also a social welfare system which provides financial and other forms of assistance for those who are unable to support themselves financially. This is covered by state or local government budgets and does not involve contributions from the individual. There are very strict policies on who is eligible to claim. Candidates are the families of the physically disabled, the elderly, and single parents.

For details on hospitals with English-speaking doctors see: Contact Addresses in Tokyo and Principal Cities.

State education is provided between the ages of five and eighteen. Most pre-school and higher education is privately funded.

11 Religion

As in most countries, religious themes are intimately linked with social, political and cultural institutions. No survey of Japan, therefore, would be complete without reference to them. The distinctive feature of religion in Japan, however, is not simply the richness and diversity of its traditions, but the way in which these traditions have interacted and transformed each other to create a religious consciousness with peculiarly Japanese traits.

Though no one religion can be viewed without reference to another, for convenience the major elements which form Japanese religion today might be broken down into Shinto, Buddhism, Confucianism, Christianity and New Religions.

SHINTO

Shinto is the term used to denote those elements of Japanese religion which are native to Japan. Unlike Buddhism, Confucianism and Christianity, it does not have a founder or commonly recognized scripture. The word Shinto is comprised of two Chinese characters. *Shin* is normally translated as god, and *tō* as way: 'the way of the gods'. The Japanese term used to denote a Shinto place of worship is *jinja*, or sometimes *jingu*, translated into English as shrine.

Early religion

Archaeological evidence suggests that the earliest form of religion in Japan involved fertility rites, and possibly rites of passage, such as birth, coming of age and death. There is also evidence of shamanistic practices. The artefacts found in the burial tombs of the next wave of settlers seem to suggest belief in an afterlife.

Greater social cohesion, associated with the development of rice farming, saw the division of society into *uji*, or groupings of clans, with a well-defined hierarchy. Each *uji* had its tutelary deity, the *ujigami*. The leader of the *uji* had an important religious function in relation to the deity and may actually have been worshipped as the deity itself. One kingdom, according to a third-century Chinese record, was governed by a queen whose task was to commune with the gods, leaving the administrative affairs to her brother.

Imperial mythology

Another, more political dimension to the native religion then emerges. The myths codified in the *Kojiki* and *Nihonshoki* of AD 712 and 720 were attempts to establish the legitimacy of the imperial lineage and to subsume the various *uji* and their *kami* (gods) under its supremacy. According to these, before the earth was formed, the god Izanagi and goddess Izanami stirred up the sea with a heavenly spear. The drops of brine which fell to the sea solidified and formed the islands of Japan. Amaterasu, the sun-goddess, who is worshipped at the Grand Ise Shrine, descended to the isles where she ordered her grandson to rule the world, presenting him with the three sacred imperial regalia: sword, curved jewel and bronze mirror, artefacts found in the tombs of earlier rulers. His great-grandson, in turn, was to become the first emperor, Jimmu. The present emperor Akihito is said to be the 125th in line from Jimmu.

The myths, as well as being an inspiration for literature and theatre, have provided for later centuries a most potent symbol and focus for national unity. It is to these myths that the Japanese have turned in times of national crisis, most notably in the imperialist era.

Interaction with Buddhism

The official acceptance of Buddhism at the imperial court in the sixth century did not meet with universal approval. Its opponents claimed it would incite the wrath of the native *kami*. However, the superior culture and magical rituals of the foreign religion attracted the ruling family, and the centuries which followed are marked by considerable communication and at times ingenious blending of the two traditions. (Attempts were made to bring these together at the official level with the Office of Shinto Worship, which sought to bring together the native traditions and Chinese accretion in the form of an official round of annual ceremonies, codified ancestral rites and even a bureau of yin and yang.) In some cases Buddhism and Shinto were to exist side by side, often physically in the form of *jinguji*, or shrine-temples (temples containing shrines). At the philosophical level, individual temples and individual shrines developed their own mythologies, relating them to Buddhism.

This resulted in a number of syncretic cults. Notable among them are those of Hachiman, the warrior god and personification of the legendary emperor Ojin, to whom a large number of shrines are dedicated today. Originally a warrior god, he was also revered as a *boddhisatva* (Buddha-to-be). Certain angry spirits of the Shinto pantheon were said to have sought salvation and been 'civilized' through refuge in Buddhism. Most well known is that of the Heian minister, Sugawara no Michizane, exiled to Kyushu, whose angry spirit, in the form of a *kami*, was pacified and worshipped as the Buddhist divinity of compassion (Avolekitesvara). Over 3,000 shrines are dedicated to him. Associations between the cosmic Buddha Vairocana, translated as Dainichi (great sun), and Amaterasu the sun-goddess lead to the belief that she too was a Buddhist divinity; likewise the spirit of Tokugawa Ieyasu, enshrined at Nikko.

All of this was supported by the doctrine of *honji suijaku* (original essence and manifest traces), favoured by the traditionally syncretic and magical nature of esoteric (Shingon) Buddhism, by which Buddhas and *boddhisatvas* were manifested as native gods in order to spread their teachings. Various schools of syncretism exist, some emphasizing the Buddhist nature of the *kami*, others starting from the creation myth, seeing Buddhas as forms of the original Shinto cosmology.

It was not until the tenth century that a coherent system of myth, ritual, priestly families and functions had emerged. There are 22 imperially patronized shrines, which still stand today as the major Japanese shrines around Nara and Kyoto. Some were specifically concerned with rites relating to the emperor, some were dedicated to important historical and mythological figures, others related to Buddhism, and still others to major agrarian and seasonal matters.

Ascendancy of Shintoism

Throughout the Edo period, Buddhism and Shintoism continued to coexist. However, there were strains of thought among samurai intellectuals which stressed the importance of strictly native traditions. Complementing Confucian reverence for the son of heaven, they drew up cosmologies on the ancient creation myths to stress the divine origins of the imperial line. This line of thought was later developed to meet the demand for a restoration of the ancient ways, with the imperial institution firmly at the centre. The new government, essentially inimical to Buddhism, sought to separate the two traditions, and confiscated many temple lands, instituting a form of state Shintoism, bringing local shrine teachings, the roles of their priests and their practices into line with them. As Japan entered the imperial phase, emperor worship was encouraged, with the emperor acting as a spiritual and moral focus: the myths of Japan were taught as history in schools, people were forced to worship at shrines, and were advised, 'in the case of emergency, offer yourselves courageously to the State . . . to guard and maintain the prosperity of Our Imperial Throne, coeval with heaven and earth' (Imperial Rescript on Education, 1890).

After defeat in World War II, the emperor formally renounced his divinity. State and religion were separated. Some argue that Shinto may still provide the occasion for a resurgence of outright national fanaticism and have speculated as to the less than symbolic overtly religious nature of the funeral of Hirohito. Extreme right-wing groups still maintain the above sentiments, but their presence is more notable in terms of noisy propaganda vans than in terms of numbers.

Shinto today

The Ministry of Cultural Affairs gives a figure of over 100 million followers: other surveys suggest that only 3 per cent identify themselves as Shinto believers and few have any interest in its tenets.

Shinto today incorporates a wide variety of beliefs, customs and practices. One could perhaps distil Shintoism, however, down to notions of sacred space, sacred time, and purity.

Kami ('god' is perhaps a little misleading), of which there are said to be 8 million (the *yaoyorozu no kami*), are a ubiquitous presence, both residing in the spatial sphere and overseeing it. Mythological and historical figures may be revered as *kami*. They may also be immanent in certain objects, such as the imperial regalia, but more importantly, in nature: trees, stones, rivers, mountains and the elements. Thus, many shrines can be found in places of scenic beauty – at the mouth of a river, or the bottom of a mountain, or by a waterfall. This keen feeling and reverence for nature, at once bountiful and fearful, is said to pervade much of the Japanese religiousness and is reflected in much of Shinto practice.

There are numerous shrines (some 80,000 registered as legal entities) which vary considerably in size and scale. These are normally denoted by a gate or *torii* made of two columns supporting two cross-beams. Passing through the *torii* one enters sacred space. This sense of entering hallowed ground is strikingly represented in the Fushimi Inari shrine near Kyoto. Hundreds of dedicated *torii*, presented by parishioners and businesses, line the path to the sanctuary, effectively forming a tunnel. Many larger shrines possess a roofed trough where one scoops up water with a bamboo ladle and washes one's hands and mouth in an act of purification. Thereafter one enters the *haiden* or place of worship. In the inner sanctuary, which is usually raised above the ground, is enshrined the *kami* (not normally represented by a figure or image). Visitors ordinarily ring a bell, bow twice and clap their hands twice, thereby summoning the *kami*. Offerings may also be made, though this is normally done by throwing coins into a box at the front of the sanctuary.

Aspects of sacred time and rituals

Sacred time is reflected in the various rituals and festivals (*matsuri*), whose origins relate either to the agricultural season or to mythological events. Each shrine has its own distinctive practices at these festivals, but essentially they involve acts of propitiation to the gods and above all acts of purification. The movements and words follow a prescribed liturgy and are performed by Shinto priests (*guji*), often with the assistance of shrine maidens (*miko*). Shinto priests can be distinguished by their white robes and black hats. Doors are symbolically opened, and ritual prayers (*norito*) are made, principally of supplication or thanksgiving. The preparation and offering of special foods forms a central aspect of the act of propitiation (the rich heritage of much of Japanese cuisine is grounded in the Shinto *matsuri*). Rice wine is also offered to the *kami* and imbibed by participants, thus symbolizing communion with them.

In addition to the festivals marking the rites of passage, there are numerous local festivals. All of the major festivals have a fête-like character, with lines of street stalls selling food, talismans, amulets, etc. These festivals may be accompanied by dancing, theatre, sumo and drinking.

Purification

The most pronounced and influential aspect of Shinto is that of purification. Ailments and misfortunes are often perceived as the result of pollution from outside. Ideas of pollution are associated with such things as death, childhood, menstruation and disease. Common symbols of purity in Shinto are salt (hence the custom of throwing salt into the centre of the sumo ring), folded pieces of paper (*shide*), which are tied to posts or sacred trees, the twisted rope (*shimenawa*) which is often seen in shrines, fire and rice. Public exorcisms (*oharai*) also form an essential part of Shinto ceremony. They usually involve the Shinto priest waving a rod with strips of white paper (*gohei*) over the participants. Misfortune is often attributed to outer pollution, and it is still not uncommon for individuals to invite a Shinto priest to perform an exorcism over the family car or the house.

Anthropologists have pointed out how notions of purification and pollution have contributed to the keen division in Japan between inner and outer. Cleanliness itself is highly valued in Japan. Sweeping and cleaning are regarded as spiritual disciplines.

It is often said: 'Born Shinto, die Buddhist'. Shinto, in the minds of most Japanese, represents life and vitality, whereas Buddhism symbolizes death.

BUDDHISM

In contrast to the other half of the equation, Buddhism possesses both a founder and scriptures. It traces its origins to the historical figure Siddharta Gautama, the prince of a small kingdom in what is now Nepal. At the age of 29 he renounced his comfortable existence and underwent a variety of ascetic practices. Six years later, sitting under a tree in Buddhagaya, he experienced enlightenment. Thereafter he travelled throughout Central India sharing his wisdom.

By the time this religion reached Japan via Korea and China, it had undergone a number of transformations and local accretions, and comprised a variety of sects and practices. The teachings which were adopted and the sects which developed and survive today in Japan may or may not reflect the flavour of Gautama's experience and his initial teachings. Nevertheless, they have shaped and been influenced by native political, social, cultural and religious factors.

These Buddhist sects of Japan belong to the Mahayana, or Greater Vehicle, form of Buddhism, as opposed to the Hinayana or Lesser Vehicle. The latter is essentially monastic and took root in Sri Lanka and the countries of southern Asia. It used the early Pali-language sutras and commentaries, venerated the Gautama Buddha only, and emphasized strict discipline and the individual attainment of liberation through observance of this discipline. The Mahayana, by contrast, which spread north of India through Tibet and China, is often called the easy path of salvation for all people. Among its various sects there developed the belief in a number of Buddhas or enlightened beings, including the historical Buddha, compassionate Buddhas-to-be (*boddhisatvas*, or *bosatsu*), kings of light and other heavenly beings.

Although Buddhist scriptures and ideas were probably brought to Japan by travellers from Korea in the fifth century, Buddhism is said to have been introduced to Japan in 552, when the king of Paekche in Korea presented the ruling court of Yamato with an image of Shakyamuni (Gautama) Buddha and a number of sutras. The devout scholar and patron saint of Japanese Buddhism, Shōtoku Taishi, set up a number of monasteries, and sent regular missions of monks and scholars to China to learn more of its beliefs. The most notable of these monasteries is Horyuji near Nara, where Prince Shotoku is said to have resided.

In the Nara period (710-794), under Emperor Shomu, Buddhism was adopted as a state religion, and temples called *kokubunji* were built in each state. Essentially a religion of the aristocracy, its appeal lay less in its teachings than in its esoteric rituals and its sophisticated architecture and sculpture, which enhanced the prestige of the ruling families and guaranteed divine protection.

Of the Six Nara Schools of academic Buddhism imported from China, few had any influence beyond the monasteries in which they were studied. The complex Chinese language of the sutras must also have been an obstacle to comprehension and their philosophical speculations about the nature of reality had little appeal. One, however, the Kegon Sutra (after which the sect is named) was adopted by Emperor Shomu. Its focus of worship is the Vairocana (Dainichi) Buddha, from which Shaka (Shakyamuni, or Gautama Buddha) is an emanation.

The grandeur of the temples is perhaps the greatest legacy of this phase of Buddhism. The best-known temples (many of their buildings date from a later period) are Yakushiji, Kofukuji and Toshodaiji. Todaiji houses an image of the Dainichi Buddha which is over 50 feet (15 metres) high. It was built, typically, after the outbreak of an epidemic.

It was the Heian (794-1185) and Kamakura (1185-1333) periods which were to produce the most important and lasting sects of Buddhism. Two major centres of Buddhism, away from Nara, were established by two key figures in Japanese Buddhist history: Saicho and Kukai.

Saicho founded a temple on Mt Hiei near Kyoto. From Mt Hiei emerged most of the subsequent strains of Japanese Buddhist thought. *Tendai*, the sect which he brought over from China, had wider appeal. Based on the Lotus sutra, its teaching is eclectic and non-exclusive, allowing for different levels of truth: it accommodates all scriptures as different stages on the way to Buddha-hood, which every person may achieve.

Kukai established the Chinese school of Shingon Buddhism at the second major centre, Mt Koya, south of Nara. Also known as Kobo Daishi, he is a legendary figure, accomplished in the arts and letters. The doctrines are complex and esoteric, centring on the theme of the omnipresence of the Dainichi Buddha. Mystical rituals, symbols, gestures, letters and mandalas provide access to, and enhance, the sense of omnipresence.

The fearsome Myo-o, deities which ward off evil spirits, are peculiar to this sect. The teachings of both these sects incorporated the Shinto *kami*. The Shinto Inari deity, for example, symbolized by a fox, acts as a protector of Toji temple in Kyoto, which belongs to the Shingon sect.

Nevertheless, it was not until the Kamakura period that Buddhism really escaped its ecclesiastical confines. The decline of law and order at the end of the Heian period lent weight to the doctrine of Mappo, which said that people were no longer able to attain salvation because of their frailty. They must rely entirely on the grace of Amida, the Buddha of the Western Paradise. The monk Honen, who trained at Mt Hiei, was the first to develop this notion into a sect, the Pure Land (Jodo) sect, distinct from *Tendai*. What was necessary for salvation was the repetition, with complete faith in his mercy, of the name of Amida, Namu Amida Butsu. This recitation is termed *nenbutsu*. This form of Buddhism had enormous popularity with the ordinary people, but aroused severe criticism from the Tendai monks. Honen was finally exiled in 1207.

One of his followers, Shinran, did much to further popularize this form of other-reliance (*tariki*) Buddhism, with some alterations. Sometimes likened to Luther, Shinran advocated marriage for the priesthood, himself marrying the daughter of an aristocratic Kyoto family. As founder of the Jodo Shinshu (True Pure Land) sect of Buddhism, Shinran stressed that the only requirement for salvation was a single, utterly sincere utterance of the Buddha's name. Morality and human effort are important for social order, but in terms of 'divine' truth what matters is grace. If Amida vows to save a good man, Shinran maintained, how much more would he save a wicked man. The headquarters of Shinshu are today located in the large Kyoto temples of Nishi-Honganji and Higashi-Honganji.

The third of the popular sects dating back to this period was founded by Nichiren, after whom it is named. Nichiren was intolerant of other sects, and in this respect is somewhat anomalous in the history of Japanese Buddhism. Salvation can come only through faith in the Lotus sutra, which he saw as the sole and complete repository of truth. Faith is expressed by invoking the help of the sutra, with a brief phrase text, not unlike the *nenbutsu* which he criticized so fiercely. Sokagakkai, a 'new' religion which gained a large number of adherents in the postwar era, is an offshoot of this sect.

In contrast with the above sects, the Zen sect of Buddhism, also introduced at this time, is often described as a religion of self-reliance, or *jiriki*. Historically, it is a form of Buddhism that was transmitted from India to China by the semi-mythological character, Bodhidharma. It first flourished in China and took root in Japan in the early thirteenth century. Doctrinally, it is difficult to say what Zen is, as it de-emphasizes dogma and scripture. Its flavour can be summed up in a quatrain attributed to Bodhidharma:

> A special transmission outside the scriptures
> Not relying on written words or letters
> Direct pointing to the human essence
> Seeing into one's nature and becoming Buddha

Meditation is central to Zen, and the master plays an important role in communicating the Way. All beings, as they are, possess the Buddha nature and are enlightened. This reality cannot be apprehended simply by the discursive, discriminating intellect. The Rinzai sect, introduced by the monk Eisai, therefore employs the *koan* as a tool for attaining this realization on an experiential level. Usually, the *koan* is a seemingly illogical account of an exchange between master and disciple, in which the latter attains realization (*satori*). One *koan* records how when the master Joshu was asked why Bodhidharma came to China, he replied, 'The cypress tree in the courtyard.' Through constant immersion in the *koan*, the practitioner transcends attachment to discriminating and delusive thought. In the Soto sect, founded by Dogen, *zazen* (sitting meditation) and having the mind of *zazen* in all activities, beyond discrimination between 'enlightened' and 'deluded', is itself the Way and notions of attainment or realization are frowned on. Soto Zen was more popular among the common man.

The large Kyoto temple complexes of the Rinzai sect in Kyoto were major seats of learning and culture, particularly for the samurai elite in pre-modern Japan. Zen has engendered many aesthetic and cultural values: economy of style, allusiveness, simplicity, egolessness and harmony with nature. These find expression in a wide variety of traditional 'arts', from flower arrangement and the tea ceremony to *haiku* poetry, Noh drama and even the martial arts.

As a practice and way of life today, however, Zen conceivably has a greater following overseas. Many of the leading monasteries are populated by shaven-headed sons of temple priests, who endure a few years of severe training, including hours on end of agonizing cross-legged meditation, before returning fully 'qualified' to take over the family temple. As with many of the established Buddhist sects today, their duties rarely go beyond the upkeep of the temple and conducting of memorial services for deceased relatives of parishioners. For most Japanese, Zen practice conjures up notions of hardship and endurance (*gaman*), which promote spiritual strength (*seishin*) – distinctively Japanese virtues highly prized today. Indeed, it is not unknown for schools and companies to send students and employees away for a brief period of such 'spiritual training'. Enforced *zazen* is also a common punishment in prisons!

A number of Zen temples will accept foreign students for a period of training or at *zazen* meetings. Some familiarity with the cultural milieu of Zen Buddhism in Japan today would be advisable.

These sects have undergone a few modifications and sub-divisions over the centuries, but form the core of 'mainstream' or 'established' Buddhism today. It is to them that the majority of Japanese families are affiliated, although only a small minority would class themselves as regular practitioners.

New religions

If the religions described above represent the less conscious influences of religion in Japan, the phenomenon of 'new religions' represents a far more conscious, volitional aspect of Japanese religiousness. As a whole they account for about 10 per cent of the population (30 per cent if one accepts the slightly inflated figures given by these religious organizations themselves).

The term 'new religions' is commonly used to denote the numerous, predominantly lay, religious organizations which have arisen in waves since the late Edo period. Some have had only a brief life-span, others have been more long-lasting. Others have divided into subsects, changing names in the process. Membership of individual organizations varies from a few hundred to several million.

Although organizationally they stand outside the 'main-stream' of established Buddhism and Shinto, the term 'new' is something of a misnomer. The vast majority (with the exception of such 'foreign' religions as Jehovah's Witnesses and the Unification Church – also considered new religions), tend to draw their influence from existing traditions, often infusing them with a new meaning or vitality. Possession by *kami* or visitation by a deity, for example, is frequently the occasion for the founding of such a religion. Thus, Tenrikyo, which dates back to 1838, was founded by a farmer's wife who, at a time of famine and hardship, was possessed by a *kami* claiming to be the true Parent-God. With a membership of up to 2 million, Tenrikyo is now one of the larger of the new religions. It has a huge headquarters in the city of Tenri (named after the religion), a reputable university and its own publishing house. Similarly, both Konkokyo and Omotokyo, founded in the late nineteenth century, derive their inspiration from visitations by a little-known folk-Taoist divinity, Konjin. A number of the so-called 'new' new religions, which have burgeoned in the past two decades, have similar origins.

Correct conduct of ceremonies for ancestors, whose unplacated souls are the source of numerous karmic hindrances, is another instance of the way in which the new religions have drawn on existing traditions. Memorial services for the deceased form a central part of the Buddhist Reiyukai sect. A more spectacular example is the regular and well-publicized fire festivals of the recently formed Agonshu sect.

Others have turned to Buddhist sutras and discovered or rediscovered in them hidden messages for modern man. Shinnyoen, another of the 'new' new religions, finds inspiration in the Nirvana sutra. The Lotus sutra re-emerges once again as the mainstay of the well-subscribed Reiyukai, Rissho Koseikai and Sokagakkai ('value-creating society'). This last is perhaps the best-known, and certainly the largest, of the new religions. With a membership of upward of 6 million, it derives from the Nichiren sect. Often characterized as exclusivist and intolerant, its somewhat aggressive proselytizing of individuals and families swept the country in the postwar period. It stresses changing one's karma in this life by spiritual effort and by repeated invocation of the Lotus sutra. From it emerged one of the larger opposition parties, the Komeito, or Clean Government Party, with which the Sokagakkai retains close links, though not officially. Like Tenrikyo it has its own university and publishing house; it also has its own newspaper and a growing overseas membership.

Some new religions emphasize symbolism and fine art as means of promoting spiritual well-being – a characteristic reminiscent of Shingon Buddhism. Notable among these is the Sekai Kyuseikyo, which boasts two sizeable museums. Others have typically syncretic tendencies. More recently, new religions have been able to draw on elements from Yoga and even Christian elements. Jesus is thus imaginatively included in the cosmologies of the Mahikari and Omoto sects today.

The primary concern of most of the new religions, however, is health and well-being in this life. The root cause of misfortune or illness is generally said to be some form of spiritual pollution. The exact form of the pollution varies from religion to religion, as do the rituals by which it is purified. But the new religions generally contain a practical and moral element, too. Tenrikyo teaches the attainment of a happy life (yokigurashi) through unselfishness. The members of another modern religion sometimes wear a T-shirt bearing the simple injunction 'Help yourself by helping others'.

In many cases the new religions have characteristics

peculiar to the modern age. In response to the approaching millennium and the widespread nuclear and ecological threat, some have developed distinct messianic and international overtones. Ultimate world destruction is to be averted by correct conduct of the liturgical and ritual practices of a particular faith. Most contain promises of a new and hopeful era and have taken practical steps in this direction. Some prescribe a healthy lifestyle and diet and warn against excess. Others, notably the Rissho Koseikai, have launched international peace movements. A common sight throughout Japan is the 'international peace poles', erected by the Byakko Shinkokai, another of the major new religions.

There is no single simple explanation for the development of these religions. Certainly, their growth has paralleled the major socio-economic shifts in Japan's recent history: the late Edo period, the depression of the 1920s and 1930s, and the immediate postwar period, when traditional family and communal ties were considerably weakened by the mass exodus to the urban areas. The fact that the new religions have very few followers in rural areas, and are increasingly popular on university campuses further suggests that their rise is due to the need for social identification beyond the company or school. But there are other reasons. The image of state religion has been tarnished since the war, and the established Buddhist priesthood has declined somewhat into a family funeral 'business'. Heavy emphasis on tradition has further sapped some of the original vitality. The new religions, by contrast, though rooted in tradition, have presented a much more approachable modern face, often through the mass media. They also provide an antidote to some of the pressures created by living in a relatively conformist, increasingly consumerist urban society, since membership is, to a large extent, a matter of personal choice. Individual frustrations and fears, ordinarily suppressed and unable to be tackled on a rational level, can be expressed and ultimately sublimated through supra-rational, even 'miraculous', means. The new member finds meaning to his life in a deeper, ancient and cosmological order.

The Japanese character of Buddhism

Perhaps the chief characteristics of the Japanese approach to Buddhism are its non-rationalistic, subjective, emotional, human and this-worldly nature. This attitude accounts for a number of things: first, the appeal of the various Buddhist deities, over and above the more philosophical and abstract teachings. As with Shinto, the emphasis is more on what the gods can do for humans than on what the teachings demand of humans, although Buddhist deities perhaps present a more gentle aspect than the *kami*. The *boddhisatvas* (*bosatsu*), who stand on this side of enlightenment, have enjoyed enormous, almost cult-like popularity in Japan. The two most important are Kannon, the goddess of mercy who hears the cries of the world, and Jizo, the guardian of travellers, whose bald-headed figure can often be seen at the side of the road. Jizo also guards the souls of young children. Yakushi, the Buddha of healing, also became a focus of cult worship in early centuries.

Second, the same non-rationalistic response facilitated the acceptance of the initial popularity of esoteric practices as well as mandalas and other potent symbols. The short Hannya, or Heart sutra, can be found inscribed on talismans. The importance of sutra chanting lies not in the profound meaning of the scripture itself, but in the mantra-like, magical power it possesses. This is most evident in the Sokagakkai, a postwar manifestation of Nichiren Buddhism, which focuses on chanting passages from the Lotus sutra.

Third, it accounts for the rise of individual charismatic leaders and sect founders. This is true in both medieval and modern forms of religion. It also explains the schismatic nature of Buddhism in Japan.

Fourth, it allows for the coexistence of diverse beliefs between sects, between *jiriki* and *tariki*, *kami* and Buddhas.

Another characteristic of Buddhism in Japan lies in its social dynamic. Some 75 per cent of the population are registered as members of Buddhist sects. For the large majority, this membership only takes on significance at funerals and memorial services, or at festivals commemorating the ancestors. It is households, rather than an individual or members, which belong as *danka* to Buddhist temples (a tradition dating back to the Edo period – see: History – when, to show their non-allegiance to Christianity, all households had to register at a Buddhist temple). Deceased relatives are also called Buddhas (*hotoke*).

The temple

The entrance to a Buddhist temple (*o-tera*), is usually marked by an elaborate gate, called a *sanmon*. The principal Buddhist image is located in the main hall, *kondo*. In large temples there is usually a lecture hall, or *kodo*, a pagoda housing a Buddhist relic and a bell tower.

The procedure when visiting a temple is similar to that for a shrine. Purification may be by incense, which is wafted by hand over the body. In front of the main hall, hands are held together in silent prayer.

CONFUCIANISM

Confucianism is not a religion in the sense that Buddhism or Shinto are. It has no priesthood, temples or adherents. It is a social and political ethos which was to dominate most of the history of China. Confucius (a Latinized version of the Chinese Kongfuzi), who lived in the fifth century BC, saw his task as one of restoring the true Way of an idealized past. The various interpretations of the Classics attributed to him can best be conceived as a socio-political philosophy. Society is a strict hierarchy made up of five basic relationships. These are between ruler and subject, father and son, husband and wife, elder brother and younger brother, and friend and friend. Given the correct conduct of these relationships, there will be harmony at the individual, social and national level. The moral qualities to make these relationships function are those of benevolence, loyalty and filial piety.

Confucianism was introduced to Japan at the same time as Buddhism. It has been used at various stages in Japanese history. At the beginning of the seventh century, Shōtoku Taishi attempted to model his various government ministries and the legal code on the Chinese system. It is likely that under Confucian influence the elements of matriarchy which had been evident in early Japanese society died out. In the Edo period it was drawn upon heavily to bolster the vassal-lord status and was used as the philosophical basis of Edo government, with the creation of clearly defined social classes: the gentry, peasants, artisans and merchants. Education for young samurai stressed the Confucian classics, and contributed greatly to the development of *bushido*, the ethical code of the samurai which centred upon loyalty (see: History).

CHRISTIANITY

Christianity has strikingly few adherents in Japan. Statistics vary regarding membership, but the total number certainly does not exceed 1 per cent of the population. This figure is not significantly higher than the number of adherents at the peak of the so-called 'Christian Century', when Christianity was first introduced to Japan. Missionary activity in Japan dates back to 1549, when a Jesuit mission, led by Francis Xavier, arrived on the shores of Kagoshima on Kyushu. The new religion quickly attracted followers, not least among the feudal barons (*daimyō*) of western Japan, who were perhaps attracted by the prospect of Portuguese trade in Chinese silk.

The division of Japan at the time into petty kingdoms, and the relative autonomy which the *daimyō* enjoyed, initially worked to the advantage of the missionaries. Their leader, Valignano, in fact obtained a number of audiences with the ruler Oda Nobunaga, resulting in a small mission of young nobles to Europe, a remarkable 'anachronism' in Japan's history. Oda's successors, however, noting the extent of support, were more suspicious. Tokugawa Ieyasu, who eventually brought the whole of Japan under his control, fearing that the Christian nobles would lend their support to his chief rival, proscribed the religion in 1614 and banished the missionaries. Nevertheless, covert missionary activity continued for some years, but eventually suffered brutal suppression, public martyrdoms, torture and persecution. By 1640, the religion was all but wiped out.

Christianity returned to Japan, however, in the mid-nineteenth century. Pockets of 'hidden Christians' (*kakure kirishitan*) were discovered in Nagasaki. There, a remarkable document was found which documented the understanding of these underground Christians. It contains a mixture of garbled Bible stories and prayers, and, somewhat typically, an admixture of Shinto and Buddhist elements.

Subsequent work by Catholic, Protestant and, to a lesser extent, Orthodox missionaries secured for Christianity a permanent foothold throughout Japan as an established religion. Roman Catholics account for approximately one-third of the Christian population, and Orthodox believers for one-tenth. The rest are various Protestant denominations, the most influential being the entirely Japanese-led United Church of Christ in Japan. The Spirit of Jesus Church has a large following, and the Anglican-Episcopal Church, the Japan Baptist Church, the Japan Evangelical Lutheran Church, the Salvation Army and the Church of Jesus Christ of the Latter Day Saints also have church buildings in most of the major cities.

Christianity's influence in Japan, however, is much greater than the small number of adherents would suggest. Christianity has made great contributions to the development of education. There are currently some 800 mission schools, and Christian universities are noted for their high educational standards, with Doshisha, Rikkyo, and the International Christian Universities representing some of the major Protestant ones. The main Catholic universities are Sophia (in Tokyo) and Nanzan (in Nagoya).

Churches have also sponsored the founding of hospitals, old people's homes and institutions for the mentally retarded. Others have been involved in aid to Vietnamese refugee camps.

Christianity has also had some impact on the intellectual sphere. In the early phase, Christianity was popular among intellectuals, partly due to its associations with the 'superior' western civilization which Japan was trying to emulate. A number of leading Christians included such figures as the educationalist Niijima Jo, and Uchimura Kanzo, who founded

113

the 'No church' (*mukyōkai*) movement, in response to the divisions he saw within western Christianity. Christianity also had considerable influence on the development of socialist and trade union movements in the early 1920s and 1930s.

JAPANESE RELIGIOSITY

A little over 30 per cent of Japanese people, when asked if they possess a personal religious belief, respond in the affirmative. This ranks somewhat lower than most countries of Western Europe and America.

Were one to draw parallels with the increasingly 'secular' societies of these latter countries, a concomitant absence of any form of religious practice might be expected. However, this does not necessarily appear to be the case. Some 60 per cent of Japanese families, for example, possess a *butsudan*, or family Buddhist altar; a similar number possess a *kamidana*, or 'god shelf'. Some 90 per cent (70 per cent on a regular basis) visit the tombs of their ancestors to make prayers and clean the graves. Visitors to Japan over New Year will be impressed by the huge crowds and generally 'carnival-like' atmosphere at major, and many minor, temples and shrines. For a week or so in mid-summer, likewise, the country seems to undergo a 'demographic shift' as people return to their home-town to celebrate *o-bon*, a festival of Buddhist origin. Annual festivals, some of Buddhist origin, some Shinto, and others of Christian, folklore and agrarian origin, have in no way lost popularity in Japan, and there is much to suggest that they are on the increase.

Events commemorating the rites of passage through life are numerous and durable, often with religious overtones: the presentation of a child at the local shrine 32 days after its birth, the Seven–Five–Three festival when boys and girls of those ages pay their respects at the local shrine, marriage and the traditionally Buddhist funeral are among the most commonly practised.

Famous tourist spots are often holy sites or originally places of pilgrimage. The Grand Shrine at Ise, for example, dedicated to the legendary progenitor of the imperial line, still attracts over 6 million tourists per year, and the 88-temple pilgrimage of Shikoku is increasingly popular among young people. Nor has the practice of invoking the protection of the gods or praying for good fortune eroded with time. A common sight in temples and shrines alike is rows upon rows of brightly coloured, small wooden plaques bearing handwritten inscriptions requesting success in entrance examinations, or for the safety of one's family, success in business, victory for one's baseball team, or success in finding a marriage partner. A number of the leading business organizations have their own shrines dedicated to the

Shinto deity Inari. Cars, trains and buses often carry a small sticker or talisman purchased at a Buddhist temple or Shinto shrine dedicated to a tutelary deity, with the inscription '*kōtsū anzen*', or 'safe travel'. Another common practice at the outset of a business venture is to acquire a '*daruma* doll', an image of Boddhidarma, with a rounded base. Not only does its legless, rounded bottom represent determination (it never falls over), but it is also customary to paint in one eye before the enterprise, or when a wish is made, and to paint in the other when the mission is accomplished.

Elements of folk religion and Taoism, and a range of ideas about auspicious dates, places, directions, numbers, etc., of various origins (Taoist, folk, Buddhist) are far from moribund. There is serious consultation about choosing a name, depending on whether the number of strokes used in writing the name is a lucky one. Attribution of misfortune to certain *yakudoshi* years (mainly 33 for women and 42 for men) is still common. All Japanese are aware of their blood type, which is used as a basis for analysing a person's character. This and other techniques (such as palm-reading, physiognomy, I-Ching and astrology) form part of the repertoire of the fortune-teller, who can often be seen sitting at a stall at the side of the road late into the night.

The picture seems more contradictory when one surveys government figures for religious membership. The postwar Constitution guarantees freedom of religion to all. Government statistics show membership of religious organizations at 218.43 million. This is almost twice that of the whole population. Statistics vary, but between 85 per cent and 95 per cent of the population are classified as Shinto, 76 per cent as Buddhist, and less than 1 per cent as Christian.

These figures suggest a number of things: first of all, the very loose sense in which membership or affiliation is measured – in terms of locality in the case of Shinto, in house-hold, rather than individual membership (once registered, always a member) in the case of Buddhism.

Second, there is the issue of double membership: it is not uncommon to be affiliated to both Shinto and Buddhism. Many people may not know to which sect of Buddhism they belong until a death occurs in the family, but membership is not denied. Figures for the number of religious adherents are not redundant. Above all they point out the role of religion as a vital element in the social fabric. In all of the functions, however, ritual bonds of membership are reaffirmed, either to a local community in local Shinto festivals, or of the larger group – indeed, the nation – at New Year or on pilgrimages. In the case of Buddhism in particular a sense of belonging, of reunion and of membership, is reaffirmed at *o-bon* or at funerals. Thus religion, while less consciously acknowledged than in many other developed countries, continues to play an important social, celebratory and purificatory role.

The gods also can be used as an emotional outlet. While most may be reluctant to affirm belief in a religion, the practice of 'turning to the gods in times of distress' (*kurushii toki no kamidanomi*) is more openly admitted. In most cases it may take the forms mentioned above, or that of purchasing one of the numerous amulets, lucky charms and o-*mamori* (talismans) available at the various temples and shrines. It may involve having one's car purified by a Shinto priest, for example, or paying a visit to the shrine dedicated to a deity of medicine or healing. In other cases it may involve membership (often temporary) of one of the ubiquitous new religions, or periodic attendance at Zen meditation meetings. For others, particularly at times of change or crisis, it might involve consultation of a consultant specializing in divination, geomancy, Taoism or the Chinese zodiac.

Many, not least the Japanese who participate in the various festivals or rites of passage, would be reluctant to admit that these practices have any real religious significance (in spite of the fact that there seems to be a lot of talisman-purchasing and head-bowing, and making of offerings), or that they necessarily 'believe in the gods'. Part of the problem is the definition and perception of religion itself. The word *shukyo* as a translation of the word 'religion' is relatively new to the Japanese vocabulary. It consists of the characters for 'sect' and 'teaching', and began to hold currency in the nineteenth century with the exposure to systems of thought alien to the Japanese experience at that time. It thus carries connotations of belief in certain dogma, probably to the exclusion of other teachings. These dogma relate to a 'supernatural' order (distinct in some way from the affairs of this world, outside the ordinary experiences of life and customary practice).

The ambivalence about the words 'religion' and 'religiosity' gives the Japanese a certain degree of flexibility when it comes to answering the question: 'What is your religion?'. For the foreign business person visiting Japan, Japanese religions provide a fascinating perspective on a culture and society often described as a mass of contradictions. Understanding something of the religious side of Japanese life is a valuable asset in understanding what makes the Japanese tick: the very flexible, and yet highly practical, nature of religion in Japan reflects some of the main characteristics of the Japanese people themselves.

12 Education

The foundations of the modern Japanese education system were laid down in 1872. It underwent substantial reform in the immediate postwar era (1947), with the aim of bringing equal educational opportunities for all citizens.

SIX-THREE-THREE-FOUR SYSTEM
The first six years of compulsory education are in elementary school (kindergartens are also available for children from the age of 3). Junior high schooling (in lower secondary schools) takes children from 12 to 15 years of age (three years). From then there is a choice of full-time, part-time or correspondence schooling at senior high-school level (upper secondary school).

From 18 years of age, students will normally follow one of the following routes: to university, to junior colleges, to a college of technology, to special training schools, or to schools for the deaf, blind and handicapped. School-age children with physical or mental disabilities are usually cared for in special classes within the framework of an ordinary junior or senior high school.

MONBUSHO (EDUCATION MINISTRY)
Monbusho's function is to advise local governments on the methodology of providing an education service to their local communities. Local governments have their own board of education whose function it is to manage the educational, cultural and science provision in their areas. Monbusho has been a traditionally powerful and controversial government department: when it attempted to rewrite certain passages in secondary school textbooks concerning the behaviour of Japanese troops in China during World War II, it not only incurred the wrath of Japan's neighbours all over East and

South-east Asia, but also the anger of the leftist teachers' union Nikkyoso, which would have had to teach the new history curriculum devised by Monbusho if the controversy had not forced the ministry to back down on its proposed editorial changes.

PROMOTION OF ENGLISH IN JAPANESE SCHOOLS

Monbusho has for some years supported various programmes to bring in young, native English-speaking teachers from the United States, the United Kingdom, Canada and Australia. These people fulfil a dual role of language teacher and local celebrity in carrying out what can be a very demanding job. Children are keen to know all about their new *gaijin* teacher, while their Japanese English teachers are either overly enthusiastic about having a native English speaker around, or very wary about being shown up in front of the students. The experience for both the teacher and the school is usually a positive one.

Overseas teachers find that in a Japanese school, teachers do not enjoy the same degree of freedom available back home: teachers in Japanese schools are required to stay on after school on Saturdays in order to run tennis clubs and other activities. The education system relies to an enormous extent on the dedication and commitment of individual teachers, without whom it could not work. Their efforts tend to keep children occupied with hobbies and club activities so that they stay off the streets and away from trouble.

All Japanese schoolchildren are required to make sure that their classroom is spotlessly clean at the end of every school day: this involves everyone mucking in with polishing, wiping and dusting. These are positive aspects of the Japanese system, as they teach children how to respect one another's property, to tidy up effectively and to get on with each other while doing the cleaning.

IJIME (BULLYING)

Ijime came to the fore in the late 1980s with a series of terrible cases involving the mental and physical abuse of young girls and boys by their classmates at school. Studies of *ijime* show that girls are particularly vindictive and psychologically nasty, whereas male bullies tend to go for more physical attacks on their weaker counterparts. There are endless reasons for a person to be bullied: among girls the main reason can be that one girl does not cut her hair the way all the other girls do, or she has a different coloured sports outfit from everyone else. Peer pressure is enormous, as is the pressure to pass exams.

Getting through all the tests is a very stressful matter for the majority of children in Japan and so it is hardly surprising that some choose to vent their anger and frustration by bullying someone else (in some cases driving them to commit suicide). The worst treatment among girls is to be shunned by one's former group (the children call this tactic *mushi suru*). For the group-oriented Japanese this is a terrible fate indeed.

THE EXAMINATION HELL

That children have to sit crucial exams in Japan throughout their most formative years is a problem well documented and discussed inside and outside Japan. Japanese children are victims of a vicious situation: the big-name companies, particularly those which can offer life-time employment to youngsters who get into the big-name universities, set the pace for a spiral of homework, tests and more homework.

Passing the exams is mainly a question of number-crunching and rote-memorizing. Japanese examinations tend to be multiple-choice-oriented so that there is little room for self-expression in a test. Most children look forward to the day when they can say they have passed their university entrance examinations, for this signals (in the cases of most Japanese university students) a period of four years doing part-time jobs and generally having fun. And who can blame them? Deprived of a real childhood, they are making up for lost time.

13 Requirements for Visitors

VISAS

Visas are required for any non-Japanese who intends working in Japan or staying longer than the tourist limit. British passport-holders going to Japan for less than six months do not require a visa, provided they can provide proof of means of exit (that is, a ticket out of Japan) and do not earn any income while in the country. New Zealanders can stay up to 30 days, Americans and Canadians 90 days. Other nationalities should check what arrangements exist with the local Japanese embassy. It is a good idea to check anyway, because the situation is always subject to change.

There are several categories of visa, depending on your residency status for being in Japan. The visa you are awarded will determine how long you can stay and what you can do while you are in the country; for example, student visa, teaching visa, spouse visa, etc.

Extensive documentation is required before any visa can be issued, and the process of application can take several months. Normally your employer will apply to the Immigration Department of the Ministry of Justice on your behalf, but be prepared for a long wait.

ALIEN REGISTRATION

If your stay in Japan is to exceed 90 days, you must register as an alien with the municipal office of the town or district where you are staying. Take your passport and up to three passport-sized photographs to the Alien Registration Office within 90 days, where you will be issued with an alien registration card. You should carry this with you at all times. Short-term visitors should carry their passport.

RE-ENTRY PERMITS

If you have to leave and return to Japan within the period of your residence, you must have a re-entry permit, or risk losing your residence visa. Permits can be applied for at your local Immigration Office and are usually issued on the spot. If you are likely to be travelling in and out of the country frequently, it is worthwhile applying for a multiple-entry permit. This can be issued at the discretion of the Immigration Office, and costs about double the fee for a single re-entry permit. Check with your Immigration Office for up-to-date information on fees.

CUSTOMS

Japan is subject to strict laws on the import of narcotics, firearms, plants, animals and plant/animal products, which are subject to strict quarantine laws. Written customs declarations are required when you arrive by ship, or if you have unaccompanied baggage.

MISCELLANEOUS

Consult your in-flight magazine or check with the retailer for details of **duty-free** allowances.

No **inoculations** are required for visitors into Japan, except that those who have come from a cholera-infested area should have been inoculated. Tap **water** in Japan is safe to drink. The standard of **medical care** in Japan is high, with English-speaking doctors available at certain hospitals in Tokyo and other cities (see: Directory). Make sure you have comprehensive **insurance**, as medical care can be extremely expensive.

The **voltage** in Japan is 100V, but two different cycles are used: 50Hz in eastern Japan and 60Hz in western Japan. Plugs are the flat, two-pin type. Hotels usually provide 110–220V outlets for shavers.

WHAT TO TAKE

Clothing and footwear

The Japanese dress very smartly. On business, men should wear suits and ties, while women should wear smart suits or dresses. As a tourist, wear clothes which you feel comfortable in, but which are fairly presentable.

You will need light cotton things for summer, but take a jacket or light sweater for air-conditioned buildings. Warm clothing is needed for the winter and an umbrella and light raincoat are essential for the rainy season. Remember that the climate varies greatly between the north and south of Japan and plan your wardrobe accordingly.

Remember too that shoes will be taken off frequently, so

slip-ons are the most convenient. Make sure that your tights or socks can stand up to inspection.

Clothes and shoes are expensive in Japan and it may be difficult to find western sizes outside Tokyo. Make sure you take enough for the length of time you intend to stay.

Presents

Take a supply of presents for your Japanese counterparts or hosts. If you are going as a representative of your company you can take a 'company' present, as a gift from one company to another. You should also take one substantial present for the most senior member of the company you are dealing with and a number of smaller presents for others you have contact with. Take extra, just in case you forget someone.

Quality name-brand goods and local or national products, such as china, crystal, designer ties or scarves, chocolates, jams, teas, etc., all make good gifts. A good whisky or cognac is also a good bet. Gifts should be nicely packaged and wrapped.

Baggage

Try to travel light if you intend doing any extensive travelling around Japan. It is difficult to find space for suitcases on trains, and stations tend to have lots of stairs but no luggage carts or porters.

If you do have a lot of luggage, and will be spending several days in different parts of Japan, it may be worth sending your luggage on ahead of you. Enquire about sending personal possessions by *takyubin* (express parcel delivery) at your hotel, 24-hour convenience store or airport information desk. Most Japanese do this and there are many companies which handle baggage delivery efficiently and at a reasonable price. Luggage is usually delivered the next day, or when specified. You can also have luggage delivered to and from the airport. Ask a Japanese colleague to help you arrange this.

Business cards

You will need a large supply of business cards, printed in Japanese on one side. There are now a number of specialist translation and printing companies that can arrange this for you. Ask your national trade and industry department for hints on which company to use. Note that Japan Airlines has a translation and printing service for their passengers. For details on the etiquette of business cards, see: Business Culture.

PART FOUR

Culture

14 The Arts

Japan has a fine artistic and cultural heritage, with painting, sculpture, theatre, dance and music all flourishing today in modern and traditional forms. The Japanese show a deep interest in artistic developments, as spectators and as practitioners. A large number of art exhibitions are held throughout the year all over Japan and are well attended. Painting and drawing are popular leisure activities. Japanese painting and sculpture owe much to Chinese techniques and traditions, with the introduction of Buddhism in AD 552 prompting an artistic flowering, which reached its peak during the Asuka period (538–645) under imperial patronage.

FINE ARTS
Ukiyoe
The most famous of the uniquely Japanese styles which have emerged is perhaps the *ukiyoe*. This style of woodblock print developed in the seventeenth century. It became immensely popular during the Tokugawa period (1600–1868) and featured brightly coloured illustrations depicting lively scenes of people, daily life, the theatre world and nature.

Ukiyoe tended to be mass-produced and sold cheaply, with several people working together to make the print. The artist would draw or paint the design, which would be placed on a wooden block and cut away, leaving only the parts which were to be printed. When more than one colour was to be used, a different block would be cut for each colour. Ink would be painted onto the blocks, which would be printed in layers of colour to make the picture.

Because the pictures were for mass consumption, the subject matter was made to appeal to the common people. The word *ukiyoe* actually means the life and manners of contemporary masses, but it has slightly risqué connotations and is sometimes translated as 'pictures of the floating world'. Popular subjects were therefore theatres and portraits of actors, sumo wrestlers and beautiful women. Often the pictures were explicitly pornographic. Sometimes they were sold in book form, called *ukiyo-zoshi*.

Originally, only simple, monochrome, black prints were available, but techniques became more and more intricate, culminating in the printing of full-colour *ukiyo-e* known as *nishiki-e*. *Ukiyoe* landscape prints were developed just at the point when the possibilities for portraits and genre subjects seemed to have been exhausted. Hokusai Katsushika's (1760–1849) 'Thirty-six Views of Mount Fuji', which includes the famous scene of Mount Fuji through a giant wave – 'Mt Fuji off Kanagawa' – and Hiroshige Ando's 'Fifty-three Stations on the Tokaido' appeared at this time. *Ukiyoe* prints also had a great influence on the Impressionist European painters of the nineteenth century, including Van Gogh, Cézanne and Renoir.

Sumie

The art of brush painting with black ink developed in the Ashikaga Muromachi period (1333–1573). It was based on the art of China's Sung dynasty period and originated with Zen Buddhists in Japan.

Emakimono

These are long hand-scrolls of pictures and writing depicting stories of battles, love-stories and folk-tales, which were popular from the eighth to the fourteenth centuries. The scroll would be read from right to left, unrolling with your right hand.

SCULPTURE

Sculpture was introduced from China during the sixth century, following the introduction of Buddhism. Many temples were built during the Asuka period (538–645) and the Buddhist influence is evident in the figurative sculpture of the period, with features idealized and the emphasis on solemnity and serenity. Indian and Chinese Buddhism continued to influence Japanese sculpture until the Heian period (794–1185), by which time contact with China had been broken and a new type of Japanese art had evolved, assimilated from the previous foreign influences. The sculpture of this period is less strong but more elegant and beautiful.

Delicacy and exquisiteness of form were the characteristics of the artistic taste of this period. During the Kamakura period (1185–1333), sculpture became more realistic in style and vigorous in expression, reflecting the austerity of the regime of the warrior class and of Zen Buddhism.

ARCHITECTURE

The artistic trends of Japan's history also influenced the architectural styles of the periods. Many Buddhist temples were built under imperial patronage during the Asuka period, including Horyuji temple near Nara, which is believed to be the oldest extant wooden building in the world.

The characteristics of delicacy and exquisiteness of form favoured in the sculpture of the Heian period are also seen in its architecture. One example of this is the Ho-o-do (Phoenix Hall) of the Byodoin temple near Kyoto. The Zen influence was likewise reflected in the purity and simplicity of the architecture of the Kamakura period (1185–1333) and traces of the influence of this tradition can be found in Japanese architecture even today.

WESTERN INFLUENCES IN JAPANESE ART

Western influences began to be felt in Japanese art from the latter half of the nineteenth century. Today, western forms and traditional Japanese styles coexist and sometimes are mingled. Since the end of World War II, there has been much artistic international exchange, with exhibitions of Japanese works of art being shown abroad and numerous exhibitions of foreign works held in Japan.

TRADITIONAL JAPANESE MUSIC

Most traditional Japanese music consists of songs with instrumental accompaniment. There are very few purely instrumental compositions. The instrumental accompaniment rarely follows the 'tune' of the song, but the 'noise' of the instrument is appreciated for the tone it gives to the music. Japanese music sometimes sounds discordant to the western ear. This is partly because the western scale of music has seven notes, whereas traditional Japanese music is based on a five-note scale and has primarily two- and four-beat rhythms, as opposed to western three-beat time.

Traditional instruments include the *koto*, a thirteen-string zither; the *shamisen*, a three-stringed long lute, and the *shakuhachi*, a vertical flute.

TRADITIONAL PERFORMING ARTS
Noh

Noh is an extremely stylized masked dance-drama in which the actor's movements, accompanied by narrative chants and songs sung by a chorus backed by flutes and drums, explain events. An occasional explanation is given between acts by the *kyogen* (comic actor). Other roles are: the *shite* (principal actor); the *tsure* (his companion); the *waki* (subordinate actor); and the chorus and musicians. Masks are sometimes worn by the *shite* and *kyogen* actors but never by the *waki*. The Noh stage has a side stage connecting it with dressing rooms and providing an entrance for actors. Very few stage props are used and there is little in the way of scenery, although a single pine tree is always painted on the back wall of the stage. There are about 250 Noh plays which continue to be performed today, and these are divided into five categories: plays about gods, warriors, women, the deranged and demons.

Noh has its origins in the dramatic performances at religious festivals in the middle of the fourteenth century. It flourished under the patronage of Shinto shrines and Buddhist temples and became a favoured entertainment of the military class during the Edo period, when it was patronized by the *daimyō* (feudal lords). Because of its association with the samurai class, it declined in popularity in the Meiji period, when the samurai lost their supremacy (see: History). Devotees have managed to keep the art alive and it is now enjoying something of a revival, as the Japanese people are starting to show an interest in their traditional arts.

Kabuki

Kabuki theatre has managed to retain its centuries'-old popularity, and the *kabuki-za* (theatres) in Tokyo and Kyoto continue to have full houses. The roots of kabuki go back to a shrine maiden in Kyoto during the Edo period, who performed *kabuki* (meaning 'to act in an unusual manner') dances. Kabuki has gone through various stages, including *onna kabuki*, with women dancing provocatively; *wakashu kabuki*, in which young men replaced the women; and *yaro kabuki*, performed by older men. Women continue to be banned in today's kabuki and the actors' skills are highly valued – graceful performances as women are particularly admired. Staging is very elaborate, with revolving stages and hoists. Individual actors may become almost cult figures. Actors have stage names – *yago* – which may be called out in appreciation by the audience during a performance, if they do something particularly striking. Kabuki skills tend to be handed down in families, and names are generally hereditary. Children in kabuki families undergo rigorous training from a very early age.

The kabuki stage has a long passageway, known as a *hanamichi*, running through the audience at the left of centre stage for principal actors to make their entrances and exits. This helps to draw the audience into the performance itself. Since the seventeenth century, playwrights have written especially for the kabuki stage, and popular themes include tales of war, court life and everyday conflicts.

Bunraku

Bunraku, the traditional Japanese puppet theatre, is not as popular as kabuki, but does have an appreciative and sizeable audience. *Bunraku* performances require close cooperation between a ballad-reciting chanter, a *shamisen* accompanist and three operators per puppet. The puppets are between 3 and 5 feet (1 and 1.5 m) high and can weigh up to 22 lb (10 kg). Each operator is responsible for different parts of the puppet's body and all have devoted many years of training to their art. The operators are visible on stage during performances, but are clothed in black to make them inconspicuous. Plays have been written specifically for the *bunraku* theatre, and themes such as romantic love, star-crossed lovers' suicide and war make them popular even with today's audiences.

TRADITIONAL JAPANESE DANCE

Buyo refers to traditional Japanese dance forms, including dances patterned on kabuki and Noh dances. Both are performed to *shamisen*-centred accompaniments. *Buyo* performers tend to move in shuffling motions and are mostly women.

TRADITIONAL ARTS

During the fifteenth century, a number of the arts which are thought of as typically Japanese were developed under the patronage of the shoguns. *Ikebana* (flower arranging) and *chanoyu* (the tea ceremony) were codified around this time and are both concerned with creating the 'small universe' – an inner harmony within the world of men. Similarly, in the art of bonsai, miniature trees are made to capture the beauty of the whole of nature.

Tea ceremony

The tea ceremony was introduced into Japan from China during the Nara period (710–84) and spread during the fifteenth century thanks to the enthusiasm of Shogun Ashikaga Yoshimasa and his tea-master. They enhanced the artistic and spiritual aspects to develop it as a discipline, known as *sado* (the way of tea).

Traditionally, the tea ceremony is held in an outdoor tea-house. The host, using stylized and codified movements, spoons some powdered green tea into a ceramic tea-bowl, adds hot water by scooping it with a bamboo dipper from the iron kettle, which is steaming on the charcoal brazier set into the *tatami* floor of the tea-house, then whisks the tea with a bamboo whisk, turning it into a vivid green froth. The guest receives the tea with his right hand, steadying it with his left palm and turning it once or twice before drinking. After drinking, the guest wipes the rim of the bowl with his finger, then his finger with a small napkin. The drinking of the tea itself is not the point of the ceremony. It is performed as an exercise in discipline and spiritual satisfaction – almost as a religious ceremony. An appreciation of the utensils, the room decor, the garden and the relationship between host and guest are all essential elements.

A knowledge of the art of the tea ceremony is regarded as essential for any well-brought-up young lady in Japan. There are a number of major schools of the tea ceremony, with branches all over the country. Although the majority of students are women, most tea-masters are men.

Shodo

Shodo is the art of writing Japanese and Chinese characters with black ink and brush. It was introduced into Japan from China in the eighth century. While it is similar to western calligraphy, it is regarded more as an art form, perhaps because of the inherently visual nature of characters and the great diversity of their shapes. There are three basic styles: *kaisho*, a block style, with little movement (sometimes called *shinsho*); *sosho*, a highly cursive style with swift strokes; and *gyosho*, less stiff than *kaisho* but not as flowing as *sosho*. *Kana*, an even more cursive and flowing style than *sosho*, is sometimes considered a fourth style. It originated as a script for Heian women and was referred to at one time as *onnade* (women's writing). It developed with the increasing popularity of Japanese poetry.

Students learn *shodo* at school, and skill in brush writing is regarded as the mark of a cultured person. As with the tea ceremony and flower arranging, there are a number of different schools of *shodo*, and a revived interest in Japan's traditional culture has meant a revival for *shodo*. An increasing number of women are masters.

Ikebana

Ikebana, also known as *kado* – the way of the flower – was also developed during the fifteenth century, and as with the tea ceremony, there is a lot more to it than simply picking flowers and arranging them prettily. Sometimes the arrangements are made to look as much like their ideal natural state as possible. At other times, the elements of the arrangements are used to represent the heavens, earth and humankind. Different schools of *ikebana* have different codes and styles. Some common styles used today are:

- *seika* – the style of using flowers as they appear naturally. In this style, the vase represents the earth and the emphasis is not on the beauty of flowers, but on their power as they grow wild.

- *nageire* – flowers are 'thrown into' a tall vase and allowed to fall naturally.

- *rikka* – a standing style whose name derives from the use of protruding branches. *Rikka* uses pine, peach, bamboo, willow, maple, cypress and other plants, plus supporting materials, to recreate a whole landscape.

- *moribana* – flowers are piled up for show in water trays or containers held in baskets. This style was developed in the last century as a reaction to the more traditional styles and makes use of western flora. Arrangements in this style are common outside the *tokonoma* – the display alcove in a Japanese-style *tatami* room – whereas most of the other style arrangements are designed to be displayed in a *tokonoma*.

Ikebana is still very popular with men and women in Japan and it is big business. New styles have been created to suit smaller and western-style housing. There are between two thousand and three thousand different schools, the largest of which is Ikenobo, which has over a million students.

Bonsai

Bonsai – the art of artificially dwarfing trees to make them look like miniature versions of the full-grown specimen – is still a popular hobby in Japan today. Exhibitions can be seen at various times of the year, particularly in the grounds of shrines.

LITERATURE

The two oldest surviving literary works in Japan are the *Kojiki* (Record of Ancient Matters), a prose work believed to have been written in AD 712, and the *Manyoshu*, a twenty-volume anthology of poems compiled around 770. This work contains over 4,000 poems covering a wide variety of subjects and written by men and women from all walks of life, from members of the imperial family down to frontier soldiers and peasants. Many of the poems are renowned for their directness and simplicity.

Until the ninth century, the literary styles of Japan emulated those of China. It was only after contact with China was broken off, and a uniquely Japanese writing system (*kana*) developed, that Japanese writers were able to develop a literature of their own.

Early novels

The *Taketori Monogatari*, written around 811, is regarded as Japan's first novel, followed by the well-known *Genji Monogatari – Tale of Genji* – written around 1010 by Murasaki Shikibu, a court lady. This 54-volume novel describes the life and loves of noblemen and ladies of the Heian court. Another famous work of the period is Sei Shonagon's *Makura no Sōshi (The Pillow Book)*.

From the end of the twelfth century for a period of about 150 years, the rise of the warrior ruling class led to the popularity of tales of war, with samurai heroes replacing the decadent courtier types of the Heian novels. Outstanding works of the period include the *Heike Monogatari (The Tale of the Heike)* and the *Taiheiki (Record of the Great Peace)*.

Essays

By contrast, the two-volume collection of essays *Tsurezuregusa (Essays in Idleness)*, written around 1335 by a Buddhist monk living in seclusion, is pensive in tone, touching on the joy of life on earth, as well as teaching the Buddhist view of the impermanence of all things. This work has had great influence on later Japanese writing and on the aesthetic ideals of the Japanese.

Tanka

During the Heian period, *waka* or *tanka* – 31-syllable poems in 5–7–5–7–7 form – became popular among the nobility. In 905, the *Kokinshu*, the first anthology of poems was compiled by imperial order. The *tanka* became the classic Japanese verse form and is still favoured by poets today. Its shortness leads to the use of suggestion as a literary device to expand the content of the lines. This has been characteristic of Japanese poetry ever since.

Haiku

In the seventeenth century the *haiku* – a three-line poem in 5–7–5 form – emerged as a new form of verse. Its greatest exponent was Basho Matsuo (1644–94), whose simplicity of style, expressing a subtle, multi-layered depth of content and meaning, continues to be the ideal form pursued by modern-day *haiku* poets.

Contemporary Japanese literature

Like much else in Japan, contemporary Japanese literature draws its strength from a variety of sources, including western thought and Japan's own traditions. Outstanding novelists of the twentieth century include Ogai Mori, whose work *Homecoming* has been translated and is widely read in the west. Other well-known writers are Soseki Natsume, who wrote *I Am a Cat*, and Yukio Mishima, who wrote *The Temple of the Golden Pavilion* and other translated works. Mishima became a bit of an embarrassment to the Japanese when his extreme right-wing views led him to commit suicide in 1970 by performing ritual *seppuku* (disembowelling) on the roof of the Diet building, as a protest in support of the return to power of the emperor.

Yasunari Kawabata (1899–1972) was the first Japanese to be awarded the Nobel Prize for Literature in 1968. His works, which are widely translated abroad, include *Yukiguni (Snow Country)* and *Senbazuru (A Thousand Cranes)*.

Japanese literature today is part of the broad stream of world literature. Nevertheless, there is a recognizably Japanese style which owes much to the traditions of Japanese aesthetics.

15 Language

Japanese is not only spoken by those living in the Japanese islands: it is rapidly developing as the lingua franca of the Pacific Rim. The hotel and leisure industry in places as far apart as Australia, Hawaii, Micronesia and Hong Kong have geared themselves up to cater, in Japanese, to the needs of their wealthy Japanese visitors. In Japan, the language occupies an almost holy place in Japanese society. Despite the fact that more non-Japanese than ever before are learning Japanese both inside and outside the country, relatively few have managed to master both the written and spoken language. As one consequence of this, there is a dearth of qualified interpreters who are not Japanese nationals. This means that the messages that pass between Japanese and non-Japanese in a negotiating situation, for example, are subject to a Japanese bias and Japanese cultural interpretation.

This causes headaches for non-Japanese companies who realize that a problem exists, but who are, in the main, reluctant to spend on the costly training of their engineers and scientists to speak and read what has been called 'the Devil's Tongue'. Several notable initiatives have been put forward in the UK and elsewhere in an effort to build up a more substantial pool of experts who can use Japanese in their work. A lot has yet to be achieved, but the signs are that the stereotypical view of Japanese as an impossible language for native English speakers to learn is gradually being broken down. So, how difficult is Japanese?

A publication (*Lingua!*) produced by the BBC attempted to rate various languages according to degree of difficulty as perceived by an ordinary British (native) English speaker. Each language, such as Chinese, Arabic, Russian, Japanese, Welsh, French, Spanish and German, was broken down into the composite elements of pronunciation, grammar, vocabulary, reading, writing and overall degree of difficulty. On the pronunciation (speaking) side of things, Japanese rates as not particularly difficult for native English speakers: it is perhaps as demanding as Spanish or Italian (both rated as relatively easy languages). The grammar of Japanese was rated as being easier than that of either Russian or German, although as being somewhat more difficult than Chinese (whose grammar is relatively simple, as it follows, for the large part, English word order). Where Japanese gains its notoriety is in the written language, which causes *Lingua*! to judge Japanese overall the hardest language of the ones featured in the book for a native English speaker to master. Why is this?

Japanese uses not only Chinese characters, called *kanji*, but also two other indigenous writing systems which are basically syllabaries (symbols representing single vowel sounds as well as combinations of consonant and vowel sounds) known as *hiragana* (cursive letters) and *katakana* (hard-edged letters). There are 1,890 basic *kanji* which need to be mastered in order to be literate: added to these are 46 basic *hiragana* and 46 *katakana*. A description of the written language is given later in this section.

THE BASIC FEATURES OF JAPANESE

Japanese people like to think of their language as unique. It does, however, have similarities with other languages which tend to be played down in the interest of making the language appear more remote to foreigners.

For the learner of Japanese, the good news is as follows: Japanese does not distinguish between gender; Japanese verbs do not inflect (the verb to be – *desu* – for example, does for 'am', 'is' and 'are'); there is no agreement of adjectives with the nouns they qualify; Japanese tenses consist basically of present and past, with a weak future tense; and there are no words for definite and indefinite articles 'the' and 'a'/'an'. The downside is that the language reflects the hierarchical nature of Japan by utilizing various levels of speech depending on who you are and whom you are talking to. This means that the personal pronoun 'I' can be rendered variously as follows: *watashi* (the polite and safe version); *boku*, which is used by men and young boys (and sometimes by young women who wish to 'make a statement'); *atashi*, which is very feminine and which some women use; *watakushi*, used by men in formal situations; *wasshi*, an older form of *watakushi* used by older men; and *ore*, which is basically a crude word used by young boys, by men among themselves, and by men with their wives or girlfriends.

Added to this, there are also alternatives to describe the

same action. Such alternatives mean that the verb 'to eat' can be rendered either by the standard, all-purpose *tabemasu*, or by *meshi agaru*, 'lift the food up' (used frequently by ladies) or by *ku*, which is what dogs do when they eat or what men do when they go for some 'grub' at a local noodle shop at lunchtime.

Most learners of Japanese will not be concerned with these variations in the early stages, as any good teacher of Japanese will introduce polite, standard Japanese which is safe and good for any situation. People learning Japanese are often worried that, given certain distinctions between male and female speech, the speech of a man learning Japanese from a Japanese lady will sound effeminate. This is another smoke-screen intended to put people off learning the language, because a woman teacher of Japanese will, if she is any good, take care to teach standard speech while at the same time alerting the student to some of the more important differences between male and female Japanese. There is usually enough to occupy beginners without adding the worries relating to male and female speech.

Finally, Japanese verbs come at the end of the sentence. This means that simultaneous interpreters need to keep their wits about them, as they juggle phrases in their heads, unsure whether they will be affirmative or negative.

THE WRITTEN LANGUAGE
One of the main challenges when contemplating learning Japanese is getting to grips with the seemingly complex, yet fascinating, written language. The three writing systems which together make up modern Japanese script are as follows.

Kanji
Kanji came to Japan from China some 1,500 years ago when Buddhism began to filter into the Japanese islands. The Buddhist scriptures were in Chinese, and the Japanese initially borrowed Chinese characters to write Japanese words. As time went on, it became clear that Chinese characters were sufficient for writing monosyllabic Chinese words such as:

来 *lài* (to come)   and 看 *kàn* (to sell)

and for conveying concepts, but were ill suited to rendering the longer, polysyllabic Japanese words with their more complex verb forms.

There are 1,890 basic *kanji* and there is no real short cut to learning them. They simply have to be memorized. The one consolation is that the more one learns, the easier it becomes to learn still more.

Hiragana

Eventually, the Japanese written language evolved a second, phonetic (sound-based) script from the *kanji*. This script is known as *hiragana*, and is used for writing particles (the key features of Japanese which show what functions a word has in a given sentence), as well as the grammatical details of verbs conceptually written in *kanji*.

Hiragana is recognizable by its smooth curves and relative simplicity. Compare the following:

$$響 \text{ and } か$$

On the left there is a *kanji* and on the right a *hiragana* character. The *kanji* here is composed of some twenty individual strokes. The *hiragana* character is made with just three strokes, and is one of 46 such characters or '*kana*' which carry sounds (in this case the sound *ka*). *Kanji*, on the other hand, represent whole concepts and do not always have the same reading. Certain *kanji* have only one reading, while most have two (the original Chinese reading, known as *onyomi*, and the Japanese pronunciation of the same character, known as *kunyomi*). Some characters have as many as twelve or more possible pronunciations, which each have to be rote-learned.

Katakana

Finally, there is a third script called *katakana*, which like *hiragana* has 46 basic *kana* representing the 46 basic Japanese sounds. The script is spikier than *hiragana* and is used to write words which are not of Japanese origin, such as *kōhī* ('coffee') or *kamera* ('camera'). *Katakana* is therefore used to write non-Japanese proper names and is also used for words equivalent to 'zap!' and 'pow!', which are often to be found in comics and cartoon films.

If you compare *katakana* with *hiragana*, the difference is quite clear:

ka	カ	か
ta	タ	た
ka	カ	か
na	ナ	な
	katakana	*hiragana*

Why the need to learn all three scripts? The reason is that modern Japanese is written in a combination of all three, as in the following sentence ('Japanese hotels are expensive.'):

日本　の　ホテル　は　高い　です。

Nihon　no　*hoteru*　wa　**taka**i　desu

Here, *kanji* words are indicated in **bold**, *katakana* in *italics*, and *hiragana* in plain script.

So, to be truly literate, it is necessary to master all of the scripts.

For more information on Japanese language learning, see: Key Phrases.

16 Sport and Recreation

TRADITIONAL SPORTS

Traditional sports in Japan include all the martial arts (collectively known as *budo*) with which the world is familiar – karate, judo, sumo and aikido as well as a few which are not as well known.

The popularity of all of these remains very high, with most of them taught at school and clubs for schoolchildren and adults. The Japanese martial arts are representative of the national character in that form is emphasized above all. What is valued is the concentration of power at the correct moment, requiring perfect management of the body and lightning speed.

Judo

In judo and karate, *kata* or standard forms are practised over and over again. Judo is a modernization of Meiji-period (1868–1912) fighting techniques in which submission was gained over opponents by throwing them, pinning them to the ground or using neck-holds and arm-locks.

Aikido

Aikido also has throwing techniques and holds, but these are based on bending and twisting the opponent's arm or leg. It is based, too, on the principle of turning the power and direction of the opponent's attack to one's own advantage and is useful for developing the ability to fend off an attacker much larger than oneself. Speed and decisiveness are therefore extremely important.

Karate

Speed and decisiveness are equally important in karate (meaning 'empty hand'), in which the only weapons are hands, arms, legs and feet. These are used in standard moves (*kata*) to block, strike and kick – very rapidly. Karate resembles boxing rather than wrestling.

Kendo

In kendo, a specially designed bamboo stave is employed to try to hit the head, torso and wrists of opponents, who wear faceguards and breast-plates. The fights climax with a 'sudden-death' mock throat-jabbing.

Sumo

Sumo wrestlers are superstars in Japan (and increasingly round the world). The thirty or so highest-ranking professionals compete in six annual fifteen-day tournaments, which are widely followed on television and radio. Sumo is a form of wrestling believed to date back to hand-to-hand combat techniques developed nearly two thousand years ago. The idea is that one of the combatants should throw or force his opponent out of the ring. Although it sounds simple, there are more than seventy techniques for doing this. Contrary to expectations, the sheer bulk of the combatants is not always a deciding factor – although in addition to the shinto rituals and ceremonies which accompany the tournaments, the hugeness of the combatants does make the sport a grand spectacle.

The average weight of a sumo wrestler is well over twenty stone (280 lb or 125 kg), but they are highly trained athletes of great discipline and extraordinary skill. The minimum height and weight requirements for entering sumo are 5ft 7in (1.70 m) and 155 lb (70 kg) if you are under 18 years old, and 5ft 8in (1.72 m) and 165 lb (75 kg) if you are over 18. The Hawaiian-born Konishiki, the heaviest sumo wrestler ever, weighs in at 547 lb (39 stone 1 lb, or 248 kg). There are no weight divisions in sumo. All sumo wrestlers (more properly *sumotori* or *rikishi*) are technically heavyweights, but the average weight of *rikishi* in the upper ranks is over 300 pounds (136 kg), with average height around 6 feet (1.80 m) tall. Top-ranking *rikishi* tend to be pear-shaped, with as much flesh as possible around the hips and thighs to provide a low centre of gravity. The training they undergo is rigorous and, despite their bulk, *rikishi* are astonishingly supple and quick and light-footed.

Adherents of the martial arts in Japan try to develop physical attributes such as strength, agility and coordination in addition to good judgement and sound character. The religious emphasis on the form of the movements and the honing of never-to-be-used skills is very revealing of the national character of Japan.

OTHER POPULAR SPORTS
Baseball
Baseball, which was introduced into Japan in 1873, is the most popular spectator sport in Japan. There are two professional leagues, each with six corporate-sponsored teams. There are also several university leagues, and a high-school league with a semi-annual tournament in Osaka, which is probably the single most popular sports event in the country. For younger children there is even a junior league. From April to October there is almost constant television and radio coverage, and the season culminates with a world series. The Yomiuri Giants in Tokyo are probably the most well-known team.

Golf
Golf is extremely popular in Japan, as both a spectator and a participant sport. For many participants, however, playing on a course can only be a pipe-dream, and they have to be content with spending hours practising on the many multi-storey golf ranges.

Golf is very expensive in Japan, with membership of private clubs costing millions of yen annually, in addition to green fees, and even public courses costing around ¥20,000 (US$186.57) per round.

Some companies may have corporate membership of clubs and will treat their own employees or visiting business people to a round of golf. Otherwise only very rich Japanese can afford to play in Japan, and golfing holidays abroad are popular.

Tennis
Tennis is a popular leisure activity for the Japanese, and during the early summer and autumn, when the weather is warm but not too hot, it can become very difficult to book a court. Weekends, holidays, early mornings and evenings are particularly popular, and municipal courts are often so heavily oversubscribed that they have a lottery system, whereby all of those who want to book a court have their names and telephone numbers put into a box and drawn out according to how many courts are available.

Skiing
Skiing is popular and there are many good ski resorts in the Nagano area of central Japan, where the 'Japan Alps' are situated, and in Hokkaidō. The skiing season lasts from January to

March in central Japan and in Hokkaidō from November/ December to April. The resorts have a good variety of practice slopes, lifts, tows and jumping facilities, and some have luxurious hotels with hot-spring baths. Equipment can be rented almost everywhere – though you may have problems if you have large feet or are particularly tall in Japanese terms. Look out too for bargain sales of last-year's ski-wear and equipment. The Japanese are as trend-conscious with their skiing as they are with everything else, and no one will buy anything that is not bang up to the minute in fashion.

Special ski-trains run during the season to the resorts. Avoid weekends and holidays if possible, as the slopes are packed at these times.

Swimming

Japan has some beautiful beaches, which are packed during 'the swimming season' – July and August. Although the weather in June and September is actually pleasantly warm, these months are considered too cold for swimming, so the beaches are empty.

Outdoor public swimming pools are open from June to August and are often crowded, though they are clean and well maintained. Hotel pools are sometimes open to the public, for a fee.

Fishing

As might be expected in a country which is surrounded by the sea and full of lakes and rivers, fishing is an extremely popular pastime in Japan. There are over 15 million sport fishermen in the country and there is intense competition among fishing-equipment manufacturers to develop high-quality equipment. Popular fishing spots are lakes Saiko and Motosu near Mt Fuji, and Lake Chuzenji at Nikko. Large cities have specially designated fishing ponds and some hotels have their own lakes, so guests can fish from their grounds. Travel agents can arrange angling holidays, which will include accommodation, travel and any permits. Fishing permits are only needed in certain places, where they are issued by the local fishermen's union.

Rugby and soccer (football)

Rugby and football are both popular team sports at university level. Large companies sometimes have their own teams or sponsor teams, which play in league matches. A football league for Japan is now on the starting blocks.

Bathing (hot springs and public baths)

A traditional and enduringly popular way to relax in Japan is to soak in a hot bath at home (see: Society – Structure), or at the local *sento* (public bath). The public bath has the advantage of being a social gathering place, as well as somewhere to enjoy the pleasure of relaxing in hot water. The *sento* is particularly popular now with old people, who use it as a place to meet and chat with friends and who also find the hot water soothes their aches and pains. A public bath is generally much larger than a home bath, so there is plenty of room to stretch out.

Visiting hot springs is a very popular weekend activity with young and old alike. Hot-spring resorts around the country offer accommodation ranging from high-class hotels, with their own indoor and outdoor spa baths, to small, reasonably priced bed-and-breakfast establishments within a short walk of the bathing places.

Some people book in just to relax and unwind in the baths, allowing the heat and the minerals in the water to treat their tired muscles. Others combine a visit to the area with daytime activities such as golf or skiing and a relaxing bath in the evening, before settling down to eat the local delicacies at dinner.

The hot springs are often situated in places of outstanding natural beauty, with outdoor baths sited in rocky mountain pools offering spectacular views. Lying in a hot mineral bath, watching the steam rise over views of autumn hillsides and distant snowy mountains, while sipping sake from a cup floated on a lacquer tray is found, by many a tired salary-man, to be one of the most refreshing experiences for body and soul.

SPORTS CLUBS AND FACILITIES
Company sports facilities

Private sports facilities in Japan tend to be expensive and public facilities crowded. One of the great benefits which large companies can offer their employees is, therefore, affordable access to sports facilities. Sometimes companies have their own sports centres, which may have tennis courts, exercise gyms, swimming pools, playing fields and sometimes golf courses or at least driving ranges. If a company is not large enough to have its own sports centre, it may make arrangements with a local private club for employees to have discounted access.

The big companies like Toyota also have training centres around the country, which the company can use for courses for their employees. They may have hostels and lodges in scenic parts of Japan, too, which employees can use at affordable rates for weekends and holidays. The use of these is usually limited to a number of days per year for each employee, and arrangements usually have to be made well in advance, but these kinds of arrangement are part of the philosophy of 'looking after employees from cradle to grave', which Japan is famed for. In fact, only the largest companies, which employ a fraction of Japan's working population, are able to offer this kind of benefit. Sometimes too this replaces other benefits, such as large salary or opportunities for promotion and responsibility, which are available with smaller companies – and which are becoming increasingly attractive to today's graduates. The 'big-name' companies, which used to have the cream of each year's crop of graduates, are now having to work harder to sell themselves to prospective recruits.

Private sports clubs

Private sports clubs often have excellent facilities, but the fees are extremely high and there may be long waiting lists. Many companies maintain corporate membership for expatriate staff, so if you are going to be living in Japan, check with your company what arrangements there are. Hotels frequently offer access to sports and health-club facilities for guests and sometimes visiting membership is possible, though again, the fees are high.

GAMES

Board games are popular in Japan. Traditional **board games** include:

- *go*, a strategic game for two players using black and white stones. The object is to see who can enclose the largest area of space with his or her stones.
- *shoji*, Chinese-style chess. Two players try to immobilize and capture each other's king.
- *mahjong*. Introduced to Japan from China in the 1920s, mahjong has become very popular and mahjong parlours can be found all over the country. It is usually played for fun or for money.

Go and *shoji* are considered intellectual games and are played professionally.

The most popular non-traditional game is **pachinko**, a vertical pin-ball game using small steel balls. Garish, neon-lit *pachinko* parlours housing rows and rows of noisy, clattering machines are a common sight all over Japan. A number of balls are bought to start off the game and then are fired into the machine, hopefully scoring by striking and catching in different parts of the machine on their way down. Depending on your score, a number of balls are then returned and you can carry on playing, or cash in the balls which you have collected for prizes. Experienced players know which machines are near to paying out and collect plastic carton-loads of steel balls which they exchange for prizes of chocolates, cigarettes, or cheap presents. These 'prizes' are then sometimes taken off the premises (usually to an anonymous shack at the rear of the parlour) where they can be exchanged for cash. This is a way of getting round Japan's gaming laws. Addicts make and lose fortunes.

Computer games such as Nintendo, Super Mario, etc., are as popular in Japan as they are in the west.

EATING AND DRINKING
Eating
In Japan, one of the most popular pastimes is eating out. Families traditionally eat out together on Sundays to give housewives a break from cooking. In addition, a lot of entertaining, both business and social, is done in restaurants. Japanese homes tend to be quite small and not able to accommodate more than a few guests, so only family and close friends are usually invited to dine at home. Restaurants often have private rooms available for hosting parties, and many companies and individuals who have to do a lot of entertaining will have accounts arranged with specific restaurants, so that no money will have to change hands in front of guests.

Office workers often go out to eat together after work or to celebrate special occasions. Even students and young people eat out a lot, either for pleasure or from expediency. Most young office workers live at home and do not have to pay rent or living expenses and therefore have a fairly high expendable income, so enjoy going out to have a good time. Students live either at home, or in dormitories where they have to cook for themselves, so going out is an easier option. There are also a large number of *tanshin funin* husbands in Japan – men who live away from their families because of work commitments – and they too frequent restaurants.

Towns and cities in Japan therefore have a proportionately high number of restaurants per capita of population. The restaurants vary widely in standard, type and price range. French restaurants tend to be the most expensive foreign restaurants and are popular for special occasions, although the recession in Japan has seen the less well-known places close down. Nouvelle cuisine enjoyed its heyday in the late 1980s but is still popular in Japan, with its emphasis on small, beautifully presented dishes of many different sorts. Italian restaurants are fairly common too and range from cheap and cheerful spaghetti and pizza joints to restaurants serving high-class cuisine. Chinese restaurants are common and popular all over Japan and also range from very cheap noodle and dumpling shops to elaborately decorated banqueting rooms. In large cities it is possible to find almost any type of cuisine and almost any price range. Fast-food chains and family restaurants such as McDonald's, Kentucky Fried Chicken, Pizza Hut and Dennys abound. Coffee-shops serve western food with a slightly Japanese flavour. Typical coffee-shop dishes include *kare raisu* (mild curry with rice), *sando* (sandwiches of various types), *sarada* (salad), etc.

Another popular option for the busy Japanese housewife who has relatives or friends to entertain at home is to order food to be delivered. All sorts of restaurants have a delivery service and popular options for this include sushi, noodles and pizza.

In addition, housewives will often pick up take-away food for home entertaining. Desserts such as ice cream and cakes are particularly popular for this option.

There are also many different kinds of Japanese food available. It is by no means all raw fish, so there is no reason to be apprehensive about eating in Japanese restaurants. (Incidentally *sashimi* – raw fish – is usually extremely tasty.) Japanese cuisine depends for its quality on the freshness of its ingredients. It is usually lightly cooked, if at all, and has a delicate, subtle flavour.

Japanese restaurants tend to specialize in one particular kind of food, such as *sushi* or *tempura*, so you have to decide what sort of thing you want to eat before selecting your restaurant. If you are on your own, it is probably best to go for a restaurant which has models of the dishes on offer in the window. That way you do not have to worry whether the menu will be in English (most unlikely outside tourist spots) and you will also get an idea about prices.

It is possible to eat quite cheaply in Japan, but it is equally possible to pay enormous amounts for a meal. Beware of restaurants which give no indication of price outside the door. You could end up with a hefty bill. Reasonable restaurants can usually be found in shopping malls and department stores – there is often a floor or two entirely devoted to restaurants of different types.

Many restaurants offer set meals for a fixed price (*teishoku*). These are usually very good value, and consist of a main dish, soup, bread or rice and a drink. Lunch-time prices tend to be much lower than evening prices.

Typical Japanese foods include:

- *sashimi*. This consists of wafer-thin slices of raw fish which is dipped in soy sauce flavoured with green horse-radish. Various types of fish and sometimes other types of meat and seafood can be served as *sashimi*. Prices depend on the type of fish and on the cut of the meat. *Sushi* chefs who prepare *sashimi* are highly trained and extremely skilled at cutting the meat so thinly that it virtually melts in the mouth. Good *sashimi* is very expensive.

- *shabu-shabu*. This dish is cooked at your table in a chafing dish over a gas burner. Thin slices of beef and vegetables are cooked in boiling stock, then dipped in a sesame paste or a soy- and lemon-flavoured dip.
- *sukiyaki*. This is another dish which is cooked at your table, but this time the beef, noodles, tofu and vegetables are braised in a sauce of soy, sake and sugar. The piping hot food is dipped in raw egg to cool it before being eaten with rice.
- *sushi*. This is thin slices of raw fish, vegetables or prawns served on bite-sized balls of vinegared rice. These may or may not be wrapped in toasted seaweed.
- *tempura*. This consists of deep-fried, battered fish, prawns and vegetables served with a soy-based dip with ground radish and ginger in it.
- *teppanyaki*. This is meat and vegetables grilled on an iron hot-plate at your table.
- *tonkatsu*. This is deep-fried breaded pork cutlet (*ton* means 'pork' and *katsu* is derived from the pronunciation of 'cutlet').
- *udon* and *soba*. These are two kinds of noodle, which can be served in various ways, including fried or served in a bowl with broth. *Soba* are thin, round noodles, usually made of buckwheat, whereas *udon* are thick, squareish noodles made of rice-flour. Noodles are one of the most economical and filling meals available in Japan.
- *yakitori*. These are small pieces of chicken and vegetables, charcoal-grilled on skewers.

Drinking

Most restaurants serve alcoholic drinks all day – there are few licensing restrictions which apply to restaurants, although in most 'family restaurants' the alcohol choice will be limited to beer and possibly wine.

Beer is the most popular alcoholic drink with either Japanese or western food. Japanese beers are most common, though international beers are also quite widely available and there is more snob value attached to drinking foreign beers. Lager is the most widely available type of beer, though a few companies make a dark beer, and 'dry' beer – a strong lager – has become quite popular in recent years. Different makes go through periods of being trendy. Popular Japanese beers include Kirin, Asahi and Sapporo. Beer is always served chilled and is available usually in bottles or draft in restaurants. It is served in small glasses with bottles, and in large mugs called *joki* if draft. The mugs come in small, medium or large size.

Cans of beer can be bought in supermarkets or from vending machines which sell beer, wines and spirits. The sizes of can available range from tiny (containing one small glassful) to enormous 3.5-pint (2-litre) cans. Officially there is an age restriction of 16 for drinking alcohol, but naturally the presence of vending machines selling alcohol renders any ruling a formality. As a gesture to licensing restrictions, the machines are programmed to stop serving alcohol at 23.00.

Sake is the generic term for 'alcohol' in Japan, and Japanese sake, made from rice, is usually known as *nihonshu* or *seishu*. It is about 17 per cent alcohol and, as it does not improve with age, is drunk the same year it is made. There are no vintage years; however, some makes are better than others and different regions are renowned. In winter, sake is usually served hot, from small china flasks warmed in boiling water, and poured into tiny cups. In summer it is generally served cold and may be drunk from small wooden boxes, which give it a pleasant, woody aroma.

Whisky is generally available in bars, but is sometimes served as an accompaniment to meals (particularly for business entertainment). It is usually drunk with water and ice (*mizu wari*). Japanese brands, being the cheapest, are most common. Popular makes include Suntory and Nikka. Scotch whisky is regarded as a preferable alternative, but though prices are coming down, it is still substantially more expensive.

Wine has become a fashionable drink recently, particularly with young people. It has also been coming down in price and is quite widely available in restaurants. European, Californian and Australian wines are popular and there are also a number of 'Japanese' wines on the market.

Drinking places range from the equivalent of a 'local pub', where the average worker stops in on his way home, to the sort of hostess bar which might cost you a month's salary for a few beers. Sometimes it is hard to tell which is which, so it's best to go with someone who knows the ropes until you find your way around. Hostess bars are often called 'snacks', so do not confuse them with a place to get a bite to eat. Generally bars with hostesses are very pricey.

If you do want somewhere to get something light and tasty to eat while having a drink in a convivial atmosphere, go to a *robatayaki*. These establishments can usually be identified by a red Japanese lantern hanging outside and a delicious smell of grilling food. You can sit around the bar and drink, snacking on any of the fresh ingredients you fancy from the display cases which the *masuta* (chef/proprietor) will charcoal-grill for you. The food is delicious and reasonably priced and the atmosphere is similar to an English pub.

Other drinking places include cocktail bars and, in the summer, beer gardens outdoors (often on the roofs of hotels or commercial buildings).

NIGHT-LIFE
In the entertainment sectors of large Japanese cities, establishments which suit any tastes can be found.

Discotheques and night-clubs with floor-shows abound. Again, beware of going anywhere without checking exactly how much it will cost you. Most of the clubs and discos, as with hostess bars, have a hefty cover charge on top of exorbitant prices for drinks, snacks, etc. Some places, particularly in Tokyo, are known to have refused entry to *gaijin* – foreigners. This may be partly due to prejudice, but is often because they have experienced trouble in the past with foreigners who have not been prepared to pay the enormous bills they have been presented with after a few drinks.

Karaoke (the word is derived from *kara okesutora* – 'empty orchestra', *kara* meaning 'empty', as in karate – 'empty hand') is of course a thriving national pastime and can be found in bars and restaurants of all types around the country. Some small establishments have a simple, basic karaoke system, with just a microphone and backing tracks. It is not uncommon to find a tired and emotional businessman propping up the bar crooning into a microphone with no one but himself and the proprietor to hear. In other places the system may be much more sophisticated, with synchronized lights, videos showing the words with a film (often pornographic, no matter what the content of the song is) to accompany them, and hundreds of people fighting to take control of the microphone. Karaoke schools and courses make a business out of the national obsession and many men and women alike spend hours practising at home in front of mirrors, preparing for their moments of glory on the karaoke machine.

FILMS
The heyday of the Japanese film industry was the early postwar period, when Akira Kurosawa gained an international reputation with films like *The Seven Samurai* and *Rashomon*, which gave another perspective on human existence.

Between 1955 and 1960, however, the emphasis in Japan's film industry switched to pure entertainment and prompted a genre of films known as '*taiyoo-zoku*' ('day in the sun') which were dominated by sex and violence. Although no memorable films of great artistic value were produced during this period, the industry prospered and cinema attendance climbed, only to decline again in the 1960s.

Attendance in the 1970s and 1980s climbed again and tapered off, with films such as the '*Tora-san*' series, developed by Yamada Yoji, successful at the box office and with the critics alike. Currently Japan's film industry has a number of home-grown, enduring heart-throbs, in addition to many more who enjoy brief periods of popularity. (Often they are teeny-bopper pop-stars, whose agents want to cash in on their short-lived stardom.)

Western films are also shown in Japan and are popular. Imported films tend to be shown rather later after their release than in New York or London, but you will be able to see most of the major releases. Foreign films tend to be subtitled in Japanese rather than dubbed. Cinema tickets are slightly more expensive than they are in the UK, but not exorbitant. They will cost more in major cities than in provincial towns.

MUSIC

Western-style music, both classical and popular, has been embraced with enthusiasm by the Japanese. Japanese **popular** music is known as *kayookyoku*, which includes *enka* (a type of mournful ballad sung to a pseudo-western-style tune – very popular for karaoke), and the term 'pops' is used to describe light, entertainment-oriented music, such as pop, jazz, rock and film sound-tracks. You can also hear *minyoo* (Japanese folk songs) and *hoogaku* (traditional Japanese music). Japan's music industry has its own superstars, usually young singers or groups who have a massive following for a brief period and then disappear. Popular singers and groups appear regularly on television and radio and on the concert circuit, drawing huge audiences.

Awards ceremonies are held to recognize people in the record industry and the year's most popular songs. Japan is also a huge market for international superstars and is a popular stop on the concert circuit with foreign artists.

Classical music is also very popular, with many Japanese children learning to play the piano and violin – the Suzuki method has become famous around the world. A number of Japanese musicians have become world famous. Seats for world-class concerts and choral performances by visiting and Japanese artists are constantly sold out. As an indication of how much western music has become part of Japanese culture, it has become a tradition that Beethoven's Ninth Symphony is performed in lavish concerts around Japan at the end of each year.

For information on traditional Japanese music and performing arts, see: The Arts.

ART GALLERIES AND MUSEUMS

The Japanese are keen appreciators and collectors of art – as many an auction house can attest. Many of the buyers of western masterpieces during the 1980s were companies, who bought art for investment purposes. Large department stores often have an art gallery on one of their floors, open to the public and usually free, where exhibitions of local, national and international work are staged.

One of the best places to see Japanese art is in the MOA Museum of Art in Atami, on the Izu peninsula. The museum is on a spectacular site overlooking the Pacific, and contains over 3,000 Japanese paintings, sculptures and other pieces of art, many of which are classified national treasures. (See also: Gazetteer.)

17 The Media

TELEVISION

Television broadcasting in Japan started in 1953 and over 99 per cent of households have at least one television set. Like the UK and Canada, Japan has a national network – Nihon Hoso Kyokai (NHK) – which is financed by viewer levies and which does not broadcast advertisements. There are two NHK channels, which are, to some extent, government controlled and tend to show more educational, documentary and news programmes than the commercial channels. Some programmes, such as the news and foreign films, are broadcast bilingually, so if you have a bilingual facility on your television, you can receive them in English.

NHK's educational network offers programmes during the day for students from elementary to university level, as well as general adult-level educational programming. Foreign language courses are popular and include English, French, German, Russian, Chinese and Korean.

In the Tokyo area, viewers can receive five commercial channels in addition to the NHK ones. All of the Tokyo channels are flagship stations for nationwide networks, but programmes may vary slightly in different areas. Some prefectures may also have their own local networks. These are supported by advertising revenues and are licensed to particular prefectures.

Most of the commercial stations operate 24 hours a day and emphasize entertainment. A typical TV day will begin at 06.00 with news and talk shows through the morning, news at noon followed by soap operas and children's programmes, then more news followed by early-evening quiz shows and dramas. Old movies and young people's music shows tend to be shown late at night.

RADIO

Radio is still a very popular medium in Japan, particularly with young people. There are numerous local and national FM music stations and late-night disc-jockey programmes (the DJs are often foreigners) catering for the youth audience. Radios can be found in 93 per cent of Japanese homes. FEN (Far East Network) broadcasts news and music in English 24 hours a day on AM 810 kHz for the United States armed services based in the area.

PUBLISHING

The Japanese are renowned for their high rate of literacy and are generally well educated (in terms of the numbers of Japanese who go on to secondary and tertiary education). Ninety-five per cent of Japanese people are high-school graduates. There are of course constant debates about the quality of the Japanese education, with recent comparisons of British, US and Japanese high-school students' reading levels showing that the Japanese students have as many reading difficulties as their English-language counterparts, if not more. None the less, as a race they are indeed voracious readers. There are approximately 4,000 publishers in Japan, ranging from firms with over 1,000 employees to tiny, one-man operations.

Newspapers

Newspapers were established in the late nineteenth century during the free-speech reforms following the downfall of the feudal system and the rise of the Meiji government. These newspapers gained the public's trust, and even today, surveys show that newspapers are the most trusted source of information (in comparison with the US and UK, where people believe more in television).

Japanese people expect newspapers to be opinion leaders. History has shown, however, that newspapers can abuse this trust and be used as a propaganda tool, so Japanese people tend to switch their subscriptions back and forth between several papers to maintain perspective. This acts as a check on the press and causes fluctuation in circulations.

There are around 165 national and local newspaper companies in Japan and over 50 million papers are printed every day (including morning and evening editions). This means that the Japanese are probably the world's most avid newspaper readers, with about half the population buying a newspaper every day – compared to about a third of the population of either the United States or Britain.

The *Yomiuri Shimbun*, established in 1874, is the most widely read newspaper in Japan and – with a circulation of more than thirteen and a half million – in the world. The four other

153

leading papers in Japan are the *Asahi Shimbun*, with a circulation of over twelve million, the *Mainichi Shimbun*, with over six and a half million, the *Sankei Shimbun* and the *Nihon Keizai Shimbun* (Japan's equivalent of the *Financial Times*). The *Yomiuri*, *Asahi* and *Nihon Keizai* also publish same-day editions in Europe and North America, which are invaluable sources of information for overseas Japanese.

There are also four English-language dailies published in Japan: the *Japan Times*, *Mainichi Daily News*, *Daily Yomiuri* and *Asahi Evening News*. These are available on subscription or in hotels, major book shops and some major stations.

Magazines and comics

It is estimated that there are over 2,500 million monthly and 1,700 million weekly magazines and comics published every year in Japan. The magazines range widely in subject matter, readership and quality, and the comics (*manga*) are read by adults and children alike. There are *manga* to cover everything from 'The Life Story of the Emperor' to 'What's Michael' (a series of stories about a cat called Michael). Sports, hobbies, history, cooking, sex and pornography are all covered by *manga*.

A number of English-language magazines are available, including the *Tokyo Journal* and *Kansai Time Out*.

Books

Despite the prevalence of *manga* in Japan, over 1,400 million books are published every year. The Japanese often read on trains to and from work and school. A glance will reveal, though, that the majority of the studious-looking types on Japan's commuter trains have their noses buried in pornographic comic books. However, there are those who still read literature, both Japanese and in translation (over 3,000 foreign titles are translated into Japanese every year, not including children's stories). Reading on trains (as well as low prices) helps to account for the popularity of the pocket-sized *bunko-bon* and *shinsho-ban* books.

18 Shopping

Japan is the ultimate consumer society, with shopping something of a national pastime. The customer truly is king and shopping can be a great pleasure. Shops are open seven days a week (not all shops are open on Sunday, but all the big department stores are). Some shops take a day off in the week in lieu of a weekend day, but there are plenty of shops open every day to make a shopping trip worthwhile. Opening hours are 10.00–18.00 or 18.30 for department stores, and 09.00 or 10.00 to 20.00 or later for small shops.

Prices are high – do not look for bargains on brand-new electronic goods or cameras (except in areas like Akihabara in Tokyo which sell duty-free goods, and even there check that you would not be better off buying at home). You can, however, sometimes get very reasonably priced electronic goods which are not the latest design. The Japanese tend to reject things if they are not state-of-the-art technology, so if you go for last year's or even last month's models you can pick up bargains. Second-hand goods can likewise be picked up cheaply, but only foreigners tend to sell their second-hand stuff. The Japanese just throw it away, and foreigners have been known to furnish their houses entirely with cast-offs filched from their local 'large rubbish' dump.

DEPARTMENT STORES

The big department-store chains are a powerful institution in Japan. The biggest names include Daimaru, Hankyu, Isetan, Tokyu, Takashimaya, Seibu, Sogo, Matsuzakaya and Mitsukoshi. The service in department stores reaches its zenith, and is very labour intensive. There are uniformed staff bowing to welcome you at the entrance and in the lift. Whatever you buy will be beautifully wrapped, and can be delivered if you wish.

Some stores provide special facilities, such as in-store baby buggies to borrow.

The stores also vie with each other for the glamour of their decor and their window displays, which can be quite spectacular. If you get tired of shopping, there will be at least one floor devoted to coffee-shops and restaurants, and many department stores have art galleries or concert halls on the top floor. Some of them also have classrooms for running language or other courses.

Food halls are usually situated in the basement of the department stores and stock an impressive variety of Japanese and international goods, all displayed in an attractive and tempting way – fresh fish, for example, may be laid out on bamboo mats, with an artificial stream running over them. There are smells of freshly ground coffee and baking bread and usually there are staff urging you to sample new products. (On selling to department stores, see: Selling.)

SUPERMARKETS

Japanese supermarkets are very similar to western ones and stock a wide variety of goods. As with food halls in department stores, the goods are attractively displayed.

In ordinary Japanese supermarkets there is a good selection of fruit and vegetables, an incredible variety of fish and seafood, and a good range of chicken, beef and pork. Lamb is difficult to get, as are large cuts of meat for doing a roast, etc. Milk, butter and yoghurts are easily available, but there is not much variety in the cheeses that are obtainable. Cheese also tends to be very expensive. For imported foods go to the department-store chains Kinokuniya or Meidiya, both of which have branches in many Japanese cities. Many familiar western brands are available in ordinary supermarkets too. (On selling to the superstores and supermarkets, see: Selling.)

MISCELLANEOUS

Flowers can be bought from street stalls, which are often situated near railway stations, or there are florists in many shopping malls. Off-the-shelf bunches can be bought very cheaply, or you can select a bouquet to be specially wrapped for you, with a choice of ribbons and paper. Flowers make a good present for a host. Most florists can also arrange for flowers to be delivered for you, and for international delivery too.

There are **bookshops** everywhere in Japan, but only a limited number will stock English or other foreign-language books. The two biggest importers of books are Maruzen and Kinokuniya, both of which have branches in many different cities.

Japanese speciality gifts

Favourite purchases in Japan are pearls, cloisonné, porcelain and lacquer ware. Mikimoto cultured **pearls** are the most famous and expensive. Good **lacquer-ware**, which is made by applying layers and layers of lacquer mixed with oil to a wood base, is very expensive, but for everyone except lacquer experts, attractive cheaper varieties are available in supermarkets and department stores and make good gifts.

Ceramic work ranges from highly decorated fine porcelain to plain, simple pottery. Prices also range widely and looks are deceptive. What to an untrained eye looks like a reject may be the most expensive piece in the store, because of its individuality. As with lacquer-ware, reasonably priced pots, dishes and tea-sets, which make good gifts, are on sale in department stores and supermarkets. A traditional set will contain five cups, not six. Some famous names are Imari, Satsuma, Kiyomizu, Arita and Hagi. Noritake is the most famous modern maker of fine china. It has its headquarters in Nagoya, where you can visit the factory, but has branches all over Japan.

Real **kimonos** are very expensive, especially silk ones, which, with all the trimmings, can cost over ¥2 million (US$18,657). You can sometimes pick up second-hand kimonos at markets for a fraction of that price, or *yukata* – summer, cotton kimonos – can be bought quite cheaply and make popular presents. *Obi* – the long, wide waist-pieces which are worn with kimonos – are often works of art themselves and make great wall-hangings.

Other good presents include dolls, fans, happi coats (short cotton jackets emblazoned with an emblem – originally these were servants' jackets), wood-block prints (originals and reproductions), scrolls and paper goods.

PART FIVE

The Economy

19 General Overview

The growth of the Japanese economy in the postwar era is one of the major phenomena of the twentieth century, elevating as it has a small, geographically isolated and devastated island country to the status of superstate, envied and feared by many of its anxious competitors. Whether Japan will continue to rank as a major force in the global economy is not in doubt: whether Japan will be a *truly* leading player or an important second-division team member has yet to be decided. The country has to make crucial decisions about its economic direction in the wake of recession, financial scandal and lack of political leadership. What has brought Japan to the crossroads of the 1990s? What does the twenty-first century hold for the economy and, more importantly, for the quality of life of the Japanese people?

THE POSTWAR PERIOD: 1945

The Pacific War left the Japanese nation in complete chaos, with over two million people dead and its major cities gutted and in ruins. To this can be added the shock of the world's first nuclear attacks, on Hiroshima and Nagasaki, and the bitter taste of defeat itself. The position of the emperor was in the balance, and the spirit of the nation on the point of being extinguished.

Into this anarchic situation came the Occupation Forces led by their supreme commander, General Douglas MacArthur (see: History). His economic vision for Japan was to give the country the kick-start it needed to get back onto the road to recovery. Apart from creating a new Constitution for the country and embarking on a wide-ranging set of reforms to turn Japan into a modern state, MacArthur is remembered for his attempts to dismantle the country's powerful industrial conglomerates, the *zaibatsu*, and to make the economic structure more open and less tied to the ambitions of a relatively small number of power-holders. He was to be unsuccessful in the former and arguably unsuccessful in the latter too: the *zaibatsu* were to be reincarnated in the *keiretsu* system of corporate Japan, and the notion that Japan might today be more democratic in its business dealings is doubtful.

INTO THE 1950s

In 1945, the idea that by 1956 Japan would have become the world's leading shipbuilding nation was quite unimaginable. No one could have predicted what a difference the Korean War of 1950–3 was to make to the Japanese economy. These were boom years when Japanese manufacturing companies were able to profit by becoming the main supplier to the American war machine on the Korean peninsula.

The boom spluttered and failed as the Korean War ground to a halt. Japan entered a period of recession, which was only checked after decisive action by the Ministry of International Trade and Industry (MITI). MITI set out plans which focused on the support of key industries in an attempt to revive the flagging economy. This signalled the start of what western observers have recognized as overt government direction for economic and business affairs. As it was to be in future years, the relationship between big business and the bureaucracy was not always cordial, and certain measures were imposed by the latter on the former.

In a short time, much of what the Americans had sought to achieve in terms of anti-monopolistic legislation was reversed. The old *zaibatsu* names – Mitsubishi, Sanwa, Mitsui, Sumitomo, Dai Ichi Kangyo and Fuji – re-emerged in the forefront of the *keiretsu* structure of Japanese business. The media, in the form of *Asahi Shimbun*, *Mainichi Shimbun* and others, joined in the general clamour for Japan to move ahead and catch up with the best of the world's industrialized nations. From 1955 to 1959 the country enjoyed over 60 months of continuous high growth, known as the Jimmu period, Jimmu being the name of the first emperor of Japan. The country was back in business.

THE 1960s

The Japanese economy outstripped the British by 1962; five years later it surpassed that of West Germany. The result of government direction, compliance and effort by big business, and the influence of the media in ensuring that the message got hammered home all meant that Japan undoubtedly achieved its goal of an economic miracle. Some Japanese uncharitably forget or marginalize the contribution of the United States to Japan's success. The US certainly provided the basis for an economic recovery which the Japanese were later to develop with great enthusiasm.

The country benefited in global economic terms, but what of the common person? The overall price of success has been the stifling of individual creativity and an over-emphasis on purely mechanical approaches to economic policy. In the 1960s the country was wracked by environmental horror stories. Pollution rose, and with it pressure on the government to do something about the unchecked pace of economic and industrial expansion.

THE 1970s

As with other critical moments in the life of the Japanese government, the administrators' response to growing ecological problems was too little too late. In this, the government of the early 1970s was no different in its response to environmental headaches from the government of the late 1980s and early 1990s in its response to the overheating of the economy and rife property speculation. In both periods, it took significant changes in the country at large to galvanize the government into action. It was the oil shock of 1973, when the OPEC countries decided to increase the price of oil radically, that forced Japan to think more creatively about energy conservation and pollution control. This came at a time when Japan was meeting in excess of 20 per cent of world demand for radios, TVs and cars.

The fact that Japan later became one of the earliest users of unleaded petrol in automobiles (a clear ten years ahead of the United Kingdom) is proof of the country's ability to adapt quickly to change when its well-being is held in jeopardy. In the early 1990s it is a post-green world, where incentives to industry to take account of its environmental record are dwindling and pollution in Japan is once again on the rise.

THE 1980s

The 1980s saw the development of what has become known as the 'bubble economy', which eventually burst in the early 1990s. The term describes, in Japan's case, a state of affairs in the domestic economy where financial institutions freely encouraged companies to borrow more and more in the name of enhanced expansion and growth, without any checks on the expansion of credit. Loans were freely available and were overwhelmingly secured by land and property. The effect of this movement into ever-greater development programmes, with land as the main source of collateral, was to send land prices soaring. Property speculation increased and ordinary citizens began to despair of ever being in a position to buy plots of land to build their own homes, thereby exacerbating the overall feeling that affluence in the true sense was slipping out of reach.

The economist Maekawa argued in his report on the state of the economy in the mid-1980s that Japan had to abandon its policy of export-led economic thinking in the interests of continued fair global trading and long-term improvements in the quality of life of the man and woman in the street. He proposed a change in economic policy to enable the main impetus of the economy to be domestic-led, with a parallel programme of increasing imports into Japan. Without such changes, Japan would risk incurring the wrath of the American protectionist lobby, which was growing ever more chary of the burgeoning trade deficit between the two countries.

Among the proposals put forward by Maekawa were the encouragement of direct investment (accompanied by an expansion overseas by Japanese industry, in order to reduce the amount of direct exports from Japan); reform of land legislation to curb the spectre of a bubble economy (caused by over-extension by companies and financial institutions), and a change in the role of the Japan External Trade Organization, to make it responsible for promoting imports into Japan, thereby helping to defuse the potentially explosive trade situation with the United States. Maekawa's proposals were noted by the government, but procrastination followed, and events began to unfold that were out of the government's power to control.

Following the Plaza Accord in 1985, the yen appreciated overnight, causing shock waves throughout Japanese industry. Japanese exports suddenly became very expensive, which prompted Japanese companies to take the initiative by moving overseas to set up manufacturing facilities inside the countries that had traditionally provided Japan with its most lucrative export markets. This occurred without prompting by the government. Inside Japan, the shock of the *endaka* (appreciation of the yen) caused companies to reassess their working practices, with the result that those corporations able to survive the yen appreciation emerged leaner and meaner than ever before, while the weaker ones simply fell out of the picture. Meanwhile, land speculation continued unchecked.

THE 1990s

Moving into the 1990s, Japan sought to escape the world recession and in some ways, due to stable domestic consumer demand, managed to escape the worst. Observers of the Japanese economic scene were divided in their interpretation of how events would unfold: some predicted that Japan would ride out the recession while others painted a gloomier picture. Putting things into perspective, it was true that the pace of growth had started to slow, but in comparison with other economies, as

TABLE 7 International comparison of Japan's economy, 1992

	Japan (%)	US (%)	UK (%)
Unemployment	2.1	7.3	9.4
Inflation	1.8	2.6	4.1
GNP growth rates	+3.1	+0.4	−1.7

Source: The Economist, 26 January 1992.

Table 7 shows, vital figures for the Japanese economy in the beginning of 1992 still showed Japan to be in a relatively strong position.

By the middle of 1992, Japan had moved, like the other major industrialized countries, deeper into recession, prompting decisive action by the Japanese government of Prime Minister Kiichi Miyazawa to counteract the worst elements of the recession, by implementing the following ¥10.7 trillion (US$86.57 billion) 'rescue plan' for the economy:

1. Expansion of public investment – general public works projects, additional appropriation for public corporations, promotion of local projects, and expansion of housing loan systems.

2. Advance procurement of land for public works projects, for government contracts (including road construction and urban development) and local government.

3. Promotion of housing investment, by expanding loan schemes – extending the upper limit on individual housing loans, and expanding the loan scheme for parking facilities – and relaxing loan conditions.

4. Private sector capital investment – giving tax incentives for investment in labour-reduction and rationalization measures; expanding loan systems for investment in labour-reduction, energy-saving and environmental measures; and requesting certain companies to implement additional capital investment and bring forward orders.

5. Small- and medium-sized businesses – expanding loan schemes.

6. Stimulating employment, by gathering, analysing and distributing information on employment trends, and

maintaining employment levels by greater flexibility in the guidelines for employment adjustment subsidies.

7. Responding to diversified consumer needs, by developing new demand, particularly in the consumer sector; promoting computerization in the public sector; and appropriate use of consumer credit.

8. Facilitation of imports, by creating an infrastructure for imports; expanding the import-promotion capacities of the Japan External Trade Organization; expanding policy financing, such as import-support financing from the Japan Development Bank; considering the import of foreign products to meet the needs of government procurement; and improving market access.

9. Stabilizing the financial system, by disposing of bad assets held by private financial institutions (by monetizing real estate used as collateral for loans); ensuring that financial institutions can respond to financial needs by means of perpetual subordinated credits at an early date; and steady implementation of the Financial System Reform Law.

10. Invigoration of the stock market, by broadening securities operations with public funds; freezing sales of government stock holdings in the Nippon Telegraph and Telephone Company and putting off sales of government stock holdings in Japan Railways (JR) and Japan Tobacco (JT); promoting securities investments by individual investors; creating an environment suitable for corporations to procure capital; and requesting companies to raise their pay-out ratio.

11. Flexible operation of financial policy.

This package, amounting to ¥10.70 trillion (US$100 billion), is the largest rescue plan mounted by the government, dwarfing previous economic packages in 1986 (¥3.64 trillion – US$33.9 billion) and 1987 (¥6.00 trillion – US$55.9 billion) by a substantial margin. A Japanese government communiqué in late 1992 stated:

The Government is confident that this package, along with the decline in interest rates following the fifth reduction of the official discount rate in late July (1992), will contribute to the achievement of sustainable economic growth based mainly on domestic demand.

Whether these measures will produce the desired effect is uncertain. Most analysts of the Japanese economy tend to think that these measures are not in themselves likely to produce the lifting of the recession which everyone is keen to see. It is Japanese domestic consumer demand, accounting for at least 60 per cent of Japanese GNP growth over the past decade, which will ultimately decide the degree and extent of the Japanese recession.

PROSPECTS FOR THE ENDING OF THE JAPANESE RECESSION

While most optimists are looking to the autumn of 1993 as the point when the economy is expected to begin to show signs of recovery, the pessimists say that it will be well into fiscal year 1994 before the situation is likely to improve. Any improvements are likely to be Japanese-consumer-driven and, with consumer spending continuing to fall throughout the early part of 1993, any forecasts must really be quite pessimistic.

The government is trying to restore confidence by attempting to be seen as providing a new and positive lead in macro-economic thinking. The markets are yet to be convinced of this and so it will be some time before the effects of the rescue package can be evaluated.

On a more general level, the instigation of the rescue package could be seen as an attempt to resuscitate the government role in what has been dubbed 'Japan Inc.' (see next section).

20 Japan Inc.

Scholars of Japan are divided as to whether Japan Inc. (the idea that government and industry work with each other in a cohesive force for the promotion of Japan in international trade and the good of the economy) actually exists. For the most part, it is clear from an examination of recent history that Japan did embark on protectionism of its key industries and did shield its newer industries from the chill winds of international competition. The period of protectionism lasted too long, with the resulting (and correct) impression being given of the Japanese market as extremely difficult to penetrate.

As tariffs (on oranges and other citrus products, beef and other foodstuffs) have been removed, there is a growing willingness to consider purchasing foreign-sourced goods, although translating this interest on the part of the Japanese consumer into cash has proved more difficult. American negotiators at the Strategic Impediments Initiative talks were convinced that the removal of tariffs and other measures was not being implemented with enough speed, and that the perceived monoliths of Japan Inc. were and continued to be resistant to change.

Unravelling the myths of Japan Inc. is a tall order, but a necessary exercise if one is to get to grips with the nature of Japan as an economic giant.

THE GOVERNMENT ROLE

When discussing the role of the Japanese government in influencing the development of the Japanese economy, it is important to distinguish between the bureaucracy, subdivided into various ministries wielding differing degrees of power and influence, and the ruling Liberal Democratic Party which has been in power almost without interruption since 1956 (see: The Bureacracy; Major Political Parties). It is worth paying particular attention to the following instruments of government and their roles in international trade:

- the Ministry of International Trade and Industry (MITI);
- the Japan External Trade Organization (JETRO);
- the Bank of Japan (BOJ).

The Ministry of International Trade and Industry (MITI)

Together with the construction ministry and the Ministry of Finance, MITI is one of the most powerful arms of the bureaucracy. It has been the main locus of governmental 'guidance' for industry and prefers to operate in a persuasive rather than an overt fashion. Its relationship with big business (see below) has not always been rosy, for as the Japanese economy has taken off, industry has become less and less inclined to toe the party line.

MITI's past function as a channel for government funding of aggressive export promotion has cast it as something of an *éminence grise* as far as western observers of the Japanese economy are concerned. Such direct involvement in export promotion has faded in line with the new economic thinking put forward by Maekawa (see: The Economy – General Overview), but MITI is by no means a spent force. The ministry is constantly monitoring trends in order to put itself in a position where it can encourage business people to look at a new or promising market. It also brings business leaders together when it appears that their particular industry is in the process of contraction: by creating a forum for discussion, it has been possible for MITI to negotiate an agreed schedule for scaling down the ailing industry while at the same time working out acceptable programmes for diversification (where appropriate).

MITI has unashamedly poured money and resources into key areas of Japanese industry such as steel and shipping, thereby earning a great deal of criticism from those who are against direct government intervention in industrial affairs. MITI has successfully weathered this criticism to enable Japanese industries to grow and to become increasingly competitive in overseas markets.

The Japan External Trade Organization (JETRO)

JETRO is a branch of MITI which was initially concerned with researching export trade issues. It was founded in 1951 as the Japan Export Trade Research Council and changed its name in 1958. Import promotion activities started back in 1971 and shifted into a higher gear from the mid-1980s. JETRO's role has now grown to encompass the promotion of imports into Japan. It is therefore a crucial organization with which to develop links if you are intending to set up business in Japan. Among other things, JETRO can be instrumental in match-making overseas companies with appropriate Japanese partners. For information on joint-venture link-ups it is advisable also to contact your own governmental department responsible for arranging introductions to Japanese corporations in Japan (see: Directory).

JETRO started staging import fairs for the United States, Europe, Korea, China and other countries in 1985 and it is worth watching out for trade fairs in Japan appropriate to your product. JETRO has offices all over the world (see: Directory).

The Bank of Japan (BOJ)

The role of the Bank of Japan has been chiefly to control the money supply and to set the official discount rate. The stock market in 1992 has looked to the bank to ease credit by cutting the rate, but with little success. The feeling in the markets in 1992 was that the cuts of that year (in April and in July) were too late in coming, and that despite the much-vaunted rescue plan announced by Prime Minister Miyazawa (see: The Economy – General Overview), the mood in the country at large was that the government had lost its way on the economy.

In November 1992 the general state of gloom in the country was exacerbated by news from the BOJ's colleagues in the Ministry of Finance of a surge in Japan's trade surplus which in that month rose to an unadjusted US$7.60 billion (compared with US$6.41 billion a year earlier).

Despite the efforts of the Japanese government in its different incarnations to achieve the opposite, imports into Japan fell by 4.8 per cent in November 1992 compared with the same period in the previous year. According to Juichi Wako of the Nomura Research Institute in December of that year, Japan's trade surplus was likely to total US$110 billion in 1992 and to rise to US$120 or US$130 billion in 1993. Exports too were up in November 1992 by 0.7 per cent on the previous year. The prospect of progress towards a reduction in the overall trade surplus for 1993 looks distinctly unlikely.

THE INDUSTRIAL ROLE

The industrial element of Japan Inc. is known as the *zaikai* (*zai* meaning 'money' and *kai* meaning 'world'). The term is used to describe the principal personalities and main organizations in industry which interface with the bureaucracy. Important *zaikai* organizations are:

- the Federation of Economic Organizations (Keidanren);
- the Japan Federation of Employers' Associations (Nikkeiren);
- the Japan Committee for Economic Development (Keizai Doyukai);
- the Japan Chamber of Commerce and Industry (Nissho).

The Federation of Economic Organizations (Keidanren)

Founded in August 1946, Keidanren is the main point of contact between the business world and the Japanese bureaucracy. Keidanren members are drawn from every sector of business and commerce (122 industrial organizations and 939 companies), so it is in a good position from which to push the interests of the business community at large. The Keidanren has attempted to play a role in easing the trade frictions existing between Japan and its major trading partners. Its leader is currently the chairman of the Tokyo Electric Power Company, Gaishi Hiraiwa. The chairman of the Keidanren is nicknamed 'the *zaikai* prime minister', since it is this individual who is entrusted to present the views of the organization to the government.

The Japan Federation of Employers' Associations (Nikkeiren)

Set up in 1948, this organization is concerned with labour and wage negotiations from the employers' viewpoint. Although the labour disputes of the 1960s are largely a thing of the past, the Nikkeiren is still instrumental in issuing guidelines on pay and conditions, which are used by the unions in their annual round of pay negotiations with management. Its membership is drawn from 47 local employers' associations and 54 industrial groups and is currently led by Takeshi Nagano, the chairman of Mitsubishi Materials Corporation.

The Japan Committee for Economic Development (Keizai Doyukai)

This organization (established in 1948) differs from the Keidanren and Nikkeiren in that its members are individuals rather than companies. The membership is largely drawn from the managing directors of major corporations, some of whom, significantly, are simultaneously members of the Keidanren. The current membership numbers 1,564 business people. The Keizai Doyukai is something of a think-tank in that it acts as a forum for individuals to put their own views on the economy to a wider audience: because of this the organization sometimes airs views which are not shared by the other main business organizations. The current chairman of the Keizai Doyukai is Masaru Hayami, chairman of Nissho Iwai Corporation.

The Japan Chamber of Commerce and Industry (Nissho)

This is the oldest of the business organizations (established in 1922) and comprises 501 chambers nationwide. It maintains overseas offices and is active on the lobbying front: it links up with the foreign chambers of commerce in Japan and arranges trade missions overseas. The president of Nissho is Rokuo Ishikawa, chairman of Kajima Corporation.

THE MEDIA ROLE

When people consider Japan Inc., they often think only of the bureaucracy and big business. Another crucial factor contributing to its past successes has been the role of the media in galvanizing the population to action: in a sense, the role of the media as a means to project government propaganda. The main elements in the propaganda machine have been:

- the press clubs;
- the newspapers.

The press clubs

All the major political parties in Japan have a tame press club to which they feed clinicized press releases. The press club passes these on to the newspapers, which until comparatively recently have run them with minimum editorial input. This meant that when you picked up your paper in the morning to read the news over breakfast, what you were reading was the unadulterated truth according to the Liberal Democratic Party – not the ideal situation for a mature democracy, but Japan's democracy is not like those of its closer trading partners (see: The System of Government; Major Political Parties). Instead, such 'clean' news has helped to create the kind of 'let's-catch-up-at-all-costs' mentality among ordinary Japanese which the government wanted and which, arguably, the country in the aftermath of the war sorely needed.

The days when Japan had no form of investigative journalism have begun to disappear at a surprisingly swift rate, thanks to the efforts of the salacious photo-journals, which in recent years have prided themselves on being the *de facto* conscience of the Japanese nation. Thus the role of the media in Japan has had to adjust itself to the demands of a changing world.

The newspapers

As mentioned above, Japan has never had the freedom of speech afforded by an unfettered press – that is, until the sex and money scandals of the late 1980s and early 1990s brought an abrupt change to the way that things are reported by the main newspapers.

In the past it was an accepted feature of Japanese society that men, and particularly men of power and influence, should take mistresses without any fear of these liaisons being reported in the press. After the 1989 scandal involving the bar-girl and Prime Minister Sosuke Uno, the Japanese people decided that enough was enough, and that those in positions of great power should also be possessed of moral integrity, and should be answerable to the electorate for their actions. Uno was exposed variously by the photo-journals and newspapers, but it was the involvement of the *Mainichi* newspaper (see: The Media) in reporting the story which really set the stage for a change. So, although the media has in the past played a vital role in the encouragement and exhortation of the Japanese people to ever greater achievement, its whole-hearted support of the official line can no longer be counted upon.

THE FUTURE

Call it what you will, the alliance between bureaucracy, big business and the media has without doubt played a deeply significant role in the development of the economy of Japan today. As hinted above, the relationships are in a constant state of flux: the shifting of the power balances within ministries, the ebb and flow of one LDP career politician from the head of one ministry to another, the ups and downs of the Japanese economy and the almost week-by-week emergence of yet another new scandal suggest that the form and shape of Japan Inc. will continue to alter – although the self-perpetuating bureaucracy, which has a life of its own, should ensure a continuity of sorts. The fabric of Japan Inc. will only really change if there is political reform of a kind which is also able to alter the core power axes which lie deep within the most powerful ministries of the land.

21 The Corporations

THE DUAL ECONOMY

Corporate Japan is characterized by the 'dual economy' – the division of Japan's corporations into the following two principal groups:

- the famous corporate giants, such as Matsushita, Toyota and Fujitsu;
- the small- and medium-sized companies which actually soak up three-quarters of the available labour market.

The **corporate giants** are the *dai kigyō* (large corporations). For details on the top 25 manufacturing companies among them, see: Key Company Histories.

The **small- and medium-sized companies** are the *chū-shō kigyō* (medium/small corporations), which typically supply the large corporations or which are engaged in new business areas, employing perhaps fewer than 100 employees.

THE *KEIRETSU* SYSTEM

Keiretsu has become something of a by-word for what Americans regard as the main obstacle standing in the way of foreign interests and corporate expansion in Japan. The dictionary defines *keiretsu* as a biological term meaning 'system, order of descent, or succession'. In the business world it is used in phrases such as *Mitsubishi keiretsu no kaisha* – 'companies affiliated to Mitsubishi' – and describes a system of interconnecting corporate links which can truly be regarded as one of the cornerstones of the Japanese business world. Calls have been made in the past to 'remove' these *keiretsu*, but in truth they cannot be removed. They are too integral a part of the system in Japan.

Understanding the system

Various types of *keiretsu* have been identified in Japan and are given different titles to indicate the category they fall into. The main one is the classic *keiretsu*, those conglomerates which had their first incarnation as *zaibatsu* (see: History). These are instantly recognizable as household Japanese company names: Mitsui, Sumitomo and Mitsubishi: a fourth, Yasuda, is now known as the Fuyo Group.

The important feature of the classic *keiretsu* is that they are usually bolstered up by a bank. They also have a strong international trading tradition: Mitsui's London office, for example, was established in 1880. Some of the classic *keiretsu* are actually centred on a bank: Dai Ichi Kangyo Bank is a good example of this kind. A subset of *keiretsu* distinct from the old *zaibatsu*-type *keiretsu*, but still connected basically by capital, is represented by companies such as Hitachi and NEC. These have grown in size to the extent that they have been able to hive off bits of themselves (in the form of research centres or actual plants), which have in turn grown into separate companies. They are nevertheless still linked to the mother organization – bound by the ties represented by capital.

Another type of *keiretsu* organization is to be found in the automotive industry. Here the bank at the centre of a spider's web of interlocking companies (the classic *keiretsu*) is replaced by a queen-bee manufacturing corporation at the top of an enormous pyramid-shaped hive. The queen bee is supported by the soldier bees – the first-tier parts suppliers – which in turn are supported by a myriad of worker bees – the small or tiny firms. It is the latter which form the crucial part of this vertically organized *keiretsu* structure. These companies are the ones which take up the slack during recession and which are generally thought to be expendable. When cost-down measures are instigated at the top of the pyramid, the pressure is passed on from level to level, from manufacturer to first-tier parts supplier and on to the lower-level *shita-uke* (subcontractors).

In the case of Toyota Motor Corporation, there are three principal Toyota Motor Corporation-affiliated company organizations (termed *kyohokai*), based on geographical areas: Tokai (Central Japan, based on the city of Nagoya), Kanto (Tokyo area) and Kansai (Osaka area). The Tokai *kyohokai* was established as far back as 1943 and comprises 141 companies which all owe allegiance to Toyota Motor Corporation. Nissan has a similar set-up with its Takarakai (104 companies) and Shohokai (70 companies which include Hitachi and Matsushita).

These last companies, Hitachi and Matsushita, also occupy a *keiretsu* grouping of their own, consisting of companies which can manufacture and then distribute their products direct to the consumer via their own distribution channels. This is the grouping which has been bitterly criticized by the outside world because it enjoys a more streamlined distribution system than its potential foreign competitors, which have to struggle with wholesalers as well as retailers to get their products to the Japanese customer.

The outside world can save its breath when it comes to complaining about the *keiretsu* groupings. The system is so much part of the fabric of the business world, if not the country, that to talk about doing away with the *keiretsu* is really to miss the point. The best way to deal with them is to try to join the club, either formally or informally. For a foreign company that is going to be no easy task. However, with patience and the right kind of attitude (see: Business Culture), the advantages of the system *when trying to operate in Japan* will become apparent.

Advantages
The advantages of the *keiretsu* system include:

- **cross-shareholding**. As the hallmark of the system, cross-shareholding makes Japanese companies extremely resistant to merger and acquisition. This was particularly useful in the hunter-killer days of the late 1980s, when it appeared that no company was immune to the dangers of the corporate raider.

- **the stability of long-term relationships**. This brings a degree of frankness to the discussions, say, between a big manufacturer and a principal parts supplier on how to instigate a design improvement or effect a quality check. The idea is that the two work together rather than one for the other – although it remains to be seen in the light of the recession in Japan how loyal these friends are likely to be.

- **the free flow of information**. This comes again from the notion of long-term relationships. It is linked to the next point.

- *amakudari* ('descending from heaven'), the term given to describe the secondment of a senior executive in his later years to a related company, where he shares his knowledge of the parent organization with new colleagues. It is also normal for senior bureaucrats to be taken on by corporations – for example, moving from the Construction Ministry to a construction company. These moves are intended as a means of sweetening relationships and promoting 'harmony' between organizations.

- **exchange of personnel**. Companies do not wait for *amakudari* before shifting staff. Moving people in order for them to carry out assignments with colleagues in other, related companies is a good way to promote the exchange of ideas and the widespread sharing of technological information, and to fine-tune already tightly coordinated production schedules, for example.

22 Natural Resources: Raw Materials, Agriculture, Forestry, Fisheries

RAW MATERIALS

Iron and steel

Annual crude steel production moved from 103.8 million tons in 1985 to 111.7 million tons in 1990 and back to an estimated 103.0 million tons in 1992. Demand in the domestic market has clearly peaked, prompting the Japanese steel manufacturers to look at speedy diversification as the only real means of survival. Examples include moving into PC production. Steel-makers have entered into discussions with the automobile manufacturers on how to reduce the weight of cars, and are talking with aluminium producers on how to reduce the weight of automotive components. Diversification is the favoured route for companies such as Sumitomo Metal Industries and Kawasaki Steel in the struggle to survive.

Non-ferrous metals

The adverse economic climate has affected this sector of industry and, with depressed commodity prices worldwide, the sector (covering aluminium, copper, lead and zinc) is not expected to see an improvement in the near future. Despite a flattening out of corporate earnings as a whole, the increasing pressure on the auto manufacturers to make lighter cars has caused renewed interest in aluminium. This has led to major steel producers linking up with the aluminium producers both inside and outside Japan. Kobe Steel, for example, has set up joint production of aluminium with the Aluminum Co. of America (Alcoa). By tying up with foreign non-ferrous metal producers, companies such as Kobe Steel will be hoping to secure supplies of ore and avoid the volatility of the market. Japanese domestic producers can supply only 1 per cent of Japan's requirement for aluminium ore.

Cement
The cement industry is dominated by Mitsubishi Materials, which currently occupies a stagnant domestic business environment. The construction boom of the late 1980s is over: projects are being shelved and apartment construction is down. Healthy exports of Japanese cement to South-east Asia provide a silver lining to the dark cloud hanging over the sector.

Glass
This is an interesting sector because it provides a good example of the kind of closed market which Japan's competitors wish to combat. The industry requires a very high initial outlay as far as set-up costs are concerned, making it difficult for a would-be foreign challenger to enter the market. As a result, it is dominated by three key players: Nippon Sheet Glass Company, Asahi Glass Company and the Central Glass Company. Ninety-five per cent of the market for sheet glass is met by the domestic producers, with only 5 per cent being imported. This in itself is not surprising, given the difficulty for any producer in shifting large quantities of sheet glass from one country to another. The Japanese government has undertaken to promote the import of foreign glass, a move that is not lost on foreign suppliers, who see a great future ahead for double-glazing in Japan.

Wood products
This sector has caused severe trade friction between Japan and its major trading partners in North America and Europe – so much so that in January 1992, the Japan Paper Association felt moved to establish the Business Global Partnership initiative (carefully timed to coincide with President Bush's visit to the country). Concerns had been raised prior to this about the extent of market share available domestically in Japan (in the case of the United States, only 4 per cent). In addition to the trade friction problem, the industry is also having to pay close attention to environmental issues. Recycling is on the increase, and the production of dioxins as a by-product of paper manufacture is being carefully monitored by the Environment Agency (see: Environmental Policy).

New materials
Among the variety of new materials being developed, engineering plastics such as PA (polyamide), which is strong as well as light, are perhaps developing at the fastest rate. Other plastics such as polybutylene terephthalate (PBT), used in electronic

devices and automobile components, are also drawing new companies into the field. In ceramics, the only drawback to more widespread use of these new materials is their high cost: nevertheless the auto industry is pressing ahead with development of silicon nitride (produced by the reaction between silicon tetrachloride and ammonia) for use in the production of engine parts.

AGRICULTURE
Rice

The key word when it comes to Japanese agriculture is 'rice'. This has become an emotive issue on both sides of the Pacific Ocean, with the United States pressing Japan for liberalization of the domestic rice market and Japan procrastinating. The issue goes back to the war years, when the Japanese government enacted the Staple Food Control Act (1942). This represented the start of major Japanese government interference in the rice markets, resulting in a complete ban on rice imports in 1969. The price paid to the rice farmers was subsequently increased, with the result that the farmers went into overdrive, producing more rice than was needed. The ministry responsible for rice (the Ministry of Agriculture, Forestry and Fisheries) cut the amount of available land for rice production in an attempt to reduce rice production, and has continued to do so. It has also made some moves towards the removal of government controls over rice distribution.

As the ruling party, the LDP, drew a significant proportion of its support from the rice farmers via the agricultural cooperative known as Nokyo, it is hardly surprising that the government dragged its feet over the rice question. The consumer continues to suffer high rice prices (see Table 8), despite the fact that, in tasting tests to ascertain whether Japanese rice is distinguishable from the same short-grained rice grown in

TABLE 8 Comparison of rice prices, 1990

Country	Price in yen of a 132-lb (60-kg) bag of brown rice
Japan	16,400
United States	2,600
Thailand	2,300

Source: OECD data.

California, consumers have been hard-pressed to identify the origin of the rice tasted.

There is also the problem of Japanese sentimentality over Japanese rice: the foodstuff enjoys a hallowed place in the Japanese diet, is said to have a 'fragrance' all its own, and is, together with the Japanese language (and its perceived uniqueness), one of the last surviving icons of Japaneseness.

While rice remains a fairly intractable hotspot, beef and citrus imports were partially liberalized in 1991.

Other agricultural products

The greenhouses of Japan produce a variety of vegetables all year round, such as lettuce, cucumbers and tomatoes. Japan also produces excellent apples, tangerines, pears (both Japanese and western types) and grapes. Exotic fruits (bananas, pineapples, etc.) are imported in abundance from countries such as the Philippines. A particular success story is the kiwi fruit, originally imported from New Zealand but now produced in Japan. Table 9 shows selected self-sufficiency rates.

FORESTRY

Over 80 per cent of the Japanese land mass is mountainous and forests cover over two-thirds of this area. Cedar is particularly valued by the Japanese. Forests are highly susceptible to damage by snow (in eastern Japan) and by typhoons. For the topography of Japan, see: Gazetteer.

TABLE 9 Self-sufficiency rates in agricultural products, 1980–9

Product	1980 (%)	1985 (%)	1989 (%)
Rice	100	107	100
Wheat	10	14	16
Fruit	81	77	67
Milk and dairy products	82	85	80
Meat:	81	81	72
Beef	72	72	54
Pork	87	86	77
Sugar	27	33	35

Source: Ministry of Agriculture, Forestry and Fisheries.

FISHERIES

Sushi and *sashimi* (raw fish on rice and raw fish by itself – see: Sport and Recreation) are synonymous with Japan. The industry which supports the Japanese love of fish is a highly sophisticated one whose activities have not made it many friends among conservationists. As the 200-mile (322-km) fishing zones imposed by many nations have obliged the Japanese and others to travel further afield to catch fish in the quantities required, so the industry has had to become more efficient. The Japanese fishing fleets have been among the most destructive with their drift-net fishing. Growing international pressure to control the excesses of the main maritime nations on the high seas will eventually result in countries such as Japan having to look more seriously to coastal and off-shore fishing as the growth area of the future. Currently, Japan fishes for a wide variety of fish, the most sought after being cod, tuna, sardine, mackerel and bonito.

For a discussion on the Japanese whaling industry, see: Environment Policy.

23 Human Resources

The one silver lining in the cloud of depression hanging over the economy is Japan's pool of human resources, an asset of tremendous energy, stamina and vitality. Although it is important to recognize that Japan has both an ageing population and a growing labour shortage, it is worth mentioning that the extant labour force is highly educated and hard-working, two factors which must underpin any successful economy.

THE LABOUR FORCE
Projections by the Ministry of Labour show that the labour force participation rate for men (the labour force population divided by the population of people aged 15 and over multiplied by 100) will drop from 63.8 per cent in 1991 to 62.3 per cent in the year 2000 and to 60.1 per cent by 2005. The rate for women will drop from 50.7 per cent to 49.2 per cent and to 47.1 per cent in the same time frame. The latest participation rate for the United States for men (1989) is 63.7 per cent (on a par with Japan at present), 61.1 per cent for the UK and 67.0 per cent for Canada. For women the picture is somewhat different: 55.5 per cent for American women (1989), 50.1 per cent for British women and 57.9 per cent for Canadian women. The message is clear: Japan is in the grip of a labour shortage which is set to increase into the next century.

FOREIGN LABOUR
Throughout 1991 and 1992 stories abounded in the Japanese press about the rising number of illegal immigrant labourers. Iranians were among the most prominent newcomers to the Japanese labour scene, drawn by the promise of the high wages to be earned on construction sites. Outstaying their tourist visas, the Iranian 'guest workers' forced the Justice Ministry to

renegotiate immigration regulations with the government of Iran in order to stem the flow of human traffic from Tehran to Tokyo. Yoyogi Park in the capital became a noted information-exchange centre for the Iranian immigrants, who came in order to share news on where jobs might be found. Unable to speak Japanese or English, the majority of these workers are consigned to a life of manual labour, with long hours and difficult working conditions.

The Japanese are pragmatists, and so the government has had to bow to the wishes of the construction companies and others by sanctioning the influx of foreigners. There are moves afoot to legitimize the standing of the new workers by insti-gating government-controlled trainee programmes specifically targeted at people from countries such as China, Thailand and the Philippines. In this way the new recruits can be better absorbed into something closer to the mainstream of the Japanese labour market, where they can enjoy better conditions and the protection of the law against unscrupulous employers.

TRADE UNION PARTICIPATION

The growth of the trade union movement in Japan was stultified as a result of the purge of left-wing activists during the Allied Occupation of Japan. Union membership has declined since 1947, when 45.3 per cent of workers were signed-up members; in 1991 the figure stood at only 24.5 per cent. One reason for the decline is that Japanese industry as a whole has been shifting away from the manufacturing industries to the service sector: the increase in part-time labour has also contributed to this effect.

Trade unions are now concerned with the issue of pro-moting the notion of shorter working hours, a move in line with current government thinking, as well as a tangible result of pressures from outside Japan. Although analysts are apt to say that shorter working hours will find favour with the younger Japanese, it is worth remembering that there is still a sizeable majority who favour more money over more free time. The reasons for this are, first, that the recession is making people more aware of the necessity to save as a hedge against worse times to come; and second, Japan is a very expensive place in which to bring up a family, see that family educated through university and ensure that, should any family member fall seriously ill, there are sufficient funds to cover potentially huge medical bills.

In an attempt to keep the employees they already have, more companies are seeking ways to improve existing benefits in the areas of childcare, company housing, etc. It should be noted that the life-time employment system is far from universal – less than 25 per cent of Japanese companies are in a position to support this kind of employment structure. In fact, the whole institution of life-time employment is currently under threat, mainly because such a system works well when times are good, but when an economy begins a prolonged recession, even the strongest corporations find it difficult to keep everyone on. This is nowhere better exemplified than in the case of IBM Japan, once thought of as one of the bastions of the life-time employment system: reports in the press in early 1993 talk of the company's decision to 'urge' up to 1,200 workers to retire or move to affiliates. Times are certainly changing.

24 Energy Resources

Japanese people think of Japan's lack of natural resources as their country's Achilles' heel. The oil shocks of the past have served to underline Japan's fundamental dependency on other countries not only for oil, but for the vast majority of its energy needs. Apart from natural hot water, of which there is an abundance, Japan today does not have the luxury of indigenous energy reserves.

COAL

In the past, coal was mined on the islands of Hokkaidō and Kyushu, but reserves are now rapidly depleting, prompting the miners to look to other industries, principally in manufacturing, for jobs. Domestic coal output has dropped from 17.4 million tons in 1982 to 8.0 million tons in 1990, and the trend is definitely downwards. There are at present six major mining facilities, four of which are scheduled to close by the year 2000, according to the Coal Mining Council.

Despite the downturn in the amount of domestically produced coal, demand within Japan is still strong, primarily from the electricity generating industry. Government forecasts show that by the year 2000, 25 per cent more coal will be required. The main supplier of coal from abroad is of course Australia, which in 1992 supplied around 70 per cent of Japan's imported coal. Joint-venture partnerships are therefore the name of the game in years to come, as the Japanese coal industry seeks to develop overseas partnerships with countries such as China, South Africa and Russia.

The signs are that the nuclear power industry will find it harder to construct new power stations and the demand for coal will remain steady, as the electricity generators look to it as a still-viable raw material for electricity generation. By the year

2010 coal is expected to account for approximately 15.7 per cent of Japan's energy needs. In 1990 it accounted for 17.3 per cent of the country's total energy requirement.

OIL

The Gulf War was a bitter reminder to the Japanese of the fragility of their overseas oil supplies. Iraq and Kuwait combined accounted for over 10 per cent of Japan's oil requirement, and the prospect of any future curtailment of that supply has, since the war, sent Japanese oil strategists scurrying in search of more stable sources of petroleum products. Despite the fact that Saudi Arabia and others were able to make up the disparity in oil which Japan suffered at the time of the Gulf War, the lesson was learned: Japanese oil companies despatched personnel post-haste to Russia and Indonesia in search of a more reliable supply. Oil reserves in Tokyo Bay are now at their highest levels ever: in 1990 there were 142 days of supply, compared with 89 in 1989, and 49 in 1973.

In 1991 Japanese companies began talks on exploration rights to oil and natural gas sources off Sakhalin.

Deregulation of the Japanese oil industry is expected to see a reduction in the number of independent petroleum wholesalers (seven in 1992). By the year 2010 Japan will have reduced its dependency on oil from the 1990 level of 57.9 per cent of total energy required to approximately 45.3 per cent. This reduction is expected to come about as a result of increases in the energy provided by nuclear, geothermal and other sources.

NATURAL GAS

Imports of LNG (liquefied natural gas) are set to increase as the power generating companies seek energy sources which give off less carbon dioxide than conventional energy sources such as coal or oil (see: Environmental Policy). Joint-venture partnerships with ASEAN countries are intended to help expand the export potential of developing countries such as Malaysia. This is a good example of Japanese know-how being traded for the lion's share of the energy resources made available. By 2010 natural gas is expected to account for 12.2 per cent of the country's energy requirement, compared with 10.0 per cent in 1990.

NUCLEAR POWER

The nuclear power industry suffered a set-back in February 1991 when the Mihama Number 2 reactor in Fukui prefecture was shut down, because of a problem in the plant's steam generator. When the same problem was discovered in another plant, that too was shut down until the appropriate corrective measures could be taken.

Nevertheless, Japan's nuclear programme is due to expand, doubling its share of the total energy required from 8.9 per cent in 1990 to 16.9 per cent in 2010.

HYDROELECTRIC POWER

Despite Japan's heavy rainfall and the abundance of natural hot water or *onsen* (hot springs), Japan's rivers are too short and the terrain too mountainous to enable hydroelectric power to take off. The proportion of power supplied by this medium in 1990 was only 4.6 per cent, and is expected to drop to around 3.7 per cent in 2010.

'NEW ENERGY'

Research is ongoing in the following areas:

- **solar energy**. The Sunshine Project (1974) signalled the start of work on this alternative energy source.
- **geothermal energy**. Scientists are investigating methods for producing electricity from magma.
- **wind energy**. Selection of suitable sites for wind generators has been ongoing since 1979.
- **hydrogen energy**. Harnessing hydrogen as an energy source is of great interest, since hydrogen fuel is clean and does not produce harmful nitrogen or sulphur oxides.
- **fuel cells**. These are under development as an efficient means of generating power.
- **non-petroleum vehicle fuels**. A number of Japanese electricity producers, such as Tohoku Electric Power Company, are active in the development of electric cars.

JAPAN'S ENERGY NEEDS TODAY

Table 10 summarizes the degree to which Japan is dependent on outside sources for its energy requirements. The factor is calculated by subtracting total energy exports (in million metric tons of oil equivalent) from total imports and dividing this sum by total indigenous production/primary sources plus imports minus exports.

TABLE 10 Degree of dependency on energy imports, 1989–90

Country	Dependency (%)
Japan	84.1
United States	17.2
United Kingdom	2.5
France	53.7
Germany	53.4
Canada	−27.6
Italy	83.9

Source: OECD, energy balances of OECD countries, 1989/90.

25 Key Industries

The fact that four of the world's top twenty companies in 1989 by total sales were Japanese attests to the fact that Japan's companies are a force to be reckoned with, by anyone's standards. The top ten for that year are shown in Table 11.

The remaining two Japanese companies in the top twenty were Matsushita Electrical Industrial Company Ltd (twelfth) and Nissan Motor Company Ltd (seventeenth). The situation altered in 1991 with Toyota moving into fifth position, Hitachi into twelfth, Matsushita into thirteenth and Nissan into nineteenth. For profiles of all these major players, see: Key Company Histories.

AUTOMOBILES

Nearly one person in ten of Japan's total working population is in some way connected with the automobile industry. It alone accounted for 75 per cent of the US$40-billion US trade deficit with Japan in 1991, so it is appropriate to begin an examination of Japan's industries with a close look at this vitally important sector.

The Japanese car industry enjoyed a heady expansion throughout the 1980s, but it is now clear that those days are over. With the encroaching recession, the Japanese consumer has reined in spending on private cars and, with the added difficulty of finding suitable parking available in the big cities, the industry is set for a period of contraction in the domestic market.

Prior to purchasing a car in Japan, the would-be buyer has to prove to the local police authorities that he or she has an approved area in which to store the car. Approval rests on submitting a document showing, on a map, where the new car will be housed. Garage rents are expensive in Tokyo and so this is

TABLE 11 World top ten companies by total sales, 1989

	Total sales (US$ million)	Profits (US$ million)
1. General Motors	126,974.3	4,224.3
2. Ford Motors	96,932.6	3,835.0
3. Exxon	86,656.0	3,510.0
4. Royal Dutch/Shell Group	85,527.9	6,482.7
5. IBM	63,438.0	3,758.0
6. Toyota Motor Corporation	**60,443.6**	**2,631.1**
7. General Electric	55,264.0	3,939.0
8. Mobil	50,976.0	1,809.0
9. Hitachi Ltd	**50,894.0**	**1,446.7**
10. British Petroleum	49,484.4	3,498.8

Japanese companies are shown in **bold type**.
Source: Fortune magazine.

now proving to be a brake on new and second car purchases. The Japanese-language press has recently published news of severe cuts in domestic car production – for example, a lead article in Japan's equivalent of the *Financial Times*, the *Nihon Keizai Shimbun*, on 22 February 1993 read in part:

> Toyota plans stringent cuts in production: vehicle production cut by 50,000 units between January and March 1993. Nissan also follows suit with plans for a reduction in annual production of cars of some 2,000,000 units.

This has been accompanied by requests to Toyota's parts suppliers to instigate drastic price reductions.

The *Japan Times* noted in an article on 19 February 1993 that Toyota had posted its first straight run of losses since the former Toyota Motor Company and Toyota Motor Sales merged in 1982 (lost profits in the last three six-month account settlements). This is bad news indeed. Stories abound of Toyota employees and staff in related parts-supplier companies who, in the light of severe cuts in their bonus payments, have been unable to keep up payments on their mortgages and are subsequently in danger of losing their homes. For a company which has been known in the past as 'Toyota Ginko' ('the Bank of Toyota'), the picture could not be more serious.

Masami Iwasaki, vice-chairman of Toyota, has said that he believes that the company's operating profits will regain a 4 per cent level inside three years, and that this will be largely as a result of more cost-cutting drives. Cost cutting is one of the company's specialities, leading some employees to boast that they can 'squeeze even a dried towel'. The company's ability to effect cost cuts will be put keenly to the test over the next few years: indeed, the aftermath of the recession may mean that Japan's major companies are left even leaner and meaner than they were before.

There is no doubt that Toyota was beginning to experience problems even before the recession started to bite. The relaunched Corolla, which was intended to take the famous family car up-market, has proved to be something of a flop: most consumers could not rid themselves of the idea that the Corolla was a cheap and cheerful family vehicle. Even with its powers of persuasion, Toyota has not managed to overcome that feeling. The result is that the company has begun to downgrade the range to bring it more in line with what the consumer had come to expect, thereby aiming to boost sales. The company had tried to cash in on a perceived move in the market towards more luxury-oriented cars, but with the tightening of the consumer belt, it is now clear that that trend has died.

Nissan too is feeling the chill winds of recession and has announced substantial cuts in staffing. Although most automotive analysts predicted a slight improvement in the domestic car market for 1992, it is still too early to say whether such optimism has been rewarded. In the light of recent announcements about job losses and cuts in production, it seems unlikely that the market will recover even in 1993. For company details on Toyota, Nissan and Honda, see: Key Company Histories.

Overseas, the picture reflects plans for all the Japanese auto makers to boost production in their traditional target markets. Toyota has tied up with General Motors in the US for joint car production (United Motor Manufacturing Inc.), with Volkswagen in Germany for joint production of pick-up trucks and for marketing VW in Japan, and with Renault to produce commercial vehicles in Colombia. Toyota also has a new car production facility in Derby in the UK, which has recently started building the Carina four-door passenger car. Nissan, in addition to its production facility in Sunderland in the north-east of England, has also been developing and producing mini-vans with Ford, and, like Toyota, has started helping to market Ford cars in Japan.

Honda's principal tie-up has been with the Rover Group in the UK, where it manufactures cars with Rover and builds engines for the UK manufacturer on a commission basis.

Mitsubishi supplies passenger and commercial vehicles as well as engines to Chrysler of the US and sells Mercedes-Benz in Japan. It is also involved in joint development of small commercial vehicles with Mercedes Benz. Mitsubishi's other main link is with Volvo in the Netherlands. Mazda supplies components and passenger cars to Ford (which has a 24 per cent share in the Japanese company). It sells Citroen cars for Peugeot and Lancia cars for Fiat in Japan. Suzuki is involved in the development and production of mini-cars in Europe with Volkswagen.

There are fears in Europe that enhanced Japanese auto manufacture in the single market will damage the market share of existing makers. Whether the Japanese auto makers continue to limit voluntarily their total production in Europe to 1.2 million units (in order to defuse any danger of protectionism in Europe) remains to be seen.

AUTOMOTIVE PARTS SUPPLIERS

The position of the auto-parts suppliers in the pyramidal structure of the domestic auto industry is an unenviable one: when Toyota sneezes, its suppliers catch the cold. The auto makers are notorious for passing the buck of cost cutting along the line to first-tier parts suppliers, who then lean on their suppliers to take the brunt of it. It is not surprising, then, to find the Japanese domestic auto-parts suppliers struggling to survive in an increasingly hard and competitive world, given the fact that the auto industry is experiencing a serious downturn in sales. In an effort to offset the decline in sales in Japan, industry analysts expect to see Japanese auto-parts suppliers upgrading their activities in North America over the next few years.

AEROSPACE

The aerospace industry in Japan is ripe for development and expansion, representing as it does one of the least developed sectors of all of Japan's industries (in comparison with Japan's performance against its main competitors in other industries).

The industry in Japan is dominated by the following companies: Kawasaki Heavy Industries, Mitsubishi Heavy Industries, Fuji Heavy Industries, Japan Aircraft Manufacturing and Shin Meiwa Industry Company. These companies currently help in the manufacture of portions of Boeing aircraft: their recent involvement in the Boeing 777 signals the first instance of participation in the actual developmental stages of a new aircraft project with the American aircraft manufacturer. Kawasaki is also involved in the production of the Airbus A321, as part of British Aerospace's interest in that project. It is likely that Japanese aerospace companies will be drawn into the project to build the next generation of super-jumbos, currently the subject of joint discussions between Boeing and Airbus Industries, the European consortium.

In the commercial satellite sector, the opening of Japan's market resulted in the American company Space Systems/Loral being awarded the contract to build the new telecommunications satellite N-STAR for NTT (Nippon Telegraph and Telephone Company). In another sector, the weapons systems market, a moratorium was slapped on the Japan Aviation Electronics company by the US State Department for illegally selling missile parts to Iran: this has resulted in weapons manufacturers (who previously sourced their parts from the Japanese company) having to look elsewhere.

ADVERTISING AND THE MASS MEDIA

Reflecting general trends within Japanese industry as a whole, the world of Japanese advertising has started to witness a slowdown in the growth of the business. Since the health of this industry is directly linked to the economic climate, the signs are there will be no drastic improvement in the near future.

The industry continues to be dominated by Dentsu Inc. and the number two, Hakuhodo. Television is the favoured medium for advertising in Japan, which is one reason why Dentsu, with its stranglehold on TV advertising, remains far and away the market leader in terms of total profits. Of total billings for TV advertising in Japan in 1991 totalling in excess of ¥5.5 trillion (US$51.3 billion), Dentsu accounted for a massive ¥1.3 trillion (US$12.1 billion). Hakuhodo, with its ¥565 billion (US$527 million) gives some indication of the magnitude of Dentsu's lead.

Now that the Japanese market is performing in a lacklustre way, the Japanese advertising houses are turning their sights on Europe, where the single market offers exciting possibilities. Dentsu is even conducting investigations of the former eastern bloc to ascertain future prospects there.

One of the main differences between advertising in Japan and in the United States and Europe is that a Japanese advertising house will not limit itself to handling the affairs of a single client: it may also handle the accounts of competing clients. This is one area where there is liable to be some friction, once Japanese advertising agencies in Europe start in head-to-head competition with European advertising agencies for business in Europe and elsewhere.

AIRLINES

In 1986 the Japanese government began a liberalization programme in the Japanese airline industry, with the aim of improving competition and enhancing service to the increasing number of Japanese travellers. The three main Japanese airlines are JAL (Japan Airlines), ANA (All Nippon Airways) and JAS (Japan Air System). Historically JAL operated international flights whereas the others were concerned with the domestic market. This has all changed, and now all routes inside and outside Japan are keenly contested. The adjudicating body is the Ministry of Transport, which awards licences to airlines for various routes and which controls the development of new airports in Japan.

There have long been problems with Tokyo's main international airport at Narita (see: Gazetteer), which is located approximately one hour away by the fastest available train from the centre of Tokyo. Farmers have fought a running battle with the authorities to prevent the completion of the second and third runways at Narita. This has put great pressure on the airport, and at the time of writing there is still no clear solution in sight. The second airport terminal has opened, which has eased congestion in the crowded north and south wings of the old Terminal One, but until there are more slots available as a result of the second runway being opened, the numbers of travellers from Japan will be strictly limited by seat capacity.

There are plans for the opening and upgrading of other airports in addition to Tokyo under the terms of the Sixth Airport Development Plan. These include major airports for Kyushu (Shin-Kyushu) and Hokkaidō (Shin-Monbetsu) in the north of the island. Feasibility studies are also under way for a new international airport to serve the central city of Nagoya.

There is in addition the famous (or infamous) New Kansai Airport near Osaka in western Japan. This project, which includes a runway which is being built out into the sea, has been beset with various problems, not least the fact that the runway has been sinking into the water. The airport is due for completion in the latter part of the 1990s.

All the airlines are busily gearing themselves up for the new era of flight in Japan. At present it is the charter market from the regional airports which is providing rich pickings for companies such as the World Air Network Company, the rather grandiosely titled charter company of ANA. The savings to passengers in the regions who do not have to travel to Narita, for example, are proving the decisive factor in making such charter deals attractive to the increasingly cost-sensitive Japanese traveller.

BIOTECHNOLOGY

The field of biotechnology is one in which Japan has yet to truly shine. Nevertheless, some significant developments are worthy of mention.

Biotechnology is said to have developed through various stages, namely fermentation, genetic engineering, protein engineering and now transgenic engineering. This latest stage aims to develop organisms which can be used to produce substances for medical purposes. Companies in Japan are now looking at what pharmaceutical products can be made through transgenic engineering. For example, research is now being conducted using mice to discover ways and means to counteract the effects of Alzheimer's disease and other conditions.

Researchers in Japan are actively involved in finding ways to produce the substance G-CSF (granulocyte-colony stimulating factor) in order to be able to use it to combat the effects of anti-cancer treatments such as radio- and chemotherapy, which can reduce the number of white blood cells present in the patient. Projections show that a successful outcome for such research would yield a potential market of some ¥100 billion (US$90 million).

In addition to this, the era of the genetically engineered tomato may not be too far away. Legislation to control such developments is also in place, in recognition of the fact that they may have a profound, and as yet not fully understood, impact on the ecosystem as a whole. The main body in Japan concerned with the regulation of biotechnological innovation is the Biotechnology Subcommittee of the Central Council for Environmental Pollution Control, which comes under the auspices of the Environment Agency (see: Environmental Policy).

CHEMICALS

Protection of the environment is a theme very much on the minds of the major Japanese chemicals manufacturers. Top of the list is a concerted effort to start mass-producing HFC-13a as a viable alternative to chlorofluorocarbon gases (CFCs). This development is in line with the 1989 Montreal Protocol, which aims to have CFC use in industrialized countries terminated by 1999. Recycling is also on the agenda, although most Japanese chemicals companies have yet to convince the general public of their commitment to the better control of effluent and of toxic waste (see: Environmental Policy).

COMPUTERS

The Japanese computer industry is now in the grip of recession and it looks as though it will suffer for some time to come. Hitachi, Fujitsu, NEC and Toshiba are all forecasting declines in revenue in the early years of the 1990s, as the industry struggles to come to terms with some quintessentially industry-specific problems.

Historically, Japan's computer industry has always been

weaker on the software side. This trend continues and, in so doing, flags up market possibilities for non-Japanese companies with an expertise in applied software production. For example, CASE tools (computer-aided software tools, which cut the number of person-hours required to write new programs) show a great deal of potential for companies such as Texas Instruments, which has a recognized edge on the Japanese competition. On the hardware side, Japanese producers are suffering from the twin problems that major client companies are now in the process of completing their computer set-ups, and others are finding that networks are a viable alternative to the purchase of substantial mainframe computers.

IBM Japan announced tough 'restructuring measures' – staff reductions – in the early part of 1993. According to the Japan Electronics Industry Development Association, sales of PCs (personal computers) declined in 1991 for the first time since records were kept – down 3.5 per cent. The only manufacturer to show signs of growth was Apple, which doubled its market share in Japan to 5 per cent in 1991. The strength of Japanese capability in the hardware side and the continuing superiority of non-Japanese companies on the software side is best exemplified by the alliance between Sony and Apple, the former now manufacturing one of the latter's notebook computers.

The PC market continues to be dominated by NEC, which has a market share of some 50 per cent of all PC sales in Japan.

CONSTRUCTION

As well as contending with a projected overall downturn in the number of construction projects to come, Japanese contractors are now having to face up to increased scrutiny by the outside world of what have been termed the closed-circle bidding practices of the past. This problem was emphasized during the SII (Structural Impediments Initiative) talks in 1990, when American negotiators homed in on the construction industry as a hot-bed of protectionism and illegal bidding practices. Added to this is the problem of a contracting labour market (see: Human Resources), which is forcing construction companies in Japan to employ an ever-increasing number of foreign contract labourers, thereby raising the spectre of instability in Japanese society as a whole.

ELECTRONICS AND ELECTRONIC COMPONENTS

As the consumer continues to tighten the purse strings, so the suffering of the electronics industry in Japan begins to worsen. Sales of televisions, camcorders, car audio and video-tape machines all registered lower sales in 1991-2. Capital investment likewise began to slow. Hitachi's plans to spend ¥280 billion (US$260 million) were reduced to ¥220 billion (US$200 million) and other similar reductions in the rest of the electronics sector have been symptomatic of the conservative and somewhat pessimistic view of planners within the industry.

On the brighter side, sales of electronics products for industrial use were expected to improve in 1992.

FOOD AND BEVERAGES

Any visitor to Japan will come away with the feeling that food is a national obsession (see: Sport and Recreation). Restaurants ranging from the cheapest fast-food joint to the most refined *kaiseki* (Japanese-style *haute cuisine*) establishment abound: visions of schoolchildren munching their way through *Makudonarudo* (McDonald's), and *sarariman* (office workers) slurping *soba* (buckwheat noodles) at busy station noodle stands, are just some of the images of food which tend to linger.

This is the face of a ¥25-trillion (US$233-billion) industry. Cramped living quarters and a propensity to entertain almost exclusively away from home are two factors which have helped Japan to develop a food and beverage industry which is second to none. As it moves into the 1990s, however, there is no doubt that consumers are beginning to spend less on dining out either for pleasure or for *tsukiai* (business socializing).

Although ground rents have started to fall in the major cities, the cost of setting up a new eating place has risen, to the extent that restaurants are either setting up or relocating in suburban areas where rents are lower, or are trying to share space with other businesses, such as music shops. Disposal of waste, particularly in the larger cities, is also helping to drive the costs of running a restaurant still higher, as the amount of available land for dumping begins to decline and waste has to be either transported further away, or disposed of in ever more sophisticated ways (again requiring more expenditure). Another problem is that of the labour shortage now facing Japan (see: Human Resources).

HOTEL AND TRAVEL

The major blot on the landscape for the hotel and travel industry worldwide in 1991 was the Gulf War. Japanese hotel and travel organizations did not escape the problem, and occupancy rates fell during and after the war, because US firms in particular were anxious about the safety of their executives in what looked like a return to the air terrorism of the 1970s. Hotels such as the prestigious Okura, New Otani and Imperial in Tokyo, which depend to a significant extent on overseas business people, suffered as a consequence of the war.

The recession has proved to be a second knock to the industry, as occupancy rates continue to be depressed. The Imperial suffered a 10 per cent occupancy rate downturn year on year from February 1991 to February 1992, and as a result decided to peg room rates at ¥34,000 (US$317.16) for a single, ¥35,000–61,000 (US$326.49–569.03) for a double or a twin, and ¥60,000–80,000 (US$559.70–746.27) for a suite. This downturn in room occupancy rates is reflected in a survey by the *Nihon Keizai Shimbun* newspaper which showed that occupancy rates at eighteen top Tokyo hotels were 74.2 per cent in 1992, down 8.6 points from 1991.

Industry specialists say that domestic use of hotels and the travel industry will expand despite the current occupancy rate drops, and most in the outward-bound travel trade are looking forward to regaining the level of business they had enjoyed during the months leading up to the outbreak of the Gulf War. Weddings are big business in Japan, as the many advertisements on the Tokyo underground prove, and signs are that there is still great potential in this area of the market.

In overseas travel too, the Japanese tourist has replaced the American as the leader in world travel, so much so that more and more operators in Europe, Australia and North America are seeking to train their employees in Japanese customer care and the Japanese language. The government's official target of 10 million Japanese overseas travellers was exceeded well in advance of forecasts, and with the continuing strength of the yen against all of the major currencies, the trend is set for Japanese consumers to take advantage of the buying power of their currency to enjoy foreign holidays to the full.

If anything, travel to Europe is set to grow, since the United States is increasingly perceived as a 'dangerous' destination. This fear is fuelled by adverse news items, such as that on the murder in the United States of a young student from the central Japanese city of Nagoya, and other horror stories. (There is in fact a book published in Japan called *Sekai no abunai tokoro* – 'A Guide to the Dangerous Places of the World' – which notes in graphic detail in what European and American cities one is likely to be robbed, raped or murdered.)

In all sectors of the travel trade, competition for Japanese custom is set to intensify, with those organizations that are 'in tune' with the needs of the Japanese consumer likely to capitalize on the growth potential in this sector. This will be at the expense of those who remained entrenched in second-class standards of customer care.

PHARMACEUTICALS

In 1976, legislation passed in Japan made it impossible for the domestic pharmaceutical companies to produce generic drugs based on those developed abroad. As a result of this, Japanese producers have been forced to take a hard look at their basic research programmes, which in turn has led them to view acquisitions of foreign pharmaceutical companies as one way to get around the changes in Japan's domestic pharmaceutical legislation. A secondary problem is that the research and development costs of creating new drugs in Japan cannot be recovered simply by relying on domestic sales of the drug: foreign markets have to be tackled. This has made Japanese companies in the field anxious to develop links with foreign producers, leading to the purchase of American and German pharmaceutical companies in particular.

Foreign companies are also seeking to expand their foothold in Japan, aware that the ageing population (one in four Japanese will be over the age of 65 in the year 2000) will require ever-increasingly sophisticated health and drug support. The market is therefore ripe for exploitation.

REAL ESTATE

Throughout the 1980s, land and property prices soared, making ordinary Japanese ever more fearful that their dreams of being able to own their own homes were turning into an ideal which could not be realized. With the bursting of the economic bubble, however (see: The Economy – General Overview), land prices have begun to fall in the heavily built-up areas of the country, and the National Land Agency predicts that this trend is set to continue.

The property price explosion is attributed to the failure of the Japanese government to develop a proper plan to overcome spiralling land prices, despite the advice of, among others, the economist Maekawa (see: The Economy – General Overview). The government finally acted in January 1992, when it decided to tax farm land in urban areas at the same rate as residential land, thereby discouraging speculation and encouraging farmers to sell their land for housing use. It remains to be seen whether this move will again turn out to be a matter of too little too late: nevertheless, the possibility of the individual looking forward to becoming a true property-owner may not be a pipe-dream after all.

26 Environmental Policy

Environmental issues affecting Japan both domestically and internationally are at the forefront of the problems which confront the country in the 1990s. A great deal of disinformation is the keynote here, for many highly charged environmental issues are subject to a lack of clear data, vested interests within Japan, misconceptions regarding what the country actually does with respect to green issues, and a blurred perception of what foreign criticism of its environmental record means. Too often, foreign criticism feeds on already rampant anti-Japanese feeling, while Japan's response to these criticisms is shakily based on half-baked notions of cultural and historical precedent, which is always used to combat aggressive foreign attempts to get Japan to 'improve'.

THE ISSUES
Perceptions of Japan's environmental record can be broadly divided into four categories:

- whaling;
- deforestation;
- air pollution;
- importation of wild animals.

Whaling
While recognizing the fact that Japan is among the world's leading whaling nations, it is important to note that it is not the only 'bad guy on the block'. Iceland, Norway and the former Soviet Union are also key players. What angers the Japanese whaling fraternity and elements of the Japanese population at large is the way that anti-whaling organizations such as

Greenpeace have chosen to portray whaling in the media by using emotive pictures of whale *sashimi* juxtaposed with pictures of a whale in the wild, as a graphic illustration of what happens to a whale once it is killed. This is clearly focusing on a Japanese cultural point, which already finds a willingly anti-Japanese audience. Why, it may be asked, are not Norwegian cultural peculiarities exploited in the same way?

Media coverage of this kind plays right into the hands of the Japanese whaling establishment, which can readily accuse the outside world of meddling in Japan's internal cultural affairs and historical heritage. It also helps the pro-Japanese lobby in Japan to activate counter-cultural arguments about the Europeans and Americans killing cows and sheep, a line which is quite clearly facile and which leads the debate nowhere. It is much better to approach the problem in the way which the UK-based Whale and Dolphin Conservation Society is doing, combining understanding of the so-called cultural angle with a strong pragmatism, which says that change in the way Japan views the killing of whales can be achieved not by raving at Japan but by effecting change from within the country, using the efforts of the Japanese people themselves.

One fine example of this approach is the encouragement of whale-watching as an alternative to whale-killing. Fishing villages and towns in Japan with a history of whaling are being asked to consider the possibility of promoting whale-watching as a recreational and scientific activity, which both contributes to the local economy and helps to preserve the tradition of 'whaling'. In a sense, whale-watching can actually revitalize local economies, and give the community the prospect of a new future. The Whale and Dolphin Conservation Society, in a document now available in Japanese, outlines how several ex-Antarctic whalers are leading the whale-watching movement, telling stories based on their own experiences.

Now, in the far south, humpback whales have become the focus of whale-watching, while the towns of Ogata and Saga provide the best starting-off point for a trip to view the little-known Bryde's whales. In the far north, off the coast of Hokkaidō, it is possible to see a rich variety of dolphins, porpoises and minke whales. This must surely be the best way to encourage change in Japan. What is most exciting is the fact that the Japanese themselves are pioneering better and more effective ways of ensuring a good whale-watching experience, and it is here that hope lies for an improved future for whales and dolphins in general.

It is crucial to note that many Japanese equate the eating of whales with the immediate postwar years, when there was almost no other available source of meat-based protein. This engenders a dangerous sentimentality and has people thinking that to eat whale in the 1990s is to take a trip down memory lane. In fact, the good old days were not good old days, and the eating of whales is a practice well past its sell-by date. The commercial killing of whales only began in Japan in the 1930s (it was learned from Europe) and so hardly merits the cachet of being tied up with Japan's traditions.

With luck the moratorium on the commercial killing of whales will survive attempts by the Japanese whalers to over-turn it. The question is whether the constructive counter-proposals can gain enough favour in a desperately short space of time.

Deforestation

That Japan destroys rainforests in the Philippines in order to use the wood for its *waribashi* (throw-away wooden chopsticks) is an often-heard criticism of Japan, which has little basis in fact. Woodchips, not whole trees, are used to make *waribashi*, and Japan is not single-mindedly destroying tropical rainforests in South-east Asia. In the 1990s it is more a question of Japanese companies helping to reforest areas devastated by the govern-ments of the countries in question.

There is no doubt that Japan is one of the world's largest consumers of wood products, such as paper and paper-board (fourth largest after the US, Canada and Sweden). In fact the country has to import 70 per cent of its wood products. Critics of Japan's wood policies wonder why it does not cut down its own forests. One explanation for this, according to Japanese authorities, is that the majority of its forests are under 35 years old and are not yet ready for felling. Figure 1 shows that Japan's record on recycling is far better than any of the other major wood users.

On a brighter note, Mitsubishi Corporation is actively replanting tropical rainforests in peninsular Malaysia, which were chopped down not by the Japanese but by the Malays themselves – an activity performed in the manic drive towards industrialization. As with most things, the Japanese are not acting here out of altruism, but in recognition of the fact that over 60 per cent of their overseas development aid (ODA) goes to the rest of Asia, and rampant industrialization without a comprehensive green policy there is likely to be to the detri-ment of Japan in the long term.

In May 1990 the Green Earth Project was launched, for which Japan has allocated ¥750 million (US$7 million) from its ODA budget. Improvements are slow in coming, but green issues are beginning to gain prominence in Japan. The biggest problem will be keeping them on the agenda, for initiatives

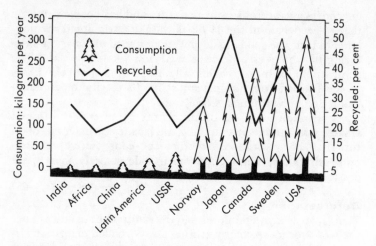

Figure 1 Paper and paper-board use per capita for selected countries in the late 1980s. Source: *New Internationalist*, April 1992 (used with permission).

accompanied by a great media fanfare in Japan are usually doomed to die a death.

Air pollution

In the 1960s and 1970s Japan's air pollution levels ran out of control: environmental catastrophes resulting from the country's rapid industrialization eventually required the government to act in an uncharacteristically decisive fashion in bringing in new laws to control air pollution. As a result, Japan now has, at least on paper, one of the strictest pieces of anti-pollution legislation in the industrialized world. Japan introduced unleaded petrol in 1978, well ahead of any of its overseas competitors, and was also keenly involved in the development of the catalytic converter in automobiles. Japanese companies are now actively involved in the development of these devices so that they can be made cheaply in newly industrialized and industrializing countries. As Mitsuo Usuki, coordinator for international affairs at the Environment Agency's Conservation Bureau, said in 1992: 'The best way for the government of Japan to play a role in the world community is to use our accumulated technical and scientific knowledge, and human resources, to overcome global environmental issues.'

The signs are that air pollution in Japan is once more on the increase and that companies will need to be brought to heel fairly soon before the excesses of the 1960s are repeated. This will require a further raising of public awareness about the extent to which there has been deterioration of air quality in the urban areas of Japan, as well as government incentives to companies to undergo green audits (as pioneered by the Body Shop) in return for tax breaks.

Although Japan has a long way to go in cleaning up its air, Japanese observers are quick to point out that it is most likely to be Japan and the European Community that will ultimately effect global changes in environmental policy, since the United States is the world's number one producer of carbon dioxide and it has refused to set specific targets for carbon-dioxide reductions in the climate change treaty.

Importation of wild animals

Japan has a notorious record with regard to the importation of wild animals, including endangered species. For too long the pet shops of Japan have competed in the procurement of strange and exotic animals and the wanton promotion of certain animals as status symbols. A walk around a Japanese pet shop in recent years would yield honey bears, frilly-necked lizards from Australia, and other similarly rare and special animals that require careful feeding and attention even when kept in captivity in their own countries, let alone within the confines of a cramped and wholly unsuitable Japanese urban apartment. The main problem is that the Japanese are slaves to fashion, and if a style magazine dictates that, to be cool, you have to own a frilly-necked lizard, it does not take much to work out that there will be a run on the market for such animals.

Japan has already signed the Washington Convention (1980), which regulates the traffic in wild animals, but it has often been criticized for not adopting sufficiently stringent measures to enforce the specified regulations. In countering criticism, Noboru Hatakeyama, the vice-minister of the Ministry of International Trade and Industry (MITI), has said that by the spring of 1996, MITI will insist that all species regulated by CITES (Convention on International Trade in Endangered Species of Wild Fauna and Flora) and products from these plants or animals will have to be accompanied by a valid export permit from their place of origin.

THE ENVIRONMENT AGENCY

One problem in effecting environmental policies in Japan is the relative weakness of the Environment Agency, which in bureaucratic terms is a comparatively young government body and one which does not come off well in policy skirmishes with the Ministry of Foreign Affairs, the Ministry of International Trade and Industry or the Ministry of Finance. Although it is required to coordinate environmental policy, the Environment

Agency finds that the multitude of programmes in progress makes this difficult. This is unlikely to change in the near future.

RECYCLING

One area where Japan is an acknowledged leader (although there are still many problems associated with it) is recycling. The country even has a National Recycling Day on 20 October: the date '1-0-2-0' (October 20 as it would be written in Japanese) symbolizes the idea of 'one cycle, two cycles'. Recycling is evident in a variety of forms, the principal ones being:

- *Chirigami kōkan* ('coarse paper recycling'). Old newspapers and cardboard are regularly collected and approximately 50 per cent of waste paper is recycled. The government has started to use recycled paper after studies showed that the bureaucracy alone was producing between 50 and 60 tons of paper per month!

- **Block collection**. Household waste is divided into combustible and non-combustible categories for disposal, while other waste products, such as batteries, glass, old refrigerators, TVs and audiovisual equipment, are put out in designated rubbish collection areas for collection by the appropriate recyclers.

- **Bottles**. Liquor-store owners return reusable containers to the original bottlers. In the same spirit, the Law for the Promotion of Utilization of Recycled Resources urges manufacturers to use more recycled materials in their products.

- **Compost recycling**. Leftovers are turned into compost for eventual use as fuel or fertilizer. In Sapporo, the capital city of the northern island of Hokkaidō, a waste-recycling plant is now in operation which can transform 200 tons of waste into 120 tons of 'refuse-derived waste'.

- **Milk cartons**. The amount of pulp in one milk carton is roughly equivalent to five rolls of toilet paper, so milk-carton recycling is particularly important.

In addition to these recycling measures, efforts are also being made to make kitchens more 'green' by ensuring that sinks have strainers and by promoting the use of new oil-absorbing sponges. The Japanese government is funding research to develop biodegradable plastic, aware that 70 per cent of plastic waste in Japan is burned as a means of disposal (compared with the United States and Europe, where 90 per cent of waste plastic is buried in landfills).

27 Finance

The world of Japanese finance has been irrevocably changed in the aftermath of what has been called the bubble economy (see: The Economy – General Overview). In the postwar period, Japanese financial institutions had become the most conservative, traditionally entrenched and arrogant of all the elements making up the Japanese system. Although the Japanese establishment is convinced that the excesses of the late 1980s, which led to the creation of the bubble economy, were an aberration and so lay outside the perimeters of the mainstream economy, as events unfold it is becoming increasingly clear that this is emphatically not the case. The best prognosis for the current ills besetting the world of Japanese finance is that banks will be forced to administer loans not on the basis of who knows whom, but on sound judgement based on a careful and thorough appraisal of the company or individual seeking financial support.

As historical precedent has it, the government, notably the Ministry of Finance, is likely to be slow to act, so that the responsibility for tidying up their act will fall fairly and squarely on the shoulders of the financial institutions. What is certain is that these institutions will have to pay dearly for their greed and arrogance.

THE STOCK MARKET

There are stock exchanges in Tokyo, Osaka, Nagoya, Kyoto, Hiroshima, Fukuoka, Niigata and Sapporo, although the three main stock markets (Tokyo, Osaka, Nagoya) account for 98 per cent of total trading volume. The Tokyo Stock Exchange itself handles 90 per cent of total trading volume.

Stock exchanges are organized on a membership basis and only the members are allowed to trade securities on the exchange. Applications to join the exchanges are via the Ministry of Finance.

On 31 December 1989, 22 foreign securities firms were given membership of the Tokyo Stock Exchange and were permitted to trade securities freely from that date on.

STOCK-HOLDING

A characteristic feature of stock-holding in Japan has been the preponderance of cross-shareholding between the banks and other financial institutions (see: The Corporations). This feature has traditionally made companies resistant to merger and acquisition, but the signs are that, as the recession in Japan deepens, many organizations will decide to relinquish their holdings in order to shore up their own financial standing. As this happens, and the truth dawns that the shares no longer match their original values, the economy as a whole will begin to suffer. This will not be limited purely to those institutions directly affected by the fall-out from the bursting of the bubble.

Another significant characteristic of the stock market to date has been the preoccupation with maximizing profits through tax-free capital gains, not through the acquisition of dividends. This made the market a very aggressive place in the mid- to late 1980s, and was one reason why it eventually overheated. The assumption was that the market could take the strain: the fact that the Nikkei continued to fall, and that institutions were gearing up for a Nikkei average of 10,000 points, shows that these assumptions were incorrect. In 1992, the economic journalist Christopher Wood stated that: 'The Nikkei could fall far lower than any conventional pundit currently expects – perhaps to 12,000, at which point the capital gains on the huge stock portfolios of the banks and insurance companies would be wiped out.'

The outlook is bleak. As a sign of the changing times, the slow market with its stagnant share prices suggests that the Big Four brokerages (Nomura, Daiwa, Nikko and Yamaichi) will turn in significant losses at the end of the year to 31 March 1993. The newspaper *Yomiuri Shimbun*, in an assessment of the performance of the top 25 listed brokerages, expects losses in the region of ¥15 billion (US$414 million) for Nomura, ¥18 billion (US$17 million) for Daiwa, ¥45 billion (US$42 million) for Yamaichi and ¥13 billion (US$12 million) for Nikko. All four brokerages have been seen to revise their out-turn forecasts downwards as the situation worsens, which suggests that the full impact of the end of the booming 1980s and the financial scandals is beginning to show.

THE BOND MARKET

The bond market in Japan has been deeply involved in the mire of the financial scandals which have come to light there in recent years. The main players in these have been the brokerages involved in the compensation of major clients for their securities-related trading losses. These organizations sold bonds at low prices to favoured clients and then bought them back at higher prices, thereby effecting a kind of 'compensation'. The brokerages are but one of the groups of players that compete in this multi-faceted market: there are national bonds, government-guaranteed bonds, general corporate bonds and yen-based foreign bonds, for which city banks, local banks, trust banks and life insurance companies expend effort in trading.

The compensation scandals have had a sobering effect on the securities companies and others in Japan. The realization that guaranteeing returns on investments and removing any risk, at least for the big-time players, runs counter to the spirit of stockbroking has been a painful experience in a country where such practices had become part of the known, if not publicized, features of the trade.

As part of a concerted effort to regulate the industry, the Japan Securities Dealers Association introduced a ruling which stated that there had to be an allowable price range for the trading of bonds. This was followed by action by the Tokyo Stock Exchange to limit the regulated price of listed bonds, so that when they are traded over the exchange they are subject to a range of 1.5 per cent above or below the market price and to a range of plus or minus 2.0 per cent for over-the-counter dealing.

THE BANKS

Apart from the Bank of Japan (see: Japan Inc.), there is a variety of banks in Japan. **City banks** are the main suppliers of funds to companies and have nationwide networks. Their principal source of funds is deposits. **Long-term credit banks**, such as the Industrial Bank of Japan, the Long-term Credit Bank of Japan and the Nippon Credit Bank, obtain funds via the issuing of debentures. These banks supply approximately 7 per cent of total capital funds supplied by all banks in Japan. **Trust banks** perform a long-term financing role and provide 10 per cent of total capital funds supplied by Japanese banks.

INSURANCE COMPANIES

Japanese life insurers, in the wake of the problems affecting the stock and bond markets, are said to be retrenching. This means that they are seeking the shelter of safer portfolios, adding to past criticisms that their asset management has been rather weak. The insurance industry has operated something of a cartel, meaning that the twenty mutual life insurance companies have tended to pay out roughly the same dividends. Deregulation planned by the Ministry of Finance may change all of this.

In non-life insurance, premiums are low. This reflects the status of Japan as a relatively low-risk country; nevertheless, the high incidence of typhoons in recent years has meant that some non-life insurance companies have begun to feel the pinch. Most of these will have to borrow from the banks to help to cover inordinately high claims in respect of the damage wreaked by the typhoons.

The 'Big One', the earthquake scheduled to hit Tokyo at any time now, is expected to exact a devastating toll on the non-life insurers.

The main players in the non-life market are Tokio Marine and Fire (with a 17 per cent share of the market), Yasuda Fire and Marine, Taisho Marine and Fire, Dai-Tokyo Fire and Marine, and Sumitomo Marine and Fire. The main life insurers are headed by Nippon Life Insurance, Dai-Ichi Mutual and Sumitomo.

28 Trade Issues and the Future

The recession in Japan will have a continuing and damaging impact on global trade relations into the 1990s. Counter to the export promotion activities of non-Japanese companies wishing to sell into Japan, and the efforts of the Japanese government to promote imports, the stagnant domestic economy is not only depressing the import side, but causing the export side to start climbing (see Figure 2). The effects of this combined development are to increase the deficits that Japan is running with its major trading partners, thereby raising the spectre of protectionism and long-term damage to the worldwide trading system.

In January 1993 the trade surplus of Japan with the United States, the EC and with Asia in general was as shown in Table 12. These figures represent record highs for the trade surplus and are fuelling calls for the government to do something about boosting domestic demand. The key to this, according to some economists, is to instigate income tax cuts in order to put more money back into the pocket of the consumer. Consumer-oriented industries such as the automobile sector are particularly keen to see this happen. Others argue that with the pessimism in Japan likely to make consumers save their money for a rainy day, introducing tax breaks will not help at all.

Against official predictions from the Ministry of Finance and analysts at the Bank of Tokyo that the surplus for the calendar year 1992–3 will break all previous records (such as the US$94.1 billion in fiscal year 1986–7) to reach an all-time high of US$107.064 billion, it is clear that something has to be done.

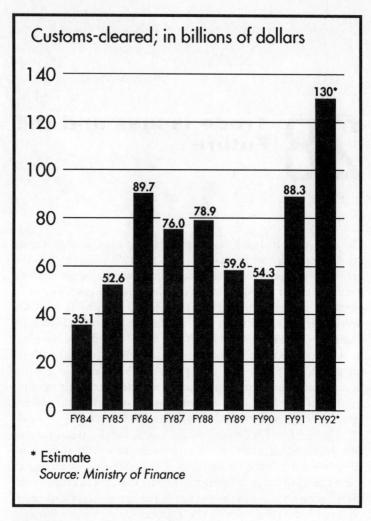

FIGURE 2 Japan's trade surplus.

THE CASE FOR TAX CUTTING

The basic assumption is that as personal consumption accounts for a full 60 per cent of the GNP of Japan, it is personal consumption which needs a shot in the arm. There is talk of one-year tax rebates and special tax reductions for those buying new houses: some are calling for tax reductions of between ¥2 trillion (US$18.7 billion) and ¥5 trillion (US$46.6 billion). According to the newspaper *Nihon Keizai Shimbun*, a tax cut of ¥4 trillion (US$37.4 billion) would yield an extra ¥100,000 (US$933) on

TABLE 12 Japan's trade surplus, January 1993

Surplus with:	Exports (US$ billion)	Imports (US$ billion)	Surplus (US$ billion)
US	7.18 (6.4%)	4.23 (−1.8%)	2.95 (21.0%)
EC	5.05 (−0.2%)	2.31 (−20.5%)	2.74 (27.0%)
Asia	7.67 (6.1%)	6.13 (−4.9%)	1.53 (96.1%)
Total	*24.17 (0.8%)*	*18.88 (−6.4%)*	*5.28 (39.4%)*

The figures in parentheses are year-on-year changes.

average for each taxpayer, although the actual amount could vary considerably from individual to individual. Whether the consumer would then spend or save is open to conjecture, but in the current climate of pessimism, it would seem logical to assume that the consumer will choose to save.

At present Japan has a five-tax-rate system in which the tax burden varies according to the amount of personal income and other factors such as the number of dependants. Taxpayers pay the government between 10 per cent and 15 per cent of their taxable income (minus calculable reductions for dependants, etc.). They also pay between 5 per cent and 15 per cent of their taxable income to their local authorities. Therefore any tinkering with the current income tax system which takes account of the needs of the economy in the current recession will have to be effected in such a way that raising the amount of taxable income in each of the five tax-rate categories (and they need to be raised) will not immediately result in a higher tax rate.

This theory, as expounded by Yukio Noguchi, Professor of Economics at Hitotsubashi University in Tokyo, would seem to be a good solution as part of a broader income-tax reform programme. Professor Noguchi also says that any proposed cuts in income tax should be part-funded by the consumption tax (currently 3 per cent) and that this should be raised to around 15 per cent by the year 2020. The rationale here is that as Japan ages, the pressure to pay for increased spending on support services for the old will inevitably fall on the shoulders of a shrinking, younger working population, and that the principal means of raising funds will necessarily be through the apparatus of income tax. Funding these increased services via an increased consumption tax will be one way to spread the tax burden more evenly.

INCREASING PUBLIC SPENDING

Those who believe that the economy can be kick-started by greater spending on public works are being overly optimistic. These projects alone will not be able to lift Japan out of the recession. It will be a combination of remedies that does the trick, if indeed the Japanese economy can be cured using conventional medicines. Some would argue that the effects of the bubble economy are going to have fundamental and structural ramifications in the economy at large, which will need a radical new approach if the problems are to be overcome.

CAPITAL SPENDING

One of the manifestations of the recession – which proves the point that the bubble economy was not just grafted onto the main body of the economy – is the fact that corporate capital investment (CCI) is slowing down. Table 13 shows projected CCI for the financial year 1993.

According to *Nihon Keizai Shimbun*, these will be the first two consecutive years of decline since the survey began in 1973. It will also be the largest since 1975, after the first oil shock. Capital spending in seventeen manufacturing industries with

TABLE 13 Projected capital corporate investment, 1993

Category	Number of firms	FY93 investment plans (¥ billion)	FY93 estimated investment (¥ billion)
All industries	1,166	13,975 (−8.4%)	15,249 (−7.6%)
All industries except electric power companies	1,154	10,134 (−12.5%)	11,581 (−12.0%)
Manufacturing industry	716	5,577 (−14.6%)	6,533 (−17.3%)
Non-manufacturing industry	450	8,397 (−3.7%)	8,715 (+1.4%)

The figures in parentheses show the change from a year earlier.
Source: Nihon Keizai Shimbun.

the exception of precision equipment is expected to drop. Declines will even be registered in the food and textile industries, sectors which are traditionally highly resistant to this kind of downturn. There will also be knock-on effects such as those to be seen in the steel industry, where the decline in car sales has caused capital investment to fall by 17.6 per cent. This slow-down in CCI will undoubtedly retard Japan's progress out of recession.

THE ECONOMIC OUTLOOK FOR THE 1990s

It will be clear from the discussions above that Japan is entering not just a problematic period of its economic history, but a crucial one. The effects of the bursting of the bubble economy are only now beginning to be fully understood (see Figure 3, on the next page). What these augur for the future of the Japanese economy cannot be said to favour optimism. The greed of the late 1980s may have cost Japan the chance to become a global player in the true sense: after all, its power in the world today rests solely on its economic prowess, and if that evaporates, or at best dissipates, Japan will ultimately find itself relegated to the second division for good.

The United States does not really need Japan in the way that Japan desperately needs the United States. The US could power its economy domestically if needs dictated this to happen: Japan on the other hand depends on the outside world for its energy needs, and increasingly for its food needs. The United States is the major provider in this sense.

On the positive side, Japan has weathered attempts by the Mongol hordes to invade, has survived the holocaust of conventional and nuclear war, has got through the oil shocks and other economic trauma such as *endaka* (the yen appreciation of the 1980s), and has a resilient and hard-working people. The country will need not only the skill and determination of its people but also a strong measure of good fortune to survive what looks like being a turbulent decade.

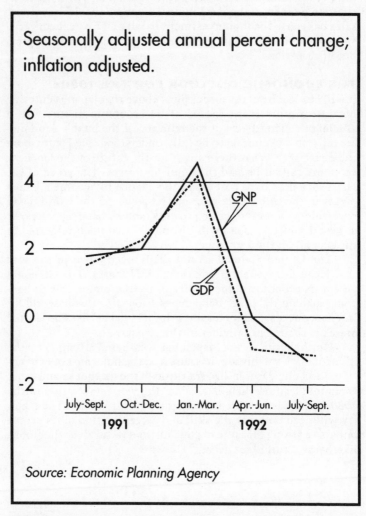

FIGURE 3 Japan's economic growth rates in 1991–2.

PART SIX

Doing Business in Japan

29 Market Entry

Gaining entry to the Japanese market and making a success of business there has in the past filled most non-Japanese companies with trepidation, not only on account of the widely recognized language and cultural barriers, but also because of what has always been regarded as a protected and restrictive place to do business.

Times are changing in Japan, as evidenced by the progressive eroding of tariffs on most goods, and because the improvement in the availability of information about Japan has helped to dispel some of the misconceptions about the place. Japan-watchers have been able to make a steady living out of highlighting the tremendous differences between Japan and the rest of the world: the time has come to realize that while there are big differences in the way things are done in Japan, there is no reason why these differences should not be understood and even a competitive advantage derived from them. Japan is a different market, but then so are all export markets. With commitment, a solid record in terms of quality of the product, and a proven ability to follow up with a reliable after-sales service, a non-Japanese company has every possibility of being successful in this rich and promising market.

According to figures from the Ministry of Finance, the main donors of foreign direct investment in Japan are, in order of magnitude in millions of US dollars: the United States (1,334), Canada (764), United Kingdom (431), the Netherlands (323), Switzerland (176) and Germany (172), as of 31 March 1991.

PREPARING FOR MARKET ENTRY

The Japanese tendency to equate business with warfare is a point which should be kept in mind. It follows that information-gathering and reconnaissance trips to learn about the market should be the first step in any approach to Japan. In this way you will be able to ascertain current fashions and get a feel for the Japanese approach to colour, form and texture of consumer goods, for example.

In the 1950s a business person wishing to do business in Japan needed to brace himself or herself for a long and arduous journey, but today it is possible to reach Japan using direct flights from Europe (10–12 hours), the west coast of the United States (7–8 hours) and Australia (8 hours from Sydney). So visiting the market in the early stages is a vital first move. It is important to *feel* the vibrancy of Tokyo and Osaka and to imbibe the atmosphere of 'get-up-and-go', while at the same time laying the foundations of friendship with potential business partners or clients in Japan. A one-off visit is seldom going to be enough: most successful non-Japanese business people see themselves on a plane to Japan at least two or more times a year. It is as essential to be seen in the market as to see the market.

Similarly, it is important to signal that your interest is in the Japanese market specifically: implying that Japan is but one destination on an Asia-Pacific business odyssey is unlikely to give your business initiatives the kind of degree of seriousness which the Japanese demand. There will always be the tempta-tion to locate a 'Far East Representative Office' in a place like Singapore, but this should, if possible, be resisted at all costs: the Japanese do not think of themselves as being in the Far East and will not look upon being lumped in with the rest of Asia with particular favour. While there is a tremendous cost impli-cation for setting up representation in Japan, if you are truly serious about getting the most out of the market, then an office in Tokyo or a link-up with a Japanese partner are really the only options.

You may be the Japan enthusiast in your company, eager to get going, but a word of caution is necessary at this point: being successful in Japan is (in nine cases out of ten) going to take a great deal of time, patience and, most importantly, money. Without the whole-hearted support of your colleagues at home base – and that means having them accept that there are unlikely to be immediate returns – you may find it difficult to count on sustained support when you really need it. This is a bit of pre-preparation which must be attended to before leaping onto a plane to Japan.

FINDING THE RIGHT PARTNER

If you have chosen in the first instance to seek a Japanese partner to take charge of importing your product, you will find a great variety of possibilities. These may mean small,

TABLE 14 Sales of Japan's Nine *Sogo Shosha*, 1991

Trading company	Total (¥ billion)	Imports into Japan (¥ billion)
Itochu	20,012	2,057
Sumitomo	18,778	2,820
Marubeni	18,241	2,506
Mitsui	16,164	2,816
Mitsubishi	15,699	3,014
Nissho Iwai	10,916	2,632
Tomen	7,256	1,157
Nichimen	6,213	499
Kanematsu	5,920	2,509

Source: Japan Foreign Trade Council.

one-man-band operations, or, if what you have to sell looks like bringing in substantial returns, you may be happier looking at one of the major trading companies. The general trading companies or *sogo shosha* wield tremendous power in international trading terms, as Table 14 shows.

Importantly, the choice of trading company may be affected by the way it plugs into a *keiretsu*. In other words, if a Japanese customer wishing to buy your products is related to a particular trading company, it may be that the choice of trading company will be decided for you (if that is what you want). You can explore possibilities with the trading companies by contacting them in your home country, where the majority will have representation.

It is by no means the case that the bigger the trading company, the bigger your sales in Japan are likely to be. A small importer may be a better bet: as the sole representative he may be inclined to push your products more assiduously. Japanese manufacturers who make products in your field may make good partners because they are intimately acquainted with the distribution system for your goods. (They may, by the same token, give priority to their own products and wish to be involved with you as a way to contain the competition.) These are all angles which need to be explored.

It is usually the case that any agent will want to be your sole representative: if you choose to change your agent at a later stage, do so with caution, as a reputation for changing agents too often (as in most markets) will get you a bad name. That is why it is crucial to spend time getting to know Japan before you make any decisions which you might regret later. Once you have decided what to do, it will be important to pay regular visits to demonstrate your commitment to the new relationship.

MANUFACTURE UNDER LICENCE (MUL)

The Japanese are active in this area, their main motives being to use any new technology acquired for their own long-term product development. Trading companies are the principal catalysts for this kind of arrangement. Royalty rates are on average in the order of 5 per cent (depending on the industrial sector in question). It is advisable to include in any MUL agreement a clause which prevents the licensee from sharing technological information with a third party. Unprotected (i.e. unpatented) know-how is fair game in Japan, so the foreign company needs to implement counter-measures to cover any possible problems here.

The Bank of Japan is the body which gives clearance to MUL arrangements: the Japanese and non-Japanese partners-to-be are required to submit a report at least three months before any agreement is signed. Provided the ministry for the particular industry does not have to be consulted, clearance is given on the day of filing (although in theory the waiting period is 30 days) if the agreement is worth ¥100 million (US$930,000) or less. Agreements including designated technologies are likely to take longer. The following products are designated: aircraft; arms; gunpowder; atomic energy; space development; electronic computers; electronic components for next-generation electronic devices; laser-beam communication devices; new materials; salt electrolysis by non-mercury techniques; offshore petroleum production; and leather and leather products.

If a ministry has to be consulted, clearance will normally be given two weeks after filing the report. When needs dictate changes or modifications to the agreement, the waiting period can run to up to five months. After signing, the agreement must be checked by the Fair Trade Commission to ensure that there are no infringements of the Anti-Monopoly Law.

PATENTS AND TRADE MARKS

It is crucial to register patents as early as possible. Japan files over double the number of patents registered each year by the United States and such patent rights are jealously guarded (and in some cases, zealously coveted).

Legal advice is an absolute must. Applications must be handled by a patent lawyer in Japan, and you should take care to see to this yourself. Allowing an agent to do it for you in the agent's name will cause obvious problems if things between you and the agent do not work out. The period of time between filing an application and obtaining registration is approximately two and a half years. The patent right is valid for fifteen years: however, it may not last more than twenty years from the initial date of filing.

The life of registered trade marks is ten years and they may be renewed for additional ten-year periods: if they are not used within three years, another party can apply for the rights, thereby invalidating yours.

IMPORT PROCEDURES

Importing goods into Japan is a relatively simple matter: there are very few restrictions and the normal documentation applies, i.e. a straightforward customs declaration, usually made by a clearing agent acting for the importer. You should check how far products have been deregularized to ascertain whether import licences or import quota allocation certificates are required for your product.

Certificates of origin may be needed for coffee, woven fabrics, silk and some sea products. Check with your local trade body about when these apply. Your product must have an origin mark on it.

Duty is payable on most goods. Average rates are lower than in the European Community. Check to see what the current rate is. Some products are subject to high customs duty (whisky, leather footwear, etc.), but it is hoped that these will come down in due course. Any concessionary prices agreed between the importer and overseas supplier have to be declared. VAT in Japan is currently pegged at 3 per cent (6 per cent for cars).

As far as standards are concerned, it is advisable to find out what the JIS (Japan Industrial Standards) or JAS (Japan Agricultural Standards) are for your product and at least follow the labelling procedures for these standards, even if your product is not JIS/JAS registered.

Cosmetics, pharmaceuticals, electrical appliances and building materials are subject to testing for compliance with Japan's national standards. Testing can be by individual testing by the appropriate body, by product type approval for registered manufacturers, or by certification by an approved Japanese testing authority.

Labelling can only be in the metric system and must be in Japanese. You will need to check with the importer to see that all requisite regulations are covered.

If you are taking samples to Japan for exhibitions, etc., these can be imported by ATA carnet (a temporary admission carnet, i.e. no duty is charged) or under special licence for display purposes. Food samples must meet regulations on additives/ingredients.

DIRECT PRESENCE IN JAPAN

If you are involved in the production of mass-produced products of a basic kind, local production in Japan is likely to be the only real option, given the fast-paced nature of the Japanese market where efficiency is all. You will need to take into account the question of economies of scale when considering this option, since for some products it may still be advisable to bulk-import and distribute. The total number of foreign-affiliated companies in Japan stood at 2,797 in 1991 (the total of companies entering Japan since 1950).

The choice of presence in Japan will be based on the kind of product or service in question and may be JV (joint venture), 100 per cent owned green field, investment in an existing company, or branch or representative office. JV has been the most common means of establishing a presence in Japan since the war, but 100 per cent subsidiaries have grown in popularity since deregulation of investment in the 1970s.

TYPES OF COMPANY

There are two main types of company worthy of close examination. These are the *yugen-gaisha* (equivalent to a limited liability corporation) and the *kabushiki-gaisha* (shareholder-owned company).

In the **yugen-gaisha**, there are 'contributors to capital' rather than shareholders as in the *kabushiki-gaisha*. The number of partners is limited to 50, whereas the number of shareholders in the *kabushiki-gaisha* is unlimited. **Kabushiki-gaisha** have authorized capital, whereas the *yugen-gaisha* has just fixed amounts of contribution (minimum contribution ¥100,000 or US$932.84). There is a board of directors and representative directors in the *yugen-gaisha*, but auditors are not required: with the *kabushiki-gaisha* the directors choose one or more representatives from among their number and of course must employ the services of an auditor. The procedural elements in the *yugen-gaisha* are more straightforward because all that is required is a general meeting of the partners: the decision-making process is easier. With the *kabushiki-gaisha* a quorum of shareholders is required before moving. The minimum capital of a *kabushiki-gaisha* is ¥10 million or US$93,284 (as of April 1991).

For these reasons, the *yugen-gaisha* is ideally suited to the smaller company. Both types of company have abbreviations following the name of the company – YK for *yugen-gaisha* and KK for *kabushiki-gaisha*.

There are also partnership companies (*gomei gaisha*), limited partnerships (*goshi gaisha*) and sole proprietorships, but these are not common among foreign companies.

PROMOTION OF FOREIGN COMPANIES IN JAPAN

Japan is clearly in favour of the promotion of foreign involvement in Japan. The Japan External Trade Organization is actively involved in the encouragement of foreign investment in Japan (see: Japan Inc.). The government is now pushing the idea of free trade zones where foreign companies can take advantage of entering Japan via provincial towns, where operating costs are cheaper and they can use specially arranged bonded warehouses. Progress on this is slow, but the signs are that they will help to lessen the burden of getting products into the marketplace, by using simplified import procedures, etc. So the situation is improving all the time.

A foreign company can start commercial activities in Japan without having a subsidiary – it is possible to set up a branch office, hire a representative and get going. A branch office needs only to be registered at the local office of the Legal Affairs Bureau of the Ministry of Justice.

The golden rule is to get professional advice throughout the setting-up period. There are foreign law firms in Japan now that can work with you through their local offices in your country.

INCENTIVES

Japan provides a variety of incentives to foreign companies. These are mainly to encourage the establishment of manufacturing facilities outside the big conurbations of Tokyo and Osaka. These incentives can take the form of tax incentives, subsidies and financial allowances. It is sometimes possible to arrange reductions or exemptions from local enterprise tax as well as fixed property tax. Depreciation is also permissible on new investments in infrastructure, i.e. new buildings, machinery and equipment.

STAFFING

The main problem associated with the setting up of a 100 per cent wholly owned apparatus or other presence has been finding appropriate Japanese staff: thankfully the situation is improving as Japanese mores on working for a foreign company continue to change.

Be careful whom you employ for your new office in Japan. You will need a combination of go-getters and networkers:

TABLE 15 Salary levels for personnel in Japan, 1991

Post	Monthly (¥ thousand)	US$	Annual bonus (¥ thousand)	US$
Director	592.8	5,530	3,270.3	30,506
Section chief	475.7	4,438	2,547.7	23,766
Chief clerk	403.5	3,759	1,802.6	16,815
Non-position	278.9	2,322	980.4	9,146

Source: Ministry of Labour, *Basic Survey on Wage Structure*.

someone with excellent English may appear to be the best choice for your company, but you should first ascertain what kind of business contacts he or she already has. Someone without *jinmyaku* (the Japanese term for a network of contacts) may not provide the results you want.

Japanese recruitment companies will be able to give you up-to-date information on the kind of conditions of service and remuneration applicable to the kind of staff you will be hiring. As a general guide, the salary levels for personnel in Japan in 1991 are detailed in Table 15.

Make sure that you stay on the right side of the unions, which may get involved if they feel you are not playing the game according to normal Japanese practice.

If you are thinking about sending expatriate staff, go for people who have prior experience of Japan and who (preferably) speak Japanese. At the very least, the candidate for a managerial position in your offices in Japan should be able to demonstrate awareness of Japanese business etiquette, customs and culture. It might be argued that such a person can acquire this kind of experience on the job, but can you really afford either the time it will take to get to that stage, or the possibility of missed chances and gaffes?

SOCIAL SECURITY
The Ministry of Health and Welfare handles health insurance and welfare pension insurance, while the Ministry of Labour oversees unemployment insurance and workers' accident compensation insurance.

Health insurance
This is pegged at 90 per cent free health insurance for the individual and 70 per cent for his or her dependants. If the

person is not in receipt of any other compensation payments, he or she will receive 60 per cent of regular salary payments for up to eighteen months. There are also payments for childbirth costs (50 per cent of the person's monthly salary) and for maternity leave (60 per cent of the monthly salary). Payments to cover expenses for home, hospital care and funerals are also made. The premium for this health insurance is 8.4 per cent of the monthly salary (up to a maximum of ¥59,640 or US$556.34) and 0.8 per cent of bonuses. These contributions are shared 50–50 with the employer: in the case of the bonus, the employer pays 0.5 per cent.

Welfare pension insurance
This is payable to men when they reach 60 years of age, and to women when they are 55 years of age. If an individual dies while in employment, the family receives a pension of 75 per cent. The monthly premium for men is 14.3 per cent (maximum premium ¥75,790 or US$707.00) and 13.3 per cent for women (maximum premium ¥73,140 or US$682.28). These are shared 50–50 with the employer.

Unemployment insurance
A person who has been employed for six months is eligible for unemployment insurance. This is 60–80 per cent of the daily salary (but not more than ¥7,330 or US$68.50 per day) and the duration of the payment period can be from 90 to 300 days, depending on the length of service. The premium totals 1.45 per cent of total compensation including bonus payments. The employer pays 0.9 per cent of the premium and the employee 0.55 per cent.

Workers' accident compensation insurance
This is 0.5 per cent of total combined salary, bonuses and all other allowances payable by the employer. If an accident occurs while the person is in employment, the person receives free medical attention. He or she also receives 60 per cent of the average salary commencing the fourth day after salary payments have been stopped by the employers. In addition to this, a pension or lump sum is payable to the individual in the event of a permanent disability, or a compensation payment paid to the family. When applicable, the employer will also provide an allowance to the cost of a funeral.

30 Selling

HUMAN RELATIONSHIPS
The basis of a good selling operation is the development of a good personal relationship with your Japanese colleagues. For hints on how to achieve this goal, see: Business Culture. In addition, an appreciation of some of the characteristics of selling in Japan is vital.

LAWYERS AND CONTRACTS
Traditionally, Japanese companies dealing with other Japanese companies have tended to base their relationships on comparatively simple contracts. If problems arise, these are normally dealt with through the offices of a third party (usually the person or company which provided the initial introduction). When dealing with non-Japanese companies, however, Japanese corporations have long realized the weight attached to the letter of the law, and are consequently very careful to go through all the fine print in an agreement with an overseas partner.

Many Japanese companies do not have external lawyers, preferring to leave the legal aspects of a business deal to their in-house legal department. This, and the traditional distrust of lawyers, plus the strict control on the numbers of lawyers qualifying in Japan in any given year, mean that there is a dearth (comparatively speaking) of lawyers in the country. (It has often been said that there are more lawyers in Washington DC than in the whole of Japan.) Do not assume that Japanese business people will take a contract lightly, however good the human relationship with the non-Japanese company is. They will go through it with a fine-tooth comb. Nevertheless, if problems do arise, resorting to the services of a lawyer will usually be something of a last-ditch attempt to sort things out.

POST-CONTRACT: UNDERSTANDING THE DISTRIBUTION SYSTEM

The distribution system is something of a bogeyman as far as many overseas business people are concerned: the fact is that there are different kinds of distribution system depending on the product in question, and not all are problematic. Getting to grips with the type of distribution system for your product is yet another good reason for visiting Japan. There is a great deal of homework that can be done before rushing off to Tokyo: letters to your national trade and industry department and to the nearest offices of the Japan External Trade Organization outlining the nature of your product and your plans to sell it in Japan will normally result in you being sent a brief summary of the market for your product together with a guide to the pros and cons associated with the market (see: Directory). It is better to write to these government bodies, as they are normally swamped with telephone enquiries: save telephoning until you have specific points to query.

Department stores and superstores

In the vast majority of cases, foreign goods will normally find their way onto department store shelves via an exclusive importer or wholesale agent. It may be appropriate, if your product is for limited sales, to sell direct to one department store which will cash in on the fact that it is the only seller of your product in Japan. If you do this you have to choose your department store very carefully. If you are going for universal distribution it is more advisable to find a wholesaler with the right kind of relationship with the department stores, i.e. one based on long-standing associations, to handle distribution nationwide from day one. You will need to check that a potential agent has these connections before signing any agreements.

While the department stores are the better choice for upmarket or speciality goods, the superstores should be considered if your product has a value-for-money appeal. Although superstores are increasing their promotion of the more famous brand-name products (as opposed to the indigenous variety), value for money is still the key here. This is likely to continue to be the case as the recession forces people to spend their money wisely.

One important point to bear in mind is that it is not possible to sell the same brand of product successfully in the department stores and the superstores simultaneously. If your products seem more appropriate to the department stores, that is where they should be sold, as this channel offers better leeway on margins.

It should go without saying that your product must be of a

high quality and attractively packaged for the Japanese market. Presentation is everything in this sophisticated and discerning marketplace.

Hempin ('return of goods')

Hempin is the so-called consignment sales system, whereby wholesalers or manufacturers take back unsold stock from their retailers.

The fickleness of the Japanese shopper has a lot to do with the evolution of this practice: with a taste for something new and different, the consumer wants and expects to have a wide variety of choice. Meeting this requirement is a constant headache for the retailers, who need to be able to cater for a wide range but who, at the same time, do not wish to stand the risk of having masses of unwanted and unsold stock. This has resulted in consignment sales contracts being concluded between wholesaler and retailer.

The signs are that the *hempin* system is not as pervasive as it once was because of the growth of large-volume outlets: it is also the case that not all goods are affected by the system. It is necessary to check what the situation will be for your company before concluding any agreements.

Tegata (promissory note)

It has long been the practice in Japan to issue *tegata* or promissory notes instead of paying COD. This has come about because, historically, Japanese companies have tended to view a business relationship as a long-term commitment where speed of payment is not an issue. It is important to clarify with your customers which way they intend to pay, as you may find yourself facing a cash-flow problem.

31 Business Culture

In 1898 the first British consul general in Osaka, Sir Rutherford Alcock, declared: 'The incorrigible tendency of the Japanese . . . is to withhold from foreigners or disguise the truth in all matters great and small' (*Japanese Things*, Basil Hall Chamberlain). This sort of remark has set the tone for a century's worth of misunderstanding between Japanese and occidentals. The image of the wily oriental with the shifty look, the dubious character who never gives a clear yes or no to any question, has persisted until comparatively recently. Now, more work is being done on cross-cultural communication than ever before, the aim being to dispel stereotyping and to attempt to arrive at something more acceptable to Japanese and westerners alike.

The current feeling is that more research is being carried out by the west about how Japanese business culture functions than by Japan with respect to foreign business cultures. In Japan the training of personnel who are to be posted abroad tends to take the form of English conversation classes. For larger corporations in Japan, more vigorous cultural awareness programmes are provided which show that not all Caucasian foreigners are from the United States, for example, or that the first language of a Caucasian person might be Spanish rather than English.

In Japan there has always been a tendency to describe foreigners as being simply one enormous group of non-Japanese. The term for this is *gaikokujin* or 'outside-country-people'. Foreign culture and travel programmes on Japanese TV still trivialize foreign countries and stereotypes (the UK capital is 'foggy London', the UK is 'the land of gentlemen', the United States is a thoroughly 'dangerous' land, and so on) still abound. It is quite a new concept in Japan to recognize that different cultural traits exist in English speakers from the

United Kingdom, the United States, Canada and Australia, and that dealing with an American business person is likely to be quite different from dealing with a British business person.

In explaining Japanese business culture to a western audience, it would be convenient to assume that there is only one kind of Japanese businessman, and that having examined how he is likely to react in any given situation, the task of understanding how a Japanese businessman thinks is done. It is possible to look at a number of important points of Japanese business etiquette and negotiating style, but as you do so you will need to bear in mind that the Japanese in general are becoming more international in their perceptions of non-Japanese thinking, and are growing more confident as contact between Japanese and non-Japanese increases. In other words, the Japanese businessman is not a creature caught in a static moment in time: he will be learning about you and how your society functions, and will continue to be ever more receptive to the subtle ways in which you think, speak and act.

For these reasons it is useful to be aware of Japanese business etiquette as practised by the following groups:

- Japanese in Japan with little experience of foreigners;
- Japanese in Japan with extensive experience of foreigners and of living overseas;
- Japanese in your country.

A fourth group of growing significance is not actually Japanese at all: this is the emerging 'Euro-Japanese' or 'Amero-Japanese', the non-Japanese workers employed by Japanese corporations in Japan or by the transplants outside Japan (such as Honda, Nissan and Toyota in the UK, US, Canada and Australia).

Like the compradors or go-betweens who linked the British and Chinese trading communities in Hong Kong and Shanghai during the latter part of the nineteenth century, these hybrid workers are a crucial bridge between the east and the west. In Japan they are normally highly proficient in the Japanese language: in Europe and North America they tend on the whole to have little or no knowledge of Japanese. What they have in common is the Japanese approach to business: they have occidental faces with a partially Japanese mind-set. In many cases, these people are the sole point of contact between, say, a western parts supplier and the Japanese OEM (original equipment manufacturer) into which the western company wishes to sell its products.

These latter-day compradors can decide how much information gets passed to their Japanese managers and decision-makers, thereby enabling them to exert a significant influence on the shape and progress of business dealings between the Japanese and non-Japanese company. For example, when a components supplier is experiencing problems selling to a Japanese OEM, the root cause of the problems lies not in the interaction between the Japanese and the non-Japanese, but in the relationship between the indigenous business people, where one party comes from a non-Japanese business culture and the other from a confusing mixture of the two cultures. Anyone selling into a Japanese company, with a non-Japanese point of contact, will need to ascertain just how much influence this Euro- or Amero-Japanese has and how long he or she has spent in the Japanese company, in order to decide how best to deal with that person.

In the late 1980s and 1990s, the majority of the Euro- or Amero-Japanese were very young, having joined their Japanese companies from school or university. This meant that the power and influence available to them has had a tendency to be disproportionate to their age or experience, a factor which can cause severe irritation to the senior executives of a major parts supplier who are more accustomed to dealing with older representatives.

MISUNDERSTANDING: REAL OR IMAGINED?

A survey conducted by *Time* magazine in the Tokyo area in mid-1992 attempted to measure whether the capital city of Japan was actually the cosmopolitan place that many people, Japanese and non-Japanese alike, insist it is, or whether the Japanese are as inward-looking as some observers have said they are. The conclusion was that, 'A survey of 2,106 Tokyo residents suggests that despite a growing non-Japanese population in the city, insularity is still strong.' Table 16 shows some of the survey results.

TABLE 16 Results of a survey of Tokyo residents, 1992

Respondents who:	%
Have no foreign friends or acquaintances	73
Have no desire to get to know foreigners[a]	58
Have never travelled outside Japan	56
Cannot speak a foreign language	70

[a] Asked of those without foreign friends/acquaintances.
Margin of error is plus or minus 3 per cent.
Source: Time, 1 June 1992.

It is difficult to draw any clear conclusions from these figures due to the absence of comparison data. Nevertheless, it would appear that Japan still has a long way to go before attitudes become truly internationalized. The lack of foreign language capability and the lack of interest in forging friendships with non-Japanese (unless absolutely necessary) underlines a deeper fact: that Japan has only been open to foreigners for a hundred and fifty years, and that psychologically the country has only begun to address the need for greater understanding of *gaikoku* (countries outside of Japan) in the last five years or so.

It is worth emphasizing that the traditional reliance on developing a warm human relationship as the basis for a successful business partnership is as true today as it was in the Japan of the past (see: Selling). What makes the difference is that in the Japan of the past, Japanese only met other Japanese: it was easier to make friends and more straightforward to develop trust. Today the Japanese find themselves thrust into an international context where they would like to continue the traditions of the old Japanese business world, but are hardpressed to achieve this given the language barrier and cultural differences. None of these problems is insurmountable, but to get over them requires Japanese people to gain a better understanding of the ground rules of western-style business, and for non-Japanese to continue to study the basics of Japanese-style business.

It must also be said that, rather than concentrating solely on understanding the differences between cultures, it is probably equally important to discover and then to build on the similarities that exist between them. Anyone who has attended a course on negotiating technique will know that it is important to establish areas of agreement before moving on to discuss areas of contention. Doing this enables the two parties to discuss points of contention in a more harmonious way. The ability to signal in a non-verbal way your understanding and sympathy for 'the Japanese way' is sure to win you the confidence of your Japanese business colleagues.

There is a glossary of key terms at the end of this section. See also: Key Phrases.

THE JAPANESE WAY: *TATEMAE* AND *HONNE*

The Japanese have traditionally projected themselves to other Japanese by making a distinction between what the hearer wants to hear or see, and what is in fact the heart of the matter, or the 'truth' (which may not always be what the hearer wants to hear). For example, a Japanese company entering into a new relationship with a foreign partner or client will strive to maintain a certain front or facade – in other words it will seek to promote an image of itself which is strong, dependable and united. This is **tatemae**, or the face which one company or individual presents to another. Most Japanese agree that this level of formality represents the mode in which they would conduct the majority of their relationships, business or otherwise. This is certainly the case when the Japanese come to deal with foreigners.

The antithesis to *tatemae* is **honne** or 'the real thing', the truth. To a Japanese person the ideal progression of a business relationship would be for it to develop from a *tatemae* to a *honne* type of relationship in which problems, disagreements and issues can be aired without undue worry to either party. It is often said that Japanese society is obsessed by the need to maintain harmony (*wa*), but it is really the maintenance of a semblance of harmony that is important. Anyone who has taken part in an internal Japanese company meeting will know that such meetings can be anything but harmonious! This is because relationships grounded in *honne* allow a high degree of confrontation and aggression.

With a *tatemae* type of relationship it is much harder to accommodate open confrontation. In this situation, the Japanese will employ a variety of verbal or non-verbal techniques to communicate disagreement or dissatisfaction without necessarily disturbing the outward appearance of harmony. If you have not studied what these techniques are, you will miss them or misinterpret them, either way creating a tricky situation for yourself.

THE RITUALS OF JAPANESE BUSINESS

Arriving at the offices of a Japanese company in Japan for the first time, you will be expected to pay your respects to the most senior person available in the company on the day of your visit. This may be the *buchō* or general manager, or even the *shachō* or president of the company. This meeting may last only ten minutes, during which time you will be asked about your journey, your impressions of Japan and perhaps about your family. There may be time to drink some tea, but in any event, this is not the time for a formal business meeting. Rather it is the formality of a ritual known as *aisatsu* (greetings). It is important to get this done at the beginning of a visit to a Japanese organization, because the senior person to whom you pay your respects is the person who will ultimately be involved in ratifying any proposal from your company or organization. The method of decision making is described below.

You may find yourself conducting a number of *aisatsu* to personnel of varying ranks within the Japanese company until

Board of directors (*torishimariyaku kai*)

Division (*jigyōhonbu*)

Department (*bu*)

Office (*shitsu*)

Section (*ka*)

Team (*kakari*)

FIGURE 4 The structure of a typical Japanese company.

you gradually arrive at the level in the partner Japanese organization which matches your own. To help this process of finding the correct level, it is essential to have your business card or *meishi* printed in Japanese on one side and English on the other. If you find your organization has an unusual structure by Japanese standards, try to provide an organizational chart, translated into Japanese if possible. Japanese companies on the whole favour a graphic presentation of facts. If you are called upon to give a verbal account of how your organization is configured, always use a whiteboard or flipchart (if these are to hand) to back up what you are saying. This will help the interpreter (if you are conducting talks in Japanese) or, if your audience understands English fairly well, it will help to relax them.

Figure 4 shows the structure of a typical Japanese company. Some companies in Japan such as Toyota are attempting to break away from this kind of structure by abolishing the *bu* and *ka* and replacing them with larger *shitsu*, which are consequently sub-divided into *gurupu*, as shown in Figure 5. These changes have been made in order to democratize the structure and help to shorten the decision-making chain.

The staff who populate both these kinds of structure have rank titles which in Japan are fairly rigid:

Chairman	(*kaichō*)
President	(*shachō*)
Vice-president	(*fukushachō*)
Senior managing director	(*senmu torishimariyaku*)
Managing director	(*jōmu torishimariyaku*)

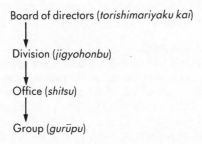

Board of directors (*torishimariyaku kai*)

Division (*jigyohonbu*)

Office (*shitsu*)

Group (*gurūpu*)

FIGURE 5 A simpler Japanese company structure.

Director	(*torishimariyaku*)
General manager	(*buchō*)
Assistant general manager	(*jichō*)
Manager	(*kachō*)
Assistant manager	(*kakarichō*)
Ordinary staff (no titles)	(*hira sha-in*)

Alternative rank titles for the newer type of structure are *shitsuchō* (office head) and *manēja* (group leader). Note that outside Japan it is rather more usual to find the rank *manēja* being used as an alternative to the rank of *kakaricho*. This title is also gaining popularity in Japan as a means to blur the area of responsibility between the ranks of *kachō* and *kakarichō* and to effect the removal of one layer in the hierarchy.

Having found the level where you belong, the next stage is to progress towards opening concrete business talks with your partners. This will begin with a ritualized self-introduction known as *jikoshokai*. Give your name, your company name, the department and section where you work, and a brief description of your duties. Depending on the degree of formality of the meeting, you may like to throw in a few words about your hobbies or interests, as this will help your Japanese colleagues to create a clearer picture of the kind of person you are. This ritual should be finished off with a pleasantry such as, 'I really look forward to working with you in the future.'

If you take the time to study some Japanese you may be able to perform this self-introduction verbatim in Japanese. Only attempt this if you are confident that you will make sense, and that the situation merits such a display! In the majority of cases, your Japanese colleagues will be only too pleased to hear you attempting to speak a few words of their language. Remember: if you find yourself facing a set of cool, impassive Japanese business people, leave your Japanese for the bar later on. In most cases though, a few words of Japanese will go down a treat (see: Key Phrases).

BUSINESS CARDS

The ritual which has just been described applies to an initial meeting with Japanese business people in Japan itself. Outside Japan it is more usual to adopt the meeting practices of that country, with the exception that the practice of *meishi kōkan* (exchange of business cards) is likely to be conducted with a higher degree of reverence than you might be used to. Do not deal your business cards out like playing cards: always keep them on the table in front of you for the duration of the meeting. When the talking has finished, collect up the cards and place them carefully in a business-card holder or similar. Do not write on the card that you have received: it is an extension of the company in question and must not be seen to be defiled in any way.

Before going to Japan, have a review of the colour and design of your business cards. Traditionally, most Japanese business cards have been printed in monochrome: garish, colourful cards for companies other than design houses or advertising agencies are regarded as frivolous and tend not to strike true to the Japanese eye. Business cards from government officials in Japan are always monochrome, for example. A set of alternative telephone numbers rather than just one may create the impression that your company is larger than it is, which is usually an advantage. It is common for Japanese business people to ask how many staff there are in your company immediately after the exchange of business cards: this is very likely to happen if your company is small and you are new to Japan.

KINEN SHASHIN (COMMEMORATIVE PHOTOGRAPHS)

Japanese visitors to your company may conclude an initial meeting with a commemorative photograph. This may seem quaint, but it has a practical purpose. After returning home, the Japanese business person will make an A3-sized 'who's who' of your company. This will consist of a succinct organizational plan, with the business card details transposed beneath the name of each key person, and either a line connecting that person to a group photograph also stuck to the page, or a numeric key. This enables any new members of the Japanese working party to 'put names to faces'. Since job rotation is particularly common in the larger Japanese companies, a chart with pictures of the main foreign business colleagues will help newcomers to get to grips with the personalities more speedily.

Japanese companies outside Japan will seldom go to this sort of trouble. However, they will generally follow the greetings ritual and the self-introductions ritual. Always remember to allow plenty of time for self-introductions if you have, for example, a group of your engineers meeting a group of their engineers. These protocols can eat up what seems like a great deal of time, but it will be well worth the effort in terms of the kick-start that it gives to the promotion of the all-important *ningen kankei*, or human relations so treasured by the Japanese.

NINGEN KANKEI (HUMAN RELATIONS)

Ningen kankei is possibly the most important aspect of business dealings Japanese-style. Whether in Japan or elsewhere, no matter how urbane your Japanese counterpart might be, making friends prior to developing a good business relationship is of paramount importance. To get yourself off to a head start in Japan or with Japanese companies in third countries, it is also essential to have had an introduction from an intermediary. Japanese companies do not appreciate cold-calling, so the better your introduction, the more likely you are to find success. Government introductions are among the best you can get. For details on Japanese government and your own government sources, see: Directory.

Intermediaries are not just important for providing an introduction: in a very real way they are considered by the Japanese to be guarantors of your company, so that if there are any initial disagreements, the intermediary is expected to intervene. In a longer-standing relationship between a Japanese and non-Japanese organization, problems should be sorted out on a bilateral basis. Obviously some problems are insurmountable without the adjudication of a third party, and here again, the intervention of the original introducer may be sought.

Making friends

In Japan you will be expected to undertake a fair amount of business socializing as a means of 'making friends'. When Japanese companies work together, it is assumed that there will be a place for after-hours socializing – a fact of business life in Japan which increasing numbers of Japanese find tedious and intrusive. This may be one reason why Japanese business people living abroad tend to take advantage of local business practice to take a kind of sabbatical from strenuous business socializing.

In Japan, the amount of time and money spent on corporate entertainment is phenomenal and reflects the need in Japanese society for an after-dark culture to cement business friendships and to allow stressed executives to let off steam. Eating and drinking, and sometimes bathing together at *onsen* (hot-spring resorts), help the Japanese to gauge whether a potential business connection is likely to work. In addition, where the success of a project is likely to involve various degrees of graft, perhaps involving government institutions, business socializing can provide a convenient platform for the practice of gift-giving, which in some cases constitutes barely disguised bribery. (For more innocent gift-giving, see below.) It is this world of after-office influence-peddling among the business community and government officials which really oils the wheels of the Japanese machine.

Understanding how 'policies', both fiscal and political, are made in the country is probably hard for the casual visitor to Japan to achieve. It involves the promotion of *kone* (connections) and the creation of myriad *jinmyaku* (networks), the mainstay of which is *ningen kankei* (human relations). Among western business schools, emphasis is placed on the tangible aspects of Japanese-style management, such as production technique and quality control, which are of course important elements in the equation. Less emphasis is currently placed on the understanding of how the process of wheeling and dealing in smoke-filled rooms works. Understanding this feature of Japanese business not only gives a clearer picture of what has moulded the Japanese success story to date, but also gives clues as to how Japanese business will adapt itself in the future. Any failures in the future will be due more to the collapse of traditional, internal Japanese decision-making style than to the collapse of the 'concrete' aspects of Japanese-style management such as TQM (total quality management).

WHEELING AND DEALING IN SMOKE-FILLED ROOMS

The prerequisite for striking deals with the Japanese is to be tough. Westerners who assume that the surface politeness of the Japanese is a mirror of their internal softness will be in for a big shock. After the niceties of the *aisatsu* ritual, getting into the nitty-gritty of business negotiations demands a tight agenda despatched to the Japanese and agreed well in advance. Any attempt to deviate from the points raised in the agenda will confuse the Japanese side and will not be worth pursuing. The reason for this is that any request for a decision on a matter not raised ahead of the meeting is going to be outside the remit of most negotiating teams.

In most cases the Japanese will want to confer with colleagues back at the company headquarters before committing themselves. When you are dealing with the *shachō* (company president) of a small- to medium-sized outfit, he may have the power to make snap decisions. In most instances, though, even the most entrepreneurial type will prefer to reserve judgement on a new proposal. If you choose to raise an issue outside those listed in the agenda and the response from the Japanese side is not very forthcoming, you will find it pointless to try to redefine your question or press it home. It is better to note it down as a point for future discussion and simply move on to another topic.

There are a number of crucial differences in the way in which Japanese business people conduct meetings. What follows is intended to show what can happen in a typical meeting between Japanese and, in this case, British business people: it is an extreme example, but shows what can go wrong when neither side is aware of the different ways in which the other side generally approaches a business meeting.

Stage 1 The opening

The Japanese side:
Wants to approach the discussion from a distance, if necessary covering ground already well-documented in previous meetings.

The British side:
Is frustrated and annoyed at going over the same ground, and sometimes feels it is being 'messed around' or not being told the truth.

Stage 2 The middle

The Japanese side:
Expects the other side to remain quiet while the point is being made;

expects the other side to make memos and to ask questions at the end;

labours points with didactic illustration and endless examples.

The British side:
Interrupts and refutes minor points before hearing the main story;

tends not to take notes and often does not listen attentively enough;

begins to switch off, thinking, 'I've heard it all before.'

Stage 3 The end

The Japanese side:
Completes *setsumei* (explanation) as part of duty, with little concern as to whether the other side is still listening or not.

The British side
Ends the meeting thinking, 'They never change!'

This is a worst-case scenario of what can happen if insufficient preparation is carried out.

NEGOTIATING TIPS

If you are selling to the Japanese it is important to adopt a humble approach. This does not mean being obsequious. The Japanese have a phrase which corresponds broadly to the notion of 'apple polishing' or 'flattery', so any heavy-handed obsequiousness will be regarded with the same suspicion as it would be anywhere in the world. The basic rule is that when you are in Japan you will have to respect the local culture if you are to make any long-lasting progress.

To take just one example of the different approach to communication in Japan: silence. Japanese people are quite at home with silence and it may be that your Japanese colleagues suddenly fall silent, making you think that you have made some sort of gaffe. It is more likely, however, that one of the following is happening:

- Your Japanese colleague is trying to understand what you just said.

- He or she is playing for time as he or she formulates a safe answer.

- He or she is deliberately putting you off your stride because it is well-known that westerners, in contrast to the Japanese, are quite ill at ease when it comes to handling a pregnant pause.

These silences are known as *ma*. You will know when you have encountered *ma* when the desire to fill an awkward gap in the conversation becomes almost overpowering. You must resist the temptation to start trying to justify what you are saying, because in so doing, you may actually start to compromise your own position without any real need to do so. The way to sit out a *ma* is to make notes, to look earnestly at your files, or to glance out of the window.

The use of silence is very common in Japan. Japanese who are new to your country will resort to it, and non-Japanese employees of Japanese companies outside Japan are also past-masters of the non-use of words. For non-Japanese used to presenting their product to a potential client against a background of polite and encouraging murmurs of appreciation, a cold, non-committal once-over of a component by a non-Japanese Japanese company employee can be extremely disconcerting. If you expect silence you will be better prepared to deal with it.

Other tips are as follows:

- **Present an overall picture of your long-term objectives**. Most Japanese negotiators will define the historical relationship between themselves and your organization.

They will also clarify in practical terms what they would like to achieve from the relationship. This scene-setting may be supported by written materials. You would do well to adopt the same approach, using a whiteboard to clarify your aims and objectives, and if possible providing the Japanese side with a written version of your introductory presentation.

- **Stress areas of agreement wherever possible**. Although it is a classic negotiating technique, flagging up those areas where both sides converge is an excellent way to start talks with Japanese partners. This is because you will succeed in creating the feeling that you are in harmony with the other party: when you come to discuss areas of potential discord, the positive atmosphere of the earlier part of the discussions may help you to get over the rougher parts of the meeting.

- **Never ask questions unless you are sure they can be answered**. Always agree an agenda beforehand and stick to it. Resist the temptation to ask questions for which the Japanese side has no prepared answers. Creating an awkward feeling just when the atmosphere has warmed up will spoil the outcome of the meeting, so it is better to have forewarned the Japanese of the questions you will be asking.

- **Listen attentively**. If a Japanese person is imparting information to you, then he or she is in the *sensei* or teacher position and it is your duty, as the *seitō* or pupil, to listen to him or her with undivided attention. It may be difficult to concentrate or to look interested all the time, especially if you are communicating through an interpreter, but you have to try to as best you can. Inattentiveness, or appearing to be inattentive, is taken as a sign of a lack of commitment to the proceedings.

- **Your body language**. Take care not to appear too relaxed when meeting your Japanese colleagues. Do not fold one leg over the other to suggest confidence (as people do in North America and elsewhere) – it is far better to keep both feet firmly on the ground, with your back straight. Eyeball to eyeball contact is not a sign of being honest in Japan: in fact close eye contact with a superior is frowned upon as being too forward. If you need to point out a detail on a drawing or indicate where something is, it is better to do so with the palm of your hand turned up, rather than pointing with your index finger.

When you hand out written materials, lay the sheets out gently in front of the reader rather than proffer them for the Japanese colleagues to take in their hands. By all means smile and laugh, but keep any hilarity for the bar. If you need to blow your nose, try to do it outside the meeting room: if you have to blow your nose during the talks, do so into a paper handkerchief, throwing it away as soon as you can. Do not blow your nose into a cloth handkerchief and put this back into your pocket: Japanese men use cloth handkerchiefs to dry their hands on, and to return a dirty handkerchief to your pocket is regarded as a disgusting thing to do.

Above all, keep to your own body bubble. Japanese people do not touch in public in the same way as people in North America, Europe and Australia might. It might be *de rigueur* to kiss the spouse of a European or North American business colleague, but to kiss a Japanese wife is not really on. Bowing is the custom in Japan, and you should work hard on a head-and-shoulders bow as early as you can. A full perpendicular bow is not required, but people in Japan with little experience of meeting foreigners will be more comfortable if you bow rather than shake hands. With Japanese people who are quite cosmopolitan, or when you meet Japanese people outside of Japan, it is probably more natural for them if you stick to shaking hands with them.

- **Japanese body language**. The Japanese business person in a meeting actually tends to be quite still; he does not gesticulate wildly, preferring to keep his hands to himself. An interested Japanese will tilt himself slightly forward in his chair; when he pushes himself back, and starts to make 'hum, hum' sounds, this is usually an indication that he has learned all he needs to know for the early stage in negotiations; if the questions dry up completely, he may be backing off.

  The Japanese group will expect to talk to your party via the most senior person, even if on their side that person's English is not as good as that of his fellows. You must resist the temptation to direct your questions at the younger, more proficient English speaker as this approach runs the risk of causing the older persons present to lose face. By all means compliment the better English speakers on their English if you want to, but bear in mind that this will be better done out of earshot of the other members of the party.

- **Some hints for the meeting room**. Japanese people often complain that western meeting rooms and restaurants are poorly lit; whereas we might favour a meal eaten under subdued lighting, this is actually a source of irritation for the Japanese. Try to make sure that wherever you hold your talks, the room is bright and cheery. If you are serving beverages during the meeting, mineral water will be acceptable. The non-gassy variety is the best choice. If you can run to providing a set of flags with the *Hinomaru* (Japanese flag) and your home country's flag, these little touches will be appreciated, particularly in the opening or concluding stages of a major business or political negotiation where there are very senior members of both sides present.

ATTENTION TO DETAIL

Much has been made of the Japanese attention to fact and to detail. What is perceived as an excessive concern for detail is often held up as a manifestation of the 'coldness' and 'logicality' of the Japanese. As Japanese decision making, and more specifically caution in decision making, is based on a principle of shared responsibility (in the best instance) or abrogated responsibility (in the worst instance), a surfeit of factual information is deemed safer than gut feeling. It has little to do with emotion. Again, much has been made of the Japanese gut feeling, but history shows that the vast majority of Japanese decisions (the better ones) tended to be made only after extensive fact-finding and consultation.

One of the few exceptions to this rule is where the autocratic, entrepreneurial or maverick businessman or woman has been able to buck the general feeling and go with his or her individual emotions, as with the decision by the Sony chairman, Akio Morita, to press ahead with the development of the Walkman, despite the protestations of almost all of his close colleagues. Mr Morita is not a typical Japanese: most Japanese are slow to take decisions, and will usually avoid any radical moves unless there is some sort of precedent which guarantees the success of a particular decision. The consumer electronics giant Matsushita, for example, has earned itself the sobriquet 'Maneshita', meaning 'copied', as testament to the company's preference for monitoring innovation by rival companies before moving in to swamp the market with its own imitations or adaptations of new products.

So, when your company is requested to submit 'further details', it is actually in your own interests to do so. You may find a Japanese company requesting information which appears extraneous to the project in hand; your bosses are reluctant to pass on any more know-how than is absolutely necessary, and you are caught between wanting to be compliant to the requests of your Japanese colleagues, and selling your company's knowledge down the river. Usually the Japanese company needs the information in order to be able to progress the project, so it is in your own interests to submit information in the spirit of trust as early on in the relationship as possible. This will help the person who is in charge of promoting your interests inside the Japanese company.

A glance at the way in which decisions are made in Japan will make you realize that you have a key role to play only at certain points in the life of a joint project.

DECISION TIME IN THE JAPANESE COMPANY: A BASIC MODEL

Many Japanese companies exercise suggestion systems as a way to guarantee that the lifeblood of ideas continues to flow. When an employee or high-ranking executive has an idea, either via the suggestion system or independently of it, that idea is subjected to a rigorous form of appraisal, adaptation and ratification. The basic model in Figure 6 shows how ideas are put into practice and how decisions are made.

Tatakidai (draft)

This is the starting point for ideas, including proposals for joint projects with foreign partners. Inside a Japanese company, ordinary workers are encouraged to pass draft ideas to their managers, who will evaluate the outline proposal and judge whether to pursue the new idea. The *tatakidai* may be a brief note on A4-sized paper, or scribbled on the back of a notebook. The form at this stage is not as important as the initial idea.

The focus is on flexibility. If the manager thinks that there is life in the proposal, he or she will invite the employee making the proposal to go away and develop the idea into a *gutai an* or concrete proposal. Importantly, an employee may be nominated to think through an idea which has actually come from higher up in the organization; a *buchō* or general manager may have an idea but he or she cannot obviously spend time developing it personally, so the germ of the idea is delegated.

Gutai an (concrete proposal)

This is usually a more formal document than the *tatakidai*, consisting of a terse summary sheet backed up by various appendices or supporting material containing empirical detail (statistics, projections, financial data, etc.). The objective is to allow people to read quickly over the main points of the

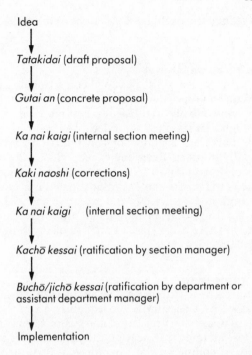

Idea

Tatakidai (draft proposal)

Gutai an (concrete proposal)

Ka nai kaigi (internal section meeting)

Kaki naoshi (corrections)

Ka nai kaigi (internal section meeting)

Kachō kessai (ratification by section manager)

Buchō/jichō kessai (ratification by department or assistant department manager)

Implementation

FIGURE 6 Decision-making in Japanese organizations.

proposal, so verbosity is clearly not acceptable. It is usual practice for the employee, seconded by his or her manager, to present the concrete proposal to colleagues at a weekly or twice-weekly internal section meeting called *ka nai kaigi*.

Ka nai kaigi (internal section meeting)
This is the venue for the main proposer of the new project to make a formal presentation of his or her findings to other colleagues in order to assess their reaction and adopt some of their suggestions for improvements. This is where the much-vaunted Japanese decision by consensus is enacted. Such meetings can be held in a very aggressive atmosphere, where the proposers are challenged to defend their idea against charges that it is too costly, or that it has been tried before, or that there is insufficient detail on which to base a meaningful decision. If it is the last of these, you can be sure that the lack of information will be attributed if at all possible to an outside party's reticence in sharing data: this is where you and your colleagues have an opportunity to expedite the project by providing the extra detail to see it through. The more you can help your Japanese

proposer to reduce the number of potential Achilles' heels, the better.

Kaki naoshi (corrections)

This is the term applied to the period of correction or enhancement of the project proposal which normally follows the presentation of the project to one's colleagues. Few proposals will ever make it through first time round: indeed, the majority of them are mauled. Therefore a period of consolidation of fact and detail is usually in order. Everyone expects this, and although it may be soul-destroying to have to rework all of your ideas, the principle is that what comes out at the end is a product of everyone's combined knowledge and expertise and is therefore superior to anything that an individual could have produced independently. There is also less likelihood of anything having been overlooked.

Kessai (ratification)

This is the term given to describe how a project proposal which has been passed by a section is subsequently given the green light by the manager of the section and his or her immediate superiors. How far up for ratification the proposal goes depends on the degree of complexity of the proposal, its cost implications and its political ramifications. Some managers may block the progress of a project merely as an exercise in power. Others may use their veto as a pawn in a broader political game. Usually, though, the veto can only be exercised for a limited period before the deadlock is broken. Projects instigated by general managers but worked out at the lower levels by the *hira sha-in* (workers without a rank title) have a smoother passage, as you would expect.

Implementation of the proposal marks the end of this decision-making process.

Ringisho and nemawashi

When a proposal affects other departments or sections, Japanese organizations will make use of a document known as a *ringisho* or 'request for decision' circular. Depending on the type of project requiring a decision, the *ringisho* will normally consist of a description of the project together with important data for the receiving party to consider. How long the receiving party has to make its decision depends again on the type of project or decision. It would not be unusual for some departments to sit on a decision for a period of up to a month or longer.

Agreement to a project proposal is given by stamping one's *inkan* or seal (name in Chinese characters) in a square space at the top or bottom of the top sheet of the document. Staff are expected to act quickly once a decision has been made.

What makes this model work so smoothly?

Nemawashi (binding the roots)

Is decision making in Japanese companies actually so straightforward and smooth? The answer quite clearly is that it is not. A great deal of effort goes into *trying* to make a decision come about as smoothly as possible, and the technique for achieving this is known as *nemawashi*.

The fact is that building a basis for the gradual ratification of a new project requires a great deal of politicking between the different parties, who, sometimes many months before a decision is finally made, will spend hours on a mixture of 'getting to know you' exercises and negotiation on a quid pro quo basis. Most of the aggression or confrontation inherent in the management of change is worked out before a formal meeting to make a decision takes place. Hence the semblance of harmony in Japanese work relationships.

Foreigners who have observed the Japanese in the workplace remark on the incredibly long hours worked and what appears to be a relative lack of result from the time put in. As distinct from desk-work, a quick chat, a shared coffee-break or a joke in the corridor are methods employed routinely to draw key people into one's own sphere of influence as a means to safeguard the success of the policy being promoted by one's own group or clique. Such canvassing can appear trivial, but it is the way things are customarily done in Japan. The situation can be further complicated by the existence of university cliques who vie with each other for ascendancy within a given department and who fight each other to support and promote certain members of particular groups.

Some Japanese business people in the 1990s doubt whether the practice of *nemawashi* (named after a gardening technique involving careful preparation of a plant's roots prior to transplantation) is still a force to be reckoned with. The majority, however, consider it to be one of the mainstays of Japanese-style business practice, particularly in Japan itself.

IMPROVING YOUR BUSINESS RELATIONSHIPS WITH JAPANESE COLLEAGUES

Gaman (perseverance)

In Japan, and among Japanese expatriates, one of the highest virtues to which one can aspire is that of *gaman* (perseverance). In Japanese society it is the mark of a truly controlled person to be able to bear adversity without complaint. The crucial thing here, though, if you are to manipulate the system successfully, is to ensure that people are aware that you are 'suffering', without ever mentioning it in an obvious way.

A group of Japanese engineers will feel challenged and exhilarated if it is presented with a set of impossible deadlines: the challenge of pulling together to try to prevail against all the odds is manifested in the notion of *yaruki* (motivation), and the main ingredient for this is the notion of putting up with pain, of enduring hardship: *gaman*. For the non-Japanese business person, it means saying, 'We'll give it a go' when presented with an enormous problem; for the expatriate in Japan who is aggravated by the pressures of life in Japanese society, it is about grinning and bearing it.

Japanese people do not respect people who bang their fists on the table when they cannot get their own way, nor do they have much time for people who in their eyes do little more than winge about this and that problem. *'Ganbarimasu!'* ('Let's do our best to succeed!') is a battlecry that you will hear from children at a school sports day, from university entrance examinees, from new recruits into the company and from workers on an assembly line who are presented with a supremely challenging production target for that day. It is this drive which has helped power Japan to its economic success (see: Human Resources).

For non-Japanese people working with the Japanese, or in Japan itself, it is important to ask yourself whether you have the stamina for a knife-edge existence: life on constant red-alert. The Japanese themselves have various ways in which to offset their very stress-inducing lifestyles, such as hot baths each night and drinking sessions.

Improving communication
Although Sir Rutherford Alcock with his remarks about the dissimulation of the Japanese set the tone for a half century of misunderstanding between Japan and the occidental world, it should be clear that the Japanese are no more and no less devious than anybody else. It is important to recognize nevertheless that their words and actions may differ quite considerably from those of North Americans, Europeans or Australasians.

Take, for example, the word *hai*. If you consult a Japanese–English dictionary, you will see that *hai* means 'yes'. In theory that should be the end of it, but in fact *hai* can have very different meanings from the English 'yes'. It is better to think of it as meaning 'I hear what you are saying' – which is a crucial distinction to make.

Imagine the hapless foreigner who has no idea how the Japanese work: if he or she is explaining the product or project to Japanese colleagues who are all nodding and saying *'hai, hai'*, it is hardly surprising that the foreign business person assumes that the Japanese side is agreeing with all that he or she is saying. In fact this kind of *'hai, hai'* is an example of what the Japanese call *aizuchi* – the noises that people make when they are listening to what another person is saying to them.

For example, a Japanese person on the telephone to another Japanese person will pepper his or her speech with words such as *'hai, hai'* or the more colloquial *'ee, ee'*, in order to signal his or her interest in what the other person is saying. Likewise, a person might use the noise *'He-e!'* (rising intonation) to express surprise, or might say *'A, so-o'* (falling intonation) to show sympathy. All these noises or *aizuchi* tell the speaker that the listener is really tuned in and interested: they do not necessarily mean that the listener agrees with everything the speaker is saying.

When a Japanese person appears to be agreeing whole-heartedly with what you are saying, and then weeks later denies that he or she ever agreed with your proposals, you may feel betrayed and misled. For his or her part, the Japanese person feels that he or she has done nothing wrong and cannot understand why he or she is accused of being two-faced.

Business dealings with the Japanese have no doubt fallen foul of this kind of misunderstanding. The best way to avoid such problems is to make a thorough agenda, to note down action points after every meeting, and to sit down (with the interpreters if appropriate) and agree what has to be done by the next time both sides meet. For information on how to use interpreters effectively, see below.

Gift-giving

A good deal of controversy surrounds the question of giving or not giving gifts nowadays: in the past it was accepted practice to take gifts for your Japanese business colleagues and to take great care over the selection of them. Some basic points to bear in mind are:

- **the tradition of gift-giving**. Gift-giving is alive and well in Japan. The only situation where it might be conceivable that gifts would not be required are in cases where the Japanese company (as Nissan has done) decides that the volume of traffic between Japan and a given country is so great, and the exchange of personnel so extensive, that the giving of gifts becomes a drain on valuable company assets and should be stopped. In all other cases you should evaluate whether a gift is appropriate. Usually some token will be required.

- **company hierarchy**. Take an impressive gift for the
  main person in the Japanese company, with a special
  present for the *tantōsha* (your main contact, the person
  you normally deal with on the telephone or by fax) and
  a large stock of smaller gifts for associates of the main
  people and their administrative support staff. All gifts
  will be very gratefully received.

- **what to take**. Take gifts which are easily transportable,
  such as prints (which can lie flat in a suitcase), scarves,
  coasters, calendars, book marks, and anything that is
  not too cumbersome but reflects the traditions and
  history of your home area. This will be of great interest
  to people in Japan, who appreciate receiving a gift with a
  story, which they can pass on to their friends and
  colleagues. It is a good idea to take your gifts along in a
  carrier-bag from a well-known department or specialist
  store so that your opposite number can see that you have
  brought gifts. This will enable him or her to arrange
  very quickly for gifts to be readied to be given to you if
  he or she has overlooked the fact that you are visiting,
  for example, or has forgotten about a gift for you. This
  will be done by asking one of the administrative support
  people to get an appropriate present out of company
  stores, thereby avoiding any loss of face.

- **wrapping**. Make sure the gifts are all neatly wrapped.
  Traditionally gifts would not normally be opened in
  front of the giver of the gift, but these days it is a nice
  touch to be able to open up a box and then discuss the
  present. This helps to cement the friendship, of course.
  If you can show that you have given a lot of thought to
  the getting of the present, so much the better.

- **giving sets of things**. Avoid giving four of anything.
  Four (*shi*) is a homonym for 'death'. This is not the kind
  of message you want to send!

THE LANGUAGE QUESTION

Is it necessary to learn Japanese in order to do good business in
Japan?

A great many business people will happily say that they do
good business in Japan without speaking a word of the language.
Others will say that knowing a few words of greeting helps to
break the ice with Japanese business colleagues, especially in
the early stages of a business relationship. This latter point
is definitely true when exercised in the proper atmosphere.
(Saying 'hello' in Japanese to someone who is quite obviously
completely fluent in English is going to appear quite ridiculous.)

However, no one has ever done good business with the Japanese without the help of someone who speaks both languages fluently *and* who knows how to operate in both a Japanese and non-Japanese business environment with confidence – despite what hearty expatriates in Japan might say.

Those people who live in *gaijin* (foreigner) areas in Tokyo and who make no effort to learn Japanese or about Japan are merely putting in time before moving on to the next foreign enclave in another distant land. The Japan that they know is a very limited and very limiting place without a knowledge of the Japanese language. It is also true that the usefulness of having these foreigners in Japan, as far as their parent companies are concerned, is quite negligible. The only real game-plan for a foreign company that is serious about Japan is to have Japan specialists working there. As a second-best alternative, it is vital for companies to ensure that the people they send to Japan have some affinity for the country (or at least the stamina to live there).

So what about just hiring Japanese nationals? Companies are divided as to the wisdom of training their employees to learn Japanese (a costly and time-consuming exercise) or hiring bilingual Japanese (a relatively cheap 'solution'). Some prestigious companies feel that they have solved the problem of the language barrier by hiring Japanese nationals to work in their American or European or Pacific Rim offices, the idea being to use these expatriate Japanese as a kind of buffer between themselves and their Japanese partners. But such moves need to be handled with very great care, for Japanese who are hired to deal with other Japanese on behalf of a foreign company can find themselves ostracized because they do not hail from any of the common in-groups in the target Japanese organization which they have been hired specifically to handle.

The fact is that until more non-Japanese learn Japanese, doing effective and long-term business with the Japanese is going to remain a very difficult thing to achieve. Further, people who simply learn Japanese because they want to make money out of the Japanese are also doomed, ultimately, to abject failure. Their *tatamae* (superficiality) will become transparently clear to the Japanese side in a short space of time, and no matter how fluent a speaker of Japanese one might become, the fruits of a business link-up with Japan will remain tantalizingly out of reach if there is no *dōjō* (empathizing) with Japan.

Interpreters

A really good interpreter is one who not only knows his or her mother tongue and target language extremely well, but who is at home with both cultures in question. He or she needs to be well read, and needs to continue to read widely in the target language in order to maintain a good vocabulary. It is not possible, however, to cover all eventualities and all technical subjects, so it is vital that you brief your interpreter as fully and as honestly as you can, well in advance of the meeting or conference day. If you anticipate a rough ride, then warn your interpreter that things might get a little acrimonious.

More often than not, if you are meeting business colleagues in Japan, it is the Japanese side that will supply an interpreter: when this happens it is obviously going to be difficult to offer the interpreter much in the way of a preparatory talk. Even a few minutes before the start of the talks is better than nothing at all.

Remember to keep your language as straightforward (not necessarily simple) as possible, and try to get into the habit of talking in sound-bites. These are much easier to deal with from the interpreter's point of view, and if the interpretation is consecutive as opposed to simultaneous, you may be able to get a kind of double-act going where the exchanges actually become quite brisk. If you are going to use a lot of jargon, make sure you supply a glossary of technical terms or give the interpreter a catalogue, guide or specifications pertaining to your product so that he or she can do some homework beforehand. You will not earn the friendship of your interpreter if you introduce technical or company-only jargon and expect him or her to be able to deal with it without offering any kind of clarification or explanation.

Above all, remember that your interpreter is a human being: he or she will need rest breaks and a chance to get something to eat. Interpreters always complain that even over lunch they are pestered to interpret jokes and trivia, without being given a chance to eat anything. This is quite clearly exploitative, and while a good interpreter will grin and bear it, he or she may not be so keen to work for you the next time around if there is an option not to do so.

It is much better to keep to the same one or two interpreters during protracted negotiations so that you do not have to keep explaining what is going on and what you expect the interpreter to do. Sometimes interpreters do not know what a crucial word is and may wait for the conversation to develop in order to get a better idea of it. If you suspect that the messages are becoming confused, suggest that you pause for five minutes to review what has been going on. This gives the interpreter a chance to clarify his or her train of thought and also avoids causing him or her to lose face. Most good interpreters will tend to take notes during a meeting, but do not expect to get these from the interpreter in place of minutes: they are likely to be written in a jumble of English and Japanese, with arrows and abbreviations that the interpreter can read back, but you cannot. Minute-taking is not the job of the interpreter. Treat your interpreter well and it will help you get the most out of your business dealings.

For a selection of useful everyday phrases, see: Key Phrases.

GLOSSARY OF KEY TERMS

aisatsu	ritual of greetings
aizuchi	term for non-verbal noises
gaikoku	foreign countries (lit.: countries outside Japan)
gai(koku)jin	foreigner (lit.: outside-country-person)
gaman	perseverance, endurance
ganbarimasu	let's do our best, our utmost
gutai an	concrete proposal
hai	yes (I hear what you are saying)
hira sha-in	employees without rank title
honne	the truth, the real thing
inkan	seal (Chinese character stamp)
jikoshōkai	self-introduction
jinmyaku	networks
kaki naoshi	correction (stage)
ka nai kaigi	internal section meeting
kessai	ratification (of a proposal)
kinen shashin	commemorative photograph
kone	connections
meishi	business card
meishi kōkan	exchange of business cards
nemawashi	preparing the groundwork
ningen kankei	human relations
ringi (sho)	circular for decision-making
seito	pupil
sensei	teacher
tatakidai	draft (proposal)
tatemae	facade, front
tantōsha	main contact
yaruki	motivation

PART SEVEN

Directory

32 Who Can Help at Home

JAPANESE EMBASSIES ABROAD

Australia
112 Empire Circuit
Yarralumla
Canberra ACT 2600

(T) 61-6-2733244,
2733686

Belgium
Avenue des Arts 58
1040 Bruxelles

(T) 32-2-513-2340

Canada
255 Sussex Drive
Ottawa
Ontario K1N 9E6

(T) 1-613-236-8541

Denmark
Pilestraede 61 1112
Copenhagen K

(T) 45-33-11-33-44

France
7 Avenue Hoche
75008 Paris

(T) 33-1-4766-02-22

Germany
Godesberger Allee 102-104
5300 Bonn 2

(T) 49-228-81910

Greece
2-4 Messoghion Avenue
Athens Tower Building, 21st Floor
Athens

(T) 30-1-775-8101-3

Luxemburg   (T) 352-464151
7 Rue Beaumont
L-1219 Luxemburg

Netherlands   (T) 31-70-3469544
Tobias Asserlaan 2
2517 KC, The Hague

New Zealand   (T) 64-4-731-540
7th Floor, Norwich Insurance House
3-11 Hunter Street
Wellington 1

Spain   (T) 34-1-562-55-46
Calle de Joaquin Costa 29
28002 Madrid

United Kingdom   (T) 071-465-6500
101-104 Piccadilly
London W1V 9FN

United States   (T) 1-202-939-6700
2520 Massachusetts Avenue NW
Washington DC 20008-2869

JAPANESE GOVERNMENT AGENCIES ABROAD
Japan External Trade Organization (JETRO)

Australia   (T) 61-2-241-1181
Level 19, Gateway
1 Macquarie Place
Sydney NSW 2000

Canada   (T) 1-416-962-5055
Suite 700 Britannica House
151 Bloor Street West
Toronto
Ontario M5S 1T7

New Zealand   (T) 64-9-797-427,
Room No. 301, Dilworth Bldg   797-428
Customs Street
East Auckland

United Kingdom   (T) 071-493-7226
Leconfield House
Curzon Street,
London W1Y 7FB

United States   (T) 1-212-997-0400
McGraw-Hill Bldg
1221 Avenue of the Americas
New York, NY 10020-1060

Manufactured Imports Promotion Organization (MIPRO)

United States   (T) 1-202-659-3729
2000 L Street, NW
Suite 808
Washington DC 20036

TRAVEL/ACCOMMODATION ORGANIZATIONS

Japan Travel Bureau (JTB)

Australia (Oceania Headquarters)   (T) 61-2-241-3466
Level 28, Gateway   (F) 61-2-241-3426
1 Macquarie Place
Sydney NSW 2000

Canada   (T) 1-416-367-5824
PO Box 70   (F) 1-416-367-0026
Dominion Bank Tower, Suite 3301
66 Wellington Street West
Toronto
Ontario M5K 1E7

New Zealand   (T) 64-9-309-7696
7th Floor, Hong Kong Bank House   (F) 64-9-309-2046
290 Queen Street
Auckland

United Kingdom (European   (T) 071-379-6244
   Headquarters)   (F) 071-240-8147
10 Maltravers Street, 2nd Floor
London WC2R 3EE

United States   (T) 1-212-247-2583
JTB International, Inc.   (F) 1-212-265-7234
Head Office
One Rockefeller Plaza
Suite 1250
New York, NY 10020-1579

Japan National Tourist Organization (JNTO)

Australia   (T) 61–2–232–4522
13th Floor
PIBA House
115 Pitt Street
Sydney NSW 2000

Canada   (T) 1–416–366–7140
165 University Avenue
Toronto
Ontario M5H 3B8

New Zealand
Refer to JNTO Sydney

United Kingdom   (T) 071–734 9638
167 Regent Street
London W1R 7FD

United States   (T) 1–212–757–5640
45 Rockefeller Plaza
630 Fifth Avenue
New York, NY 10111

33 Who Can Help in Japan

Telephone numbers in Japan are listed here without the country prefix (81). The city prefix (e.g. 03 for Tokyo) is used for calls made within Japan; if you are calling from abroad, omit the zero.

EMBASSIES IN JAPAN

Australia
2-1-14 Mita   (T) 03–5232–4111
Minato-ku, Tokyo 108

Belgium
5 Niban-cho   (T) 03–3262–0191/5
Chiyoda-ku, Tokyo 102

Canada
7-3-38 Akasaka   (T) 03–3408–2101/8
Minato-ku,Tokyo 170

Denmark
29-6 Sarugaku-cho   (T) 03–3496–3001
Shibuya-ku, Tokyo 150

France
4-11-44 Minami-Azabu   (T) 03–3473–0171/9
Minato-ku, Tokyo 106

Germany   (T) 03–3473–0151/7
4-5-10 Minami-Azabu
Minato-ku, Tokyo 106

Greece
3–16–30 Nishi-Azabu   (T) 03–3403–0871/2
Minato-ku, Tokyo 106

Luxemburg
Niban-cho, TS Bldg   (T) 03–3265–9621
2–1 Niban-cho
Chiyoda-ku, Tokyo 102

Netherlands
3–6–3 Shibakoen   (T) 03–5401–0411
Minato-ku, Tokyo 105

New Zealand
20–40 Kamiyama-cho   (T) 03–3467–2271/5
Shibuya-ku, Tokyo 150

Spain
1–3–29 Roppongi   (T) 03–3583–8531/3
Minato-ku, Tokyo 106

United Kingdom
1 Ichibancho   (T) 03–3265–5511
Chiyoda-ku, Tokyo 102

United States
1–10–5 Akasaka   (T) 03–3224–5000
Minato-ku, Tokyo 107

JAPANESE GOVERNMENT AGENCIES

**Japan External Trade
  Organization (JETRO)**
2–2–5 Toranomon 2-chome   (T) 03–3582–5511
Minato-ku, Tokyo 105   (F) 03–3585–3628

**Manufactured Imports Promotion
  Organization (MIPRO)**
6th Floor, World Import Mart   (T) 03–3988–2791
  Bldg   (F) 03–3988–1629
1–3 Higashi-Ikebukuro 3-chome
Toshima-ku, Tokyo 170

**Ministry of International Trade
and Industry (MITI)**
1-3-1 Kasumigaseki
Chiyoda-ku, Tokyo 100

(T) 03-3501-1511
(Switchboard)
03-3501-2082
(Trade Affairs Section)
(F) 03-3501-2028

34 Contact Addresses

INDUSTRIAL AND COMMERCIAL ORGANIZATIONS IN JAPAN

Fair Trade Commission
2-2-1 Kasumigaseki   (T) 03-3581-5471
Chiyoda-ku, Tokyo 100   (F) 03-3581-1963

Japan Chamber of Commerce and Industry
2-2 Marunouchi 3-chome   (T) 03-3283-7866
Chiyoda-ku, Tokyo 100

The Japanese Development Bank (International Department)
1-9-1 Otemachi   (T) 03-3244-1770
Chiyoda-ku, Tokyo 100   (F) 03-3245-1938

Japanese Trade Union Confederation
1-10-3 Mita-ku   (T) 03-3456-3856
Tokyo 108

Technology Transfer Information

Japan Industrial Technology Association (JITA)
Mori Bldg, 5th Floor   (T) 03-3591-6271
Toranomon 1-chome   (F) 03-3592-1368
Minato-ku, Tokyo 105

TRAVEL ORGANIZATIONS

Airlines

Aeroflot
Dai-ni Matsuda Building   (T) 03–3434–9681
Toranomon 3–4–8   (F) 03–3434–9669
Minato-ku, Tokyo 105

Air New Zealand
Room 131, Shin-kokusai Building (T) 03–3284–1291
3–4–1 Marunouchi
Chiyoda-ku, Tokyo 100

Alitalia Italian Airlines
Tokyo Club Building   (T) 03–3592–3970
2–6 Kasumigaseki 3-chome
Chiyoda-ku, Tokyo 100

All Nippon Airways
Kasumigaseki Buildings   (T) 03–3592–3430
3–2–5 Kasumigaseki   (F) 03–3592–3349
Chiyoda-ku, Tokyo 100

British Airways
Sanshin Building   (T) 03–3593–8811
1–4–1 Yuraku-cho   (F) 03–3214–7827
Chiyoda-ku, Tokyo 100

Cathay Pacific Airways Ltd
Toho Twin Tower Bldg   (T) 03–3504–1531
5–2 Yurakucho 1-chome   (F) 03–3595–8185
Chiyoda-ku, Tokyo 100

Canadian Airlines International
Hibiya Park Building   (T) 03–3281–7426
1–8–1 Yuraku-cho   (F) 03–3212–4029
Chiyoda-ku, Tokyo 100

Japan Airlines
Tokyo Buildings   (T) 03–3284–2646
Chiyoda-ku, Tokyo 100   (F) 03–3284–2860

KLM Royal Dutch Airlines
Yurakucho Denki Building   (T) 03–3216–0771
7–1 Yurakucho 1-chome   (F) 03–3211–5479/
Tokyo 100   5340

267

Lufthansa German Airlines
Tokyo Club Building   (T) 03–3580–2121
3-2-6 Kasumigaseki   (F) 03–3580–6485
Chiyoda-ku, Tokyo 100

Northwest Airlines
Fourfront Tower   (T) 03–3532–7100
12-1 Kachidoki 3-chome   (F) 03–7632–7460
Chuo-ku, Tokyo 104

Qantas
c/o Qantas Travel Centre   (T) 03–3593–7000
4th Floor, Urban Toranomon Building (F) 03–3597–5591
16-4 Toranomon 1-chome
Minato-ku, Tokyo 103

Sabena World Airlines
Akasaka 2-2-19   (T) 03–3585–6151
Minato-ku, Tokyo 107   (F) 03–3585–6550

Scandinavian Airline System
Toho Twin Tower Bldg   (T) 03–3503–8101/5
5-2 Yurakucho 1-chome
Chiyoda-ku, Tokyo 100

Swissair
Hibiya Park Building 4F   (T) 03–3212–1014
Yurakucho 1-8-1   (F) 03–3212–4802
Chiyoda-ku, Tokyo 100

United Airlines
Nihon Seimei Koishikawa Bldg   (T) 03–3817–4411
12-14 Koishikawa 1-chome   (F) 03–3817–4387
Bunkyo-ku, Tokyo 112

Virgin Atlantic Airways
13 Yotsuya 3-chome   (T) 03–5269–2861
Shinjuku-ku, Tokyo 160   (F) 03–5269–2877

HOTELS

First-class hotels (selection)

Asakusa View Hotel
Nishiasakusa 3-17-1   (T) 03–3847–1111
Daito-ku, Tokyo 111   (F) 03–3842–2117

Ginza Marunouchi Hotel
Ginza 8–7–13   (T) 03–3574–1121
Chuo-ku, Tokyo 104   (F) 03–3289–0478

Hilton Hotel
Nishishinjuku 6–6–2   (T) 03–3344–5111
Shinjuku-ku, Tokyo 160   (F) 03–3342–6094

Hotel Okura
Uchisaiwai-cho 1–1–1   (T) 03–3504–1111
Chiyoda-ku, Tokyo 100   (F) 03–3581–9146

Yaesu Fujiya Hotel
Yaesu 2–9–1   (T) 03–3273–2111
Chuo-ku, Tokyo 104   (F) 03–3273–2180

Business hotels (selection)

Ikebukuro Centre City Hotel
Ikebukuro 2–62–14   (T) 03–3985–1311
Toshima-ku, Tokyo 171   (F) 03–3980–7011

Kayabacho Pearl Hotel
Shinkawa 1–2–5   (T) 03–3553–2211
Chuo-ku, Tokyo 104   (F) 03–3555–1849

Tokyo Green Hotel Suidobashi
Misaki-cho 1–1–16   (T) 03–3847–1111
Chiyoda-ku, Tokyo 101   (F) 03–3295–8764

Other services for travellers

Japan Travel-Phone
In Tokyo: (T) 03–3502–1461
                                  (F) 03–3504–0564

In Kyoto: (T) 075–371–5649
                                  (F) 075–343–6847

Tokyo City Air Terminal   (T) 03–3665–7111
   Information Centre   (F) 03–3665–7175

JR Tokyo Station   (T) 03–3231–0034

JR Shinjuku Station   (T) 03–3354–4015

JR Ueno Station   (T) 03–3841–0031

FOREIGN BUSINESS ORGANIZATIONS

Australian Chamber of Commerce in Japan (and **New Zealand Chamber of Commerce in Japan**)
PO Box 1096, Chuo Post Office   (T) 03–3212–8787
Chiyoda-ku, Tokyo 100–91   (F) 03–3201–2592

American Chamber of Commerce in Japan
7th Floor, No 2 Fukide Bldg   (T) 03–3433–5381
1–21 Toranomon 4-chome   (F) 03–3436–1446
Minato-ku, Tokyo 105

British Chamber of Commerce in Japan
N16, Kowa Bldg, 3F   (T) 03–3505–1734
9–20 Akasaka 1-chome   (F) 03–3505–2680
Minato-ku, Tokyo 107

Canadian Chamber of Commerce in Japan
PO Box 79   (T) 03–3408–4311
Akasaka Post Office   (F) 03–3408–4190
Minato-ku, Tokyo 107

French Chamber of Commerce in Japan
Hanzomon MK Bldg, 8–1   (T) 03–3288–9621
Kojimachi 1-chome   (F) 03–3288–9558
Chiyoda-ku, Tokyo 102

German Chamber of Commerce in Japan
7th Floor, Akasaka Tokyu Bldg, 14–3   (T) 03–3581–9881
Nagatacho 2-chome   (F) 03–3593–1350
Chiyoda-ku, Tokyo 100

New Zealand Chamber of Commerce in Japan
(See **Australian Chamber of Commerce**)

TRANSLATION AGENCIES (SELECTION)

Adia Staff

Sanpo Akasaka Bldg, 5F	(T) 03–3505–3241
Akasaka 2–5–7	(F) 03–3505–3248
Minato-ku, Tokyo 107	

Alpa Corp

Hirikuresuto Hirakawa-cho 201	(T) 03–3230–0090
Hirakawa-cho 2–5–7	(F) 03–3234–5336
Chiyoda-ku, Tokyo 102	

Japan Translation Centre

Todoroki Kanda Bldg	(T) 03–3291–0655
Kanda Nishiki-cho 1–21	(F) 03–3294–0660
Chiyoda-ku, Tokyo 101	

Pasona Inc.

Pasona Hiro	(T) 03–5421–8023
Hiro 5–6–6	(F) 03–5421–8037
Shibuya-ku, Tokyo 150	

POST OFFICES

Tokyo Central Post Office

7–2 Marunouchi 2-chome	(T) Domestic mail
Chiyoda-ku, Tokyo 100	03–3284–9539
	Foreign mail
	03–3284–9540
	Delivery
	03–3284–9556

Tokyo International Post Office

3–3 Otemachi 2-chome	(T) General
Chiyoda-ku, Tokyo 100	information
	03–3241–4891
	Sea mail letters
	03–3241–5902
	Sea mail parcels
	03–3241–5908
	Air mail 03–3241–3544
	Business post
	03–3241–4840

OTHER USEFUL NUMBERS (IN TOKYO)

Metropolitan Police Lost Property Office	(T) 03–3814–4151

Tourist Information Centre   (T) 03–3502–1461

Tokyo Immigration Service Centre   (T) 03–3664–3046

English-speaking Baby-sitting Service   (T) 03–3368–0007

Legal Assistance for Foreign Workers   (T) 03–3368–8855

HOSPITALS
The following have doctors and nurses who can speak English.

International Catholic Hospital
  (Seibo Byoin)
5–1 Naka-Ochiai 2-chome   (T) 03–3951–1111
Shinjuku-ku, Tokyo 161   (F) 03–3954–7091

International Clinic
5–9 Azabudai 1-chome   (T) 03–3582–2646
Minato-ku, Tokyo 106   (F) 03–3583–8199

Tokyo Maternity Clinic
20–8 Sendagaya 1-chome   (T) 03–3403–1861
Shibuya-ku, Tokyo 151   (F) 03–3403–1869

Appendix

35 Key Company Histories

The companies selected for special examination are those from the *Fortune* ranking of Japanese manufacturing companies (the top 25) for 1991.

1. Company name: Toyota Motor Corporation

   Fortune ranking: 5

   Headquarters: 1, Toyota-cho
   Toyota City,
   Aichi Prefecture 471

   (T) 0565-28-2121
   (F) 0565-23-5721

Toyota is probably Japan's premier company, having won worldwide recognition for its development of JIT, the just-in-time system of lean production known as TMS within the company (Toyota management system). Nicknamed *Toyota Ginkō* (the Bank of Toyota), the company has in the past maintained a core capital which, if Toyota decided to cease production tomorrow, could pay the salaries of its 71,934 employees for the next 25 years.

Toyota enjoys approximately 40 per cent of the domestic car market: overseas it is pushing forward with its General Motors joint venture and its new manufacturing plant at Burnaston in Derbyshire, England. Because of the labour shortage in the company's home area of Mikawa in Aichi prefecture, the company has had to set up plants elsewhere in Japan (on Hokkaidō and Kyushu) where it can take advantage of the relatively improved labour situation.

Toyota is gearing up to the adverse economic situation in Japan and dwindling new car sales by instituting a new set of cost-cutting programmes. The situation is serious: the company's operating profit fell from ¥538.7 billion (US$503 million) for the year ending in June 1990 to ¥124.9 billion (US$116 million) for the year ending in June 1992. Forecasts for the year end to June 1993 put total operating profit at ¥100 billion (US$90 million). Of the five main Japanese car manufacturers, however, only Toyota's sales look firm.

2. Company name: Hitachi;   *Fortune* ranking: 12
    Hitachi Electronics Ltd

    Headquarters: Hitachi, 4–6   (T) 03–3258–1111
    Kanda-Surugadai,   (F) 03–3258–5480
    Chiyoda-ku, Tokyo

    Hitachi Electronics, 1–23–2   (T) 03–3255–8411
    Kanda-Sudacho, Chiyoda-ku,   (F) 03–3251–1366
    Tokyo

Hitachi is Japan's largest electrical machinery manufacturer. It produces information systems and electric power equipment as well as traffic systems and consumer electronics. Hitachi Electronics is also at the core of the Hitachi *keiretsu*, its main business being the development and production of video, communications equipment and sophisticated measuring and information systems.

3. Company name: Matsushita   *Fortune* ranking: 13
    Electric Industries

    Headquarters: 1006, Kadoma,   (T) 06–908–1121
    Kadoma City, Osaka   (F) 06–908–2351
    Prefecture

Founded by the patriarch Konosuke Matsushita in 1935, Matsushita is the Toyota of the consumer electronics industry. Following the death of the founder, the company was guided by the charismatic Akio Tanii, one of the leading spokesmen of the business world in Japan, until on 23 February 1993 he resigned to take responsibility for the company's disappointing results.

The company produces a range of products in the video, audio, information and electronic components fields. Reflecting its 35 per cent export ratio, this part of the Matsushita empire is perhaps better known outside Japan under its National and Panasonic brand names. In common with the other leading players in the sector, Matsushita is bracing itself for worse to come as the recession deepens in Japan. Consumers have changed their fickle buying patterns of the 1980s to reflect a more cautious approach to the acquisition of luxury goods. There also appears to be something of an over-sophistication in the market which means that people are now looking for more streamlined products and less gadgetry.

Despite this, the company is embarking on an aggressive marketing drive in HDTV (high definition TV) with the intention of maximizing market share. Its biggest rival here is Sony. The main strategy appears to be to cut the price of the principal HDTV model in an effort to gain sales. The original intention was to introduce a gradual price decrease, but the strong lead taken by Sony in introducing a markedly competitively priced model has set the pace for something of a price war. In addition to HDTV, Matsushita has also developed a camera and video-cassette recorder which can reproduce HDTV images. This will be for professional use by TV companies etc.

In the long term, the company is aiming to make itself leaner by moving to greater specialization in production. A large-scale restructuring programme is also under way, which will involve enhancing production methodology for computers, word-processors and fax machines. Loss-making divisions will be liquidated.

4. Company name: Nissan Motor   *Fortune* ranking: 19

    Headquarters: 6–17–1, Ginza,   (T) 03–3543–5523
    Chuo-ku, Tokyo 104–23   (F) 03–3544–0109

As Japan's number 2 in the automotive sector, Nissan has traditionally fought a hard battle with Toyota to improve market share. Compared with its biggest rival, it has been quicker off the mark in expanding its offshore production capability (although Toyota is now catching up quickly). Nissan is in the process of cutting down its labour force of 55,566 in an attempt to improve its performance in the current recession. Nevertheless profits are plunging, and projected sales in a sluggish market are no better. Cheap investment funds are harder to come by now, which means that a strategy to improve the performance of the company by investing in new technologies is going to be badly affected.

While the company's main business is cars and auto parts, it also has an interest in aviation.

5. Company name: Toshiba   *Fortune* ranking: 27
   Corporation

    Headquarters: 1–1–1 Shibaura,   (T) 03–3457–4511
    Minato-ku, Tokyo 105–01   (F) 03–3456–4776

Toshiba has made a name for itself in the field of consumer electronics, but its actual strengths lie in the area of data-communications systems. It has actively promoted overseas ties with American (General Electric), Italian (Olivetti) and German (Siemens) companies. Profitability, however, is dropping, with current profit for the year end in March 1993 estimated at ¥7 billion (US$6.5 million), down year on year from ¥114 billion (US$106 million).

From 1994 the company will commence production of TVs in the United States which will feature the American high-definition TV system. This project will be a joint venture with the Chicago-based company General Instruments Corp. Actual production will take place at the Toshiba America Consumer Products plant in Tennessee. In addition to this, Toshiba will be entering a three-way multimedia project with NEC and the American Telephone and Telegraph Company (AT&T) to develop mobile, hand-held communication devices based on AT&T's new Hobbit microprocessor. The 32-bit Hobbit is five times faster than Intel Corp.'s 486 DX chip.

6. Company name: Honda   *Fortune* ranking: 28

   Headquarters: 2–1–1 Minami   (T) 03–3423–1111
   Aoyama, Minato-ku, Tokyo   (F) 03–3423–8947

Honda's collaboration around the world with other automotive companies, such as Rover in the United Kingdom, has proved successful in recent years. Honda remains the world's leading manufacturer of motorcycles, a fact which accounts for the other Japanese automakers nicknaming the company 'the bike dealer'. Motorcycles now account for 11 per cent of Honda's total sales breakdown, with cars on 78 per cent and parts on 12 per cent. The motorcycle side of the business looks healthy, with expansion programmes centred on Asia (China in particular). Honda has built a reputation for concentrating on the development of fast cars (it has a remarkable history in Formula One), but this has been at the expense of developing other mainstream models such as recreational vehicles. While Honda has been actively promoting its activities abroad, it has a relatively weak domestic sales network: factors such as these plus the lack of a truly integrated range of vehicles will make it hard for the company to compete in future years.

7. Company name: NEC   *Fortune* ranking: 39

   Headquarters: 5–7–1 Shiba,   (T) 03–3454–1111
   Minato-ku, Tokyo 108–01   (F) 03–3457–7249

NEC's main business is in computers and communications equipment. It maintains the largest share of the personal computer (PC) market in Japan. In the late 1980s the company invested heavily in the development of high-tech products, which must now be paid for: this is no easy task given the slump in sales of PCs and other key NEC products. The company expects a 25 per cent drop in pre-tax profits for the year ending in 1993, down to ¥60 billion (US$55 million). Equipment investment for the end of the 1992 financial year is also expected to drop by 26 per cent. The successor to the chairman of the past thirteen years, Sekimoto Tadahiro, due in post in June 1993, will have his work cut out to turn the company around and make it more responsive to the changing nature of the consumer electronics market.

8. Company name: Sony   *Fortune* ranking: 40

   Headquarters: 6–7–35   (T) 03–3448–2111
     Kita-shinagawa,   (F) 03–3448–2183
     Shinagawa-ku, Tokyo 141

Sony is one of the world's leading manufacturers of electronic systems, including audio, video and televisual equipment. Recently the corporation has branched out and acquired the CBS Records group in addition to buying Columbia Pictures. The reasoning behind this move is to complement the existing production of hardware by the Sony Corporation with a wide variety and catalogue of musical software. Akio Morita is the company's chairman and visionary. Sony's sales in the United States currently outstrip those in Japan itself.

9. Company name: Mitsubishi   *Fortune* ranking: 46
   Electric

   Headquarters: 2–2–3   (T) 03–3218–2111
     Marunouchi, Chiyoda-ku,   (F) 03–5252–7119
     Tokyo 100

Mitsubishi Electric is the top Japanese producer of defence electronics. This is reflected in the company's overall sales profile – 37 per cent for data-communications systems and electronic devices.

10. Company name: Nippon Steel   *Fortune* ranking: 47

   Headquarters: 2–6–3   (T) 03–3242–4111
     Otemachi, Chiyoda-ku,   (F) 03–3275–5611
     Tokyo 100–71

Currently the largest producer of steel in the world, Nippon Steel was formed in 1970 with the merger of Fuji Steel and

Yahata Steel. The company's activities in the steel-producing sector are wide-ranging: apart from pig iron and ingots the company also produces flat-rolled and tubular products. However, due to the shifting nature of the demand for steel on a worldwide scale, diversification is taking place into such other activities as building construction, engineering and information technology areas. Nippon Steel has a joint venture with Inland Steel in the United States.

11. Company name: Fujitsu   *Fortune* ranking: 51

    Headquarters: 1–6–1   (T) 03–3216–3211
    Marunouchi, Chiyoda-ku,   (F) 03–3216–9365
    Tokyo 100

Fujitsu is the world's second largest computer manufacturer. It is primarily concerned with dataprocessing equipment, with interests in communication equipment and other electronic devices. Fujitsu is famous for buying the UK's ICL as well as Amdahl of the United States. Acquisitions such as these have strengthened the company's international profile.

12. Company name: Mitsubishi   *Fortune* ranking: 53
    Motors

    Headquarters: 5–33–8 Shiba,   (T) 03–3456–1111
    Minato-ku, Tokyo 108   (F) 03–5232–7743

Mitsubishi Motors has a tie-up with Chrysler of the US in that the American auto maker has a 6.3 per cent share in the company. Mitsubishi competes with Mazda and Honda for the third position in the domestic market after Toyota and Nissan. Rising labour costs are beginning to make their mark and it looks unlikely that the company will be able to improve profits in the short term. The one saving grace has been the success of the Pajero recreation vehicle (known as the Montero in the United States). Analysts are doubtful as to whether the company will be able to maintain its independent status. More tie-ups in the future with other companies look increasingly likely.

13. Company name: Mazda Motor   *Fortune* ranking: 57

    Headquarters: 3–1 Shinchi,   (T) 082–282–1111
    Fuchu-cho, Aki-gun,   (F) 082–287–5237
    Hiroshima

Mazda has close connections with Ford and ties up with Suzuki for the sale of mini-cars. Mazda has achieved great success in the past with its Familia (323) range. In recent years Mazda has shifted its design centre away from the home base of Hiroshima to Yokohama, where it was hoped that proximity to the capital would help to invigorate the creativity of its designers.

14. Company name: Mitsubishi   *Fortune* ranking: 63
     Heavy Industries

     Headquarters: 2–5–1   (T) 03–3212–3111
     Marunouchi, Chiyoda-ku,   (F) 03–3212–9860
     Tokyo 100

Mitsubishi Heavy Industries is Japan's largest heavy machinery manufacturer and shipbuilder. It forms the core of the Mitsubishi *keiretsu*. Much of its work is provided by the Defence Agency.

15. Company name: Nippon Oil   *Fortune* ranking: 65

     Headquarters: 1–3–12   (T) 03–3502–1111
     Nishi-Shinbashi, Minato-ku,   (F) 03–3502–9352
     Tokyo

Nippon Oil is Japan's primary distributor of petroleum products, 50 per cent of which are purchased from Caltex, and has a tie-up with Mitsubishi Oil. It is actively engaged in prospecting and the development of sources in the United States and South-east Asia, for example.

16. Company name: Idemitsu   *Fortune* ranking: 77
     Kosan

     Headquarters: 3–1–1   (T) 03–3213–3111
     Marunouchi, Chiyoda-ku,   (F) 03–3213–9354
     Tokyo 100

Idemitsu is Japan's largest domestically owned petroleum company. Unlike those detailed above, this is an unlisted company, with interests in gasoline, jet fuels, kerosene and lubricant oil.

17. Company name: Canon   *Fortune* ranking: 83

     Headquarters: 2–7–1   (T) 03–3348–2121
     Nishi-Shinjuku,   (F) 03–3349–8519
     Shinjuku-ku, Tokyo 163-07

Canon is a leading manufacturer of camera equipment worldwide. In recent years the company has switched its emphasis to include areas such as fax machines, photocopiers and computer peripherals as demand for cameras begins to slow down. Tie-ups include joint ventures with IBM to produce notepad PCs plus bubblejet printers.

18. Company name: NKK (Nippon   *Fortune* ranking: 87
     Kokan)

     Headquarters: 1–1–2   (T) 03–3212–7111
     Marunouchi, Chiyoda-ku,   (F) 03–3214–8428
     Tokyo 100

This is one of the world's main steelmakers in terms of crude steel production. As for Nippon Steel, the changing business environment has meant diversification. This has been into electronics and chemicals.

19. Company name: Bridgestone   *Fortune* ranking: 93

     Headquarters: 1–10–1   (T) 03–3567–0111
     Kyobashi, Chuo-ku,   (F) 03–3567–4615
     Tokyo 104

Bridgestone is the second largest tyre manufacturer in the world and supplies 50 per cent of domestic market needs.

20. Company name: Sumitomo   *Fortune* ranking: 97
     Metal Industries

     Headquarters: 4–5–33   (T) 06–220–5111
     Kitahama, Chuo-ku,   (F) 06–223–0563
     Osaka 541

Part of the large Sumitomo conglomerate, Sumitomo Metal Industries is the third most significant provider of crude steel after Nippon Steel and NKK.

21. Company name: Sanyo   *Fortune* ranking: 107
     Electric

     Headquarters: 2–18   (T) 06–991–1181
     Keihan-Hondori, Moriguchi   (F) 06–992–0009
     City, Osaka Prefecture 570

Sanyo Electric is the core company of the Sanyo group and is a manufacturer of a wide variety of consumer electronic products. The company has joint venture projects in Italy with Olivetti, and in China. Sanyo's videocassette-recorder business is suffering at home due to the adverse economic environment and depressed consumer demand.

22. Company name: Isuzu Motors   *Fortune* ranking: 120

    Headquarters: 6-26-1   (T) 03-5471-1111
      Minami-Ohi, Shinagawa-ku,   (F) 03-5471-1036
      Tokyo 140

Isuzu has an illustrious history as far as commercial vehicle production is concerned. General Motors (GM) has a 37.4 per cent stake in the company, which brings it clearly into the GM global strategy. The majority of the company's sales are in light trucks and buses. In 1991 the company had accumulated debts of ¥51.5 billion (US$48 million) with car sales dropping to only 90,000 units in the year (production break-even being 240,000 units) – hence the decision to concentrate on trucks. This strategy may be the only one available if the company is to survive.

23. Company name: Nippondenso   *Fortune* ranking: 123

    Headquarters: 1-1 Showa-cho,   (T) 0566-25-5511
      Kariya City, Aichi   (F) 0566-25-4509
      Prefecture 448

Nippondenso is probably the most famous Japanese automotive parts supplier. Geographically close to Toyota City and Toyota Motor Corporation, Nippondenso in Kariya City is a staunch Toyota affiliate. It also has links with Bosch and supplies all of the major car manufacturers with the exception of Nissan Motor Corporation. As might be anticipated, the chill winds from the recession and the depressed domestic car market are having an adverse effect on the company's performance: cost-cutting and parts rationalization programmes are therefore to be expected.

24. Company name: Sharp   *Fortune* ranking: 126

    Headquarters: 22-22   (T) 06-621-1221
      Nagaike-cho, Abeno-ku,   (F) 06-628-1653
      Osaka 545

Sharp is a major player in the field of consumer electronics and an industry leader in liquid crystal development.

25. Company name: Kobe Steel   *Fortune* ranking: 129

    Headquarters: 1-3-18   (T) 078-261-5111
      Wakinohama-cho, Chuo-ku,   (F) 03-5252-7961
      Kobe 651

Kobe Steel is the fourth Japanese steel producer in this line-up of Japan's top 25 companies. One of the company's specialities is rolled copper products: it is also diversifying into engineering.

36 Key Political Personalities

TANAKA KAKUEI

Tanaka Kakuei will be remembered as the most dominant Japanese politician of the entire postwar era. In the murky world of factional politics he was a past master at 'playing the game'. A self-made man, having worked his way up from being a construction-site worker, Tanaka became prime minister of Japan in 1972. He had no university background, which actually served as an advantage: he was not aligned to any particular university clique and had great flexibility to develop his own independent networks with no allegiances other than to himself.

Following revelations about some of his dubious financial dealings, Tanaka was forced to resign in 1974. Thereafter the Lockheed affair broke and he was indicted on bribery charges in 1976. Incapacitation from 1985 onwards as a result of a stroke marked the end of Tanaka's behind-the-scenes working of the system. His contribution to the political life of Japan was to show that in a supposedly group-oriented society it is still possible to exploit the status quo in such a way as to enable the fast and furious networking of a single individual to bring about enormous personal power.

NAKASONE YASUHIRO

The former Prime Minister Nakasone is perhaps the best-known of Japan's premiers as far as the international arena is concerned. While he tried to project a prime ministership with which Americans and Europeans could readily identify, the tactic caused a great deal of animosity in Japan itself, where the role of the individual is subjugated to the will of the group and the political system does not nurture individual 'star' politicians, in the mould of a Margaret Thatcher, for example. Many

Japanese despised the so-called Ron–Yasu special relationship (Nakasone's relationship with former US President Ronald Reagan), denouncing him rather as the 'weathervane', a reference to Nakasone's ability to change political conviction at will (depending on the prevailing political conditions at any given time).

In September 1986 Nakasone created a storm of controversy over his assertion that the United States was a less intelligent society on account of its black and Hispanic population. This betrayed a tremendous naivety on Nakasone's behalf as well as corroborating his beliefs in *Nihonjinron* (the theory of being Japanese).

Following the expiration of his term as prime minister in October 1987 (he was succeeded by Takeshita), Nakasone was implicated in the Recruit (stock-for-favours) scandal of the late 1980s. It has taken until the early 1990s for this 'problem' to begin to wear off, but there are definite indications that the 74-year-old Nakasone is beginning to exercise his political muscle again, prompting speculation that he will try to perform a more influential behind-the-scenes role instead of continuing with his rather low-key style of recent years.

TAKESHITA NOBORU

Takeshita Noboru is one of the best examples of a Japanese politician's politician: domestically oriented and consensus-led (in contrast to the Nakasone style detailed above). Takeshita was the son of a Shimane Prefecture sake-maker; he came into national politics via the prefectural assembly and rose to the very top of the political pyramid as prime minister, only to be forced out of office as a result of his involvement in the Sagawa Kyubin (Sagawa Parcel Delivery Company) scandal. His Takeshita faction has long been the dominant force in Liberal Democratic Party internal power-broking (see: Major Political Parties), but this is set to change following the fall from favour of Shin Kanemaru, who, with Takeshita and Ichiro Ozawa, formed a powerful triumvirate. The Takeshita faction split in December 1992, a development which has led political observers to assume that the relationship between Takeshita and Ozawa will sour.

MIYAZAWA KIICHI

Miyazawa had to wait a comparatively long time before it was his turn to be the prime minister of Japan. He succeeded Kaifu Toshiki and formed his first cabinet on 5 November 1991. Miyazawa's factional base is comparatively weak, which started rumours that his was likely to be a lame-duck prime ministership. Since landing the job, Miyazawa has had a rough time weathering the fall-out from the Sagawa Kyubin affair (see above), presiding over a faltering economy and watching the trade deficits with Japan's major trading partners start ballooning once again. Added to this are the tough issues of rice import deregulation and political reform. The one silver lining in the storm clouds gathering is the marriage between Crown Prince Naruhito and the former diplomat Masako Owada, an event which is expected to give the ailing economy a shot in the arm.

KANEMARU SHIN

Kanemaru was known in Japan as the LDP (Liberal Democratic Party) king-pin, or king-maker. A skilful politician, Kanemaru's luck finally ran out on 14 October 1992 when he was forced to resign in the aftermath of the Sagawa Kyubin scandal (see above). Observers of the Japanese political scene doubted that the veteran networker would survive the scandal after being fined ¥200,000 (US$1,865) for accepting ¥500 million (US$4.6 million) in illegal donations from Sagawa Kyubin (a major parcel delivery company). Nevertheless he did attempt to hold on to the chairmanship of the LDP: a move doomed to failure, since public opinion had gone so firmly against him as a symbol of the corrupt Japanese political system. Significantly, Kanemaru was also the chairman of the 111-member Takeshita faction, which he managed jointly with the former prime minister and Ichiro Ozawa, his protegé, who now finds himself pushed to the outer boundaries of the party. His resignation has caused tidal waves within the faction-bound LDP as the various cliques set about redefining their complex allegiances (see: Major Political Parties).

The feeling in Japan now is that the ousting of the 78-year-old Kanemaru may provide a long-awaited opportunity to institute real political change in Japan. His influence in recent years was all pervasive, in terms of both domestic policy (hardly any major public works projects were started without his prior approval) and international affairs (Kanemaru, along with Takeshita and Ozawa, were the three politicians with whom foreign diplomats sought audiences, not the prime minister, Miyazawa).

37 Miscellaneous

BASIC ETIQUETTE

Do not worry about behaving exactly as a Japanese. Polite western behaviour showing a degree of cultural sensitivity should be perfectly acceptable. If in doubt, take a cue from your host, or ask what you should do.

A few dos and don'ts include:

- Don't keep your shoes on if everyone else is taking theirs off.

- Don't leave your chopsticks sticking upright in your rice. This is only done if making offerings to the dead, and so is considered bad luck.

- Don't pass food from chopsticks to chopsticks – this also has funereal connotations.

- Don't blow your nose at the table, or anywhere in public, if avoidable. This is considered quite disgusting. The Japanese will sniff and snuffle rather than blowing their noses. Sticking a tissue on which you have just blown your nose up your sleeve is considered particularly revolting.

- Don't pour your own drink. Someone will pour for you and you can pour for someone else. Raise your glass and tilt it slightly if someone offers to pour for you.

- Don't start drinking before your host has said 'Kampai!' – 'Cheers!'

- If you don't drink, ask for orange juice and take part in the toasts. If you don't want to drink any more, leave your glass almost full, and let your hosts go through the ritual of filling it up a tiny bit.

- There is no stigma attached to women drinking – though it is probably not done to get absolutely plastered!

For further details on business etiquette and the business psychology of the Japanese, see: Business Culture.

FESTIVALS

Japan is a land of festivals, with probably a festival somewhere in the country every day of the year. Most festivals have their origin in religion and centre on shrines.

Some of the major festivals of the year include:

- **Seijin no Hi** (Coming-of-age Day) – 15 January. This is celebrated by young men and women who are in the year of their twentieth birthday, and involves visits to the local shrine, wearing traditional dress.
- **Setsubun** – 3 February. This marks the end of winter. Participants throw beans at homes, shrines and temples, to drive out evil spirits.
- **Hina Matsuri** – 3 March. This is sometimes known as 'Girls' Day'. Dolls representing the emperor and court are put on display in homes. The dolls are often quite old, having been passed down through families as heirlooms.
- **O Higan** – (March and September); **O Bon** (13–16 July and August). At O Higan people visit family graves to pay their respects. At O Bon people return to their home towns to remember dead ancestors. It is believed that their spirits return to the earth at this time and people may light a small fire or lantern outside the house to guide them home.
- **Boys' Festival**. Colourful carp streamers (*koinobori*) are hung from the houses which have boys in the family in the weeks leading up to this festival, and boys are treated to special foods and sometimes presents.
- **Shichi Go San Festival** (Seven-Five-Three) – 15 November. This is held in honour of boys who are 5 and girls who are 3 and 7. The children are dressed in their kimonos or Sunday best and taken to the local shrine to ask for blessing.

See also: Religion.

NATIONAL HOLIDAYS

January	1	New Year's Day
	15	Coming-of-age Day
February	11	National Foundation Day
March	25	Vernal Equinox Day
April	29	Green Day
May	3	Constitution Day
	4	People's Day
	5	Children's Day
September	15	Senior Citizens' Day
	29	Autumnal Equinox
October	10	Health-Sports Day
November	3	Culture Day
	23	Labour Day
December	23	Emperor's Birthday

CONVERSION CHARTS

The metric system of weights and measures is dominant throughout Japan. However, there are a few additional units which are maintained for historical reasons. One of these is *tsubo*, one *tsubo* being equal to the area of two *tatami* mats. One *tatami* mat is approximately 3 feet by 6 feet (91.5 cm by 183 cm). Another such unit is *i-sho*, equal to half a gallon (2.28 l), which is used to measure sake.

TEMPERATURE

The general formulas are:

$$\text{Celsius} = (\text{Fahrenheit} - 32) \times \frac{5}{9}$$

and

$$\text{Fahrenheit} = \frac{9 \times \text{Celsius}}{5} + 32$$

°C	°F
−10	14
−5	23
0	32
5	41
10	50
15	59
20	68
25	77
30	86
35	95

CLIMATE

The year average temperature for Tokyo is 15.3°C/59.5°F. Temperatures throughout the year are:

	Jan.	Feb.	Mar.	Apr.	May	June	July	Aug.	Sep.	Oct.	Nov.	Dec.
°C	04.7	05.4	08.4	13.9	18.4	21.5	25.2	26.7	22.9	17.3	12.3	07.4
°F	40.5	41.7	47.1	57.0	65.1	70.7	77.4	80.1	73.2	63.1	54.1	45.3

38 Further Reading

GENERAL
Ruth Benedict, *The Chrysanthemum and the Sword*. Tokyo, Tuttle, 1954. Classic anthropological study on what makes the Japanese tick. Available mainly in Japan.

Basil Hall Chamberlain, *Japanese Things*. Tokyo, Tuttle, 1971. A seminal work first published at the turn of the century, this book offers an insight into Japanese society which is still of great value today.

Joy Hendry, *Understanding Japanese Society*. Beckenham, Croom Helm, 1987. A valuable anthropological work on key aspects of the workings of Japanese society.

Chie Nakane, *Japanese Society*. Tokyo, Tuttle, 1984. This book contains valuable and sometimes controversial observations of Japanese life, and was the first to discuss at length the vertical nature in which Japanese society is organized.

Peter Tasker, *Inside Japan*. Harmondsworth, Penguin, 1989. Very informative examination of Japanese attitudes to work, politics, education, crime and domestic life.

Karen van Wolferen, *The Enigma of Japanese Power*. Basingstoke, Macmillan, 1989. A controversial but very readable study of the System in Japan.

LANGUAGE
Association for Japanese Language Teaching, *Japanese for Busy People*. Tokyo and New York, Kodansha International, 1984. The most popular classroom textbook for adult learners of Japanese.

Michael Jenkins and Lynne Strugnell, *Teach Yourself Business Japanese*. London, Hodder and Stoughton, 1992. Part of the established series of Teach Yourself books, this is an elementary text for the independent business learner based on the experiences of a European businessman in Japan and the everyday lives of Japanese workers in a Japanese trading company.

Osamu and Nobuko Mizutani, *Introduction to Modern Japanese*. Tokyo, Japan Times, 1977. Another popular introductory textbook for learning the language. Introduces the *hiragana*, *katakana* and *kanji* scripts.

BUSINESS AND ECONOMICS

James Abegglen and George Stalk, *Kaisha – The Japanese Company*. Tokyo, Tuttle, 1985. A look at the real strengths and weaknesses of the Japanese corporation.

Ronald Dore, *Taking Japan Seriously*. London, Athlone Press, 1987. A serious study of Japanese economic organization which examines which aspects are worthy of 'imitation' by non-Japanese companies and which can be tailored to a non-Japanese corporate framework.

Bill Emmott, *Japan's Global Reach*. London, Century, 1992. Another incisive work by the former Tokyo correspondent of *The Economist*, this book examines the influences, strategies and weaknesses of Japan's multinational companies.

Bill Emmott, *The Sun Also Sets*. London, Simon and Schuster, 1989. The *LA Times* called Emmott: 'way ahead of the pack in thoughtfulness, originality and recognition of dynamic social, economic and political forces'. This is one of the few works to have examined Japan in a really objective way.

Robert M. March, *The Japanese Negotiator*. Tokyo and New York, Kodansha International, 1988. A fascinating and perceptive look at the differences and similarities in Japanese and non-Japanese negotiating style.

Michio Morishima, *Why Has Japan Succeeded?* Cambridge, Cambridge University Press, 1982. A useful contribution to the debate on the reasons for Japan's economic rise.

Dick Wilson, *The Sun at Noon*. London, Hamish Hamilton, 1986. A prophetic work which was highly controversial when it was first published in 1986. Useful to read in conjunction with other more recent works on the reasons for Japan's economic ills.

Christopher Wood, *The Bubble Economy: The Japanese Economic Collapse*. London, Sidgwick and Jackson, 1992. A very insightful and fascinating exposé of the factors behind the bursting of the Japanese economic bubble and the prospects for the future of the Japanese economy.

Mark A. Zimmerman, *Dealing with the Japanese*. London, Unwin Paperbacks, 1988. One of the best books ever written about dealing with the Japanese in a business context.

EXPATRIATE LIFE

Janet Ashby, *Gaijin's Guide: Practical Help for Everyday Life in Japan*. Tokyo, Japan Times, 1988. A useful guide on living in Japan which looks at a range of subjects from getting around on foot to medical care and leisure facilities.

Nancy Hartzenbusch and Alice Shabecoff, *A Parents' Guide to Tokyo*. Tokyo, Shufunotomo Ltd, 1989. A handy little book with lots of valuable information on Tokyo for 'tots, teens and tourists'.

Philip J. Hinder, *Let's Eat Out: How to Read Menus in Japanese*. Tokyo, Japan Times, 1988. A useful little guide to getting the best out of eating out.

Japan – A Bilingual Atlas. Tokyo, Kodansha International, 1991. An excellent collection of 21 large-scale maps, 19 maps of major metropolitan areas, 7 maps of tourist areas and 9 transport maps in both Japanese and English.

Carolyn R. Krouse, *A Guide to Food Buying in Japan*. Tokyo, Tuttle, 1986. A thorough guide to supermarkets and food stores in Japan, complete with sections on working out the meaning on Japanese labels, etc.

Ian McQueen, *Budget Travel Guide*. Tokyo, Kodansha International, 1992. A comprehensive guidebook first published as *Japan – A Travel Survival Kit*, and now completely revised and updated. A must for tourists and long-term visitors.

Jean Pearce, *Footloose in Tokyo*. New York and Tokyo, John Weatherhill, 1984. A guidebook with a difference, this takes the stations of the Yamanote Line in Tokyo as its starting point for a trail of discovery around the capital city.

John Randle with Mariko Watanabe, *Coping with Japan*. Oxford,

Blackwell, 1987. An excellent guide to learning the ropes in Japan.

Research Committee for Bicultural Life in Japan, *Now You Live in Japan*. Tokyo, Japan Times, 1985. A useful handbook for the newly arrived long-term resident of Japan.

39 Key Phrases

These phrases have been selected on the basis that they can be used to break the ice when conducting a first meeting with Japanese business colleagues or to get a subsequent meeting off to a good start, or to help you to get around in Japan.

WHEN MEETING SOMEONE FOR THE FIRST TIME

Hajimemashite	How do you do?
(BP) no (Kenedi) desu	I'm (Kennedy), from (BP).
Dōzo yoroshiku onegaishimasu	Pleased to meet you.

Remember that you will need to ascertain in advance (if possible) whether the people you are meeting can speak English. If they can, it might not be appropriate to speak any Japanese. However, if you are going to be speaking through an interpreter, it might be a good idea to say *'Hajimemashite'*, just to show you have made an effort to prepare for your visit to Japan.

GREETINGS
As you can only use *hajimemashite* for a very first meeting, other expressions are necessary when visiting a second time.

O-hisashiburi desu ne	It's been quite a while (since we last met).
or (as appropriate):	
Ohayō gozaimasu	Good morning.
Konnichiwa	Hello, good day.

Konbanwa	Good evening.

and then:

O-genki desu ka	How are you?

The appropriate answer to the above is:

Hai, genki desu	I'm fine, thank you.

PARTING

Ki o tsukete kudasai	Please take care of yourself.

Note that *sayōnara* (goodbye) is seldom appropriate at the end of a business meeting. *Ki o tsukete kudasai* is warmer and good for any situation.

THANKS

Dōmo arigatō	Thanks.
Dōmo arigatō gozaimasu	Thank you very much.
Dōmo arigatō gozaimashita	Thank you very much (for all you have done).

If someone says any of the above to you:

Dō itashimashite	Don't mention it.

or:

Kochira koso	It's my pleasure.

ASKING FOR THINGS AND MAKING REQUESTS

(Kōhī) o kudasai	I'd like (some coffee) please.
(Hiruton hoteru) made onegaishimasu	*(to a taxi driver)* To the (Hilton Hotel) please.

AT MEALTIMES

Itadakimasu	Bon appetit. *(a set phrase always said before eating)*
Kampai!	Cheers!
Oishii desu	It's delicious.

Go-chisō sama deshita	Thank you for the meal. *(always said after the meal)*

AT THE END OF AN EVENING'S SOCIALIZING

Tanoshikatta desu	I enjoyed myself.
O-yasumi nasai!	Good night!

and if appropriate:

Mata ashita	See you tomorrow.

SAYING YOU'RE SORRY

to people you know quite well:

Gomen nasai	Sorry (about that).

to people you don't know well,
or who are in a superior
position to you, or when you
bump into someone, or if you
want to push past a person to
get on or off a train or bus:

Sumimasen	Sorry (excuse me).

ON THE TELEPHONE

Moshi moshi	Hello?
Naisen (124*) onegaishimasu	Could I have extension (124) please?
(Tanaka) san onegaishimasu	Could I speak to Mr/Ms Tanaka please?

*For Japanese numbers, see below.

IF IN DOUBT

Sumimasen, chotto wakarimasen	I'm sorry, I don't understand.

THE NUMBERS

The numbers given below are the ones you would use for telephone digits.

0	*zero* ('ze' as in zen)
1	*ichi*
2	*ni*
3	*san*
4	*yon*
5	*go*
6	*roku*
7	*nana*
8	*hachi*
9	*kyu*
10	*ju*

For example:

Naisen ichi-ni-yon   Could I have extension
onegaishimasu   124, please?

LEARNING JAPANESE

For information on Japanese language learning in your country or in Japan, contact:

Australia
Embassy of Japan   (T) 61–6–27332444,
112 Empire Circuit   27333686
Yarralumla
Canberra ACT 2600

Canada
Embassy of Japan   (T) 1–613–236–8541
255 Sussex Drive
Ottawa
Ontario K1N 9E6

Japan
AJALT (Association for Japanese   (T) 03–3400–9031
   Language Teaching)   (F) 03–3797–0176
Kowa International 6F
12–24, 4-chome
Nishiazabu
Minato-ku
Tokyo 108

New Zealand
Embassy of Japan   (T) 64–4–731–540
7th Floor, Norwich Insurance House
3–11 Hunter Street
Wellington 1

United States
Embassy of Japan   (T) 1–202–939–6700
2520 Massachusetts Avenue NW
Washington DC 20008–2869

United Kingdom
The Japanese Language Association   (T) 0225 483913
  (JLA)   (F) 0225 484594
Bath College of Higher Education
19/20 Somerset Place
Bath BA1 5SF

Callers to the Japanese Embassy wishing to find out about Japanese language courses in the UK will be referred to the JLA in Bath.

40 GNP Growth Rates of Selected Countries

	Inflation (annual change, %)		Interest rates (3-m'th money mkt, %)		GNP/GDP growth (annual change, %)		Industrial prod'n (annual change, %)		Unemployment rate (%)		Current account (last 12 months, $bn)	
	Latest	Year ago	Latest	Year ago	Latest	Year ago	Latest	Year ago	Latest	Year ago	Latest	Year ago
UK	1.3	4.3	5.94	10.00	0.6	−1.2	1.5	−1.6	10.5	9.5	−20.8	−11.6
Australia	1.2	1.7	5.17	6.48	3.6	1.0	−1.3	−2.2	10.7	10.4	−11.1	−9.0
Belgium	2.7	2.8	7.12	9.62	2.5	3.0	0.6	−1.4	8.7	7.6	3.9	4.0
Canada	1.8	1.7	4.88	6.12	1.3	−0.0	6.2	1.1	11.4	11.1	23.6	−25.5
France	2.1	3.1	7.62	10.06	0.4	1.1	−2.8	3.1	10.7	10.1	2.9	−6.5
Germany	4.2	4.6	7.61	9.75	−3.4	1.2	−7.7	−0.1	8.0	6.5	27.2	−23.1
Italy	4.0	5.7	10.63	12.50	−0.3	1.7	−4.9	0.4	9.1	9.9	−16.6	−30.0
Japan	1.0	2.3	3.25	4.69	0.6	3.2	−3.8	−6.4	2.3	2.0	126.5	91.4
Netherlands	2.3	4.4	6.80	9.53	2.1	3.9	0.2	−1.3	8.2	7.0	8.9	10.7
Spain	4.0	6.8	14.64	12.57	4.9	5.0	−8.9	−3.9	19.5	16.5	−24.7	−17.0
Sweden	5.0	2.4	8.40	11.60	2.1	2.3	−4.6	−6.7	7.1	4.2	−4.9	−3.3
USA	3.2	3.2	3.31	4.06	2.6	1.4	3.5	3.6	6.9	7.4	−62.4	−3.7
OECD	3.7	4.3	–	–	3.5	4.5	−1.1	0.1	7.5	7.2	–	–

Source: Independent, 6 June 1993.

41 Index